HAWTHORNE AS EDITOR

HAWTHORNE

AS EDITOR

Selections from His Writings in

THE AMERICAN MAGAZINE

OF USEFUL AND ENTERTAINING

KNOWLEDGE

by Arlin Turner

KENNIKAT PRESS
Port Washington, N. Y./London

HAWTHORNE AS EDITOR

Copyright 1941 by Louisiana State University Press
Reissued in 1972 by Kennikat Press by arrangement
Library of Congress Catalog Card No: 71-86068
ISBN 0-8046-1577-2

Manufactured by Taylor Publishing Company   Dallas, Texas

Preface

The purpose of this volume is to make available the most significant of Hawthorne's writings for *The American Magazine of Useful and Entertaining Knowledge* during his six months as editor. Only five of the articles, I believe, have been reprinted heretofore. In the choice of selections for this book, the plan has been to include those essays and briefer items which have some intrinsic merit or throw light on what Hawthorne was reading and thinking; also those reflecting his interest in the world about him or bearing some relation to his other writings. The task of distinguishing the articles written by Hawthorne from those by his sister Elizabeth has proved less difficult than was first expected. The chief guide has been internal evidence, since Elizabeth signed none of her contributions; but Hawthorne's letters have supplied a few clues. In the biographical sketch of Alexander Hamilton, in which both had a hand, there are several apparent differences in style and method that seem dependable enough as criteria for fixing the authorship of the other pieces. Except for a few of the very short notes, only selections with recognizable Hawthornesque qualities have been included. But it must be admitted that some of the articles reprinted here may have come mainly from the pen of Elizabeth; if such is true, though, it seems that Hawthorne added something to each, perhaps a moral or a generalization, which brands it as at least partially his own.

It is a pleasure to express here my thanks to Professor Randall Stewart for looking over the manuscript of this volume and giving me the benefit of his judgment. He and Professors Manning Hawthorne and Norman Holmes Pearson have given me access to their copies of the Hawthorne correspondence, and Professor Richard Manning has generously allowed me to quote from letters in his possession. Dean Charles W. Pipkin has made the publication of this volume possible by giving it a place among the *Louisiana State University Studies,* and Professor Marcus Wilkerson, Director of the Louisiana State University Press, has been liberal with his assistance. Professor H. B. Woolf, my colleague, has read the introduction in manuscript, and Professors D. M. McKeithan and Grady·D. Price have aided me in identifying some of the books Hawthorne alluded to. Thelma Sherrill Turner, my wife, has been a faithful and generous helper in the work that has gone into this volume.

A. T.

June, 1940

Table of Contents

Introduction

Hawthorne became editor of *The American Magazine of Useful and Entertaining Knowledge* [1] with the issue of March, 1836, and with some help from his sister Elizabeth prepared the contents of six numbers. Though the editorship held no great promise, Pierce, Cilley, Bridge, and others of Hawthorne's friends were gratified to see him find profitable employment without turning his back on authorship. [2] But the optimism was short-lived. The nature of the publication and the restrictions under which Hawthorne had to work began to gall him early; and further, his meager salary of $500 a year immediately became delinquent. [3] Samuel G. Goodrich, who had secured the position for him through his own connection with the publishers, the Bewick Company of Boston, made promises in regard

[1] The magazine was first issued in September, 1834, and, except for September, 1836, when a fire at the plant of the publishers interfered with publication, it appeared monthly through September, 1837. The publishers first called themselves the American Engraving and Printing Company, and then the Bewick Company of Boston, taking the new name from Thomas Bewick (1753–1828), the celebrated English wood-engraver (see a note in the magazine for August, 1835 [I, 507–8]). The Bewick Company was under the superintendence of Abel Bowen (see the issue for August, 1835 [I, 508]) and had as members several men who were interested primarily in engraving: Samuel G. Goodrich, Freeman Hunt, J. L. Sibley, William Croome, Alonzo Hartwell, John H. Hall, John C. Crossman, and others. As a consequence the magazine was always in the minds of the proprietors little more than a vehicle for carrying their engravings. The custom seems to have been for some member of the company to serve as editor; and at different times Hunt, Sibley, Goodrich, and possibly others of the proprietors occupied the editorial chair.

[2] See George Edward Woodberry, *Nathaniel Hawthorne,* Boston, 1902, pp. 58–59; Julian Hawthorne, *Nathaniel Hawthorne and His Wife,* Boston, 1884, I, 133–35.

[3] James T. Fields (*Yesterdays with Authors,* Boston, 1872, p. 68) mistakenly sets the salary at $600.

to the salary which—so Hawthorne became convinced even before his first issue of the magazine appeared—he made no serious effort to fulfill.

A letter to his sister Louisa on February 15 [4] bears ample testimony to the intensity of Hawthorne's feelings:

I came here trusting to Goodrich's positive promise to pay me 45 dollars as soon as I arrived; and he has kept promising from one day to another; till I do not see that he means to pay me at all. I have now broke off all intercourse with him, and never think of going near him. In the first place, he had no business ever to have received the money. I never authorized Bowen to pay it to him; and he must have got it by telling some lie. My mind is pretty much made up about this Goodrich. He is a good-natured sort of man enough; but rather an unscrupulous one in money matters, and not particularly trustworthy in anything. I don't feel at all obliged to him about this Editorship; for he is a stock holder and director in the Bewick Co; and of course it was his interest to get the best man he could; and I defy them to get another to do for a thousand dollars what I do for 500; and furthermore, I have no doubt that Goodrich was authorized to give me 500. He made the best bargain with me he could, and a hard bargain too. This world is as full of rogues as Beelzebub is of fleas.[5]

Whether or not Hawthorne was right in concluding that Goodrich had been actuated only by selfish motives in procuring the editorship for him, it is significant to note that Alden Bradford, Hawthorne's immediate predecessor and successor as editor, thought Hawthorne had been given the position out of personal friendship. In an introductory note to the first number after he took over the editorship following Hawthorne's resignation, Bradford wrote in explanation of his absence of six months from the magazine: "The principal reason for leaving it, in February last, was, the owners of the work were changed,

---

[4] This letter and others cited in the following pages are in the possession of Professor Richard C. Manning and are used here with his permission. Professor Manning Hawthorne has printed most of these letters in *The Colophon* for September, 1939, in a valuable article entitled "Nathaniel and Elizabeth Hawthorne, Editors."

[5] This letter was quoted in part by George Parsons Lathrop (*A Study of Hawthorne*, Boston, 1876, p. 171), with the severest strictures on Goodrich deleted. The Beelzebub mentioned in the last line was the cat of the Hawthorne household.

and they had made arrangements for another editor, from among their particular friends." [6]

Four months passed before Hawthorne received any pay from Goodrich or the Bewick Company. He stuck to his work and needed only a few dollars, but on February 15 he wrote to Louisa for help:

> For the Devil's sake, if you have any money, send me a little. It is now a month since I left Salem, and not a damned cent have I had, except five dollars that I borrowed of Uncle Robert—and out of that I paid my stage fare and other expenses. . . .
>
> I don't want but two or three dollars. Till I receive some of my own, I shall continue to live as I have done. It is well that I have enough to do; or I should have had the blues most damnably here; for of course I have no amusement. My present stock is precisely 34 cts. You must pay for the letter, as my pockets may be entirely empty when it comes. They made me pay for the trunk. . . . I shall come down when I am rich enough. All that I have spent in Boston, except for absolute necessaries has been 9 cents on the first day I came—6 for a glass of wine and three for a cigar. Don't send more than 2 or 3 dollars. Unless I receive a supply, I can send again.

On May 12 Hawthorne wrote to Elizabeth: "I did not receive a cent of money until last Saturday, and then only twenty dollars; and, as you may well suppose, I have undergone very grievous vexations. Unless they pay me the whole amount shortly, I shall return to Salem, and stay till they do."

But Hawthorne came to resent his employment on other scores. "The Bewick Co. are a damned sneaking set," he wrote to Elizabeth on February 10, "or they would have a share in the Athenaeum for the use of the Editor *ex officio*. I have now the liberty of reading there but not taking out books." The books he asked his family to send from Salem did not always reach him on time, if at all; and twice,[7] at least, he wrote in desperation to urge that certain books he had requested be hurried on to him. Hawthorne's letters show, too, that he made a major issue of getting his laundry bundles back from Salem in time to keep his supply of clean shirts and collars from becoming exhausted.[8]

---

[6] III (Oct., 1836), 1.   [7] To Louisa, March 3; to Elizabeth, n.d.

[8] See letters to Louisa, Jan. 21, Feb. 17, March 3; and to Elizabeth, Jan. 25, May 5.

By the first of June the Bewick Company had assigned their property to Samuel Blake to meet the demands of their creditors, and Hawthorne could see no reason for continuing in a position that had become distasteful in every way and held no promise for the future. He stayed to see the August number through the press and then said farewell. The change in his attitude toward the magazine that had come about during his term as editor is pointedly evident when his remarks on his predecessor, Bradford, appended to the March issue are set beside his note of abdication in the August number.[9] At first he had an abundance of praise for Bradford and the policies of the magazine;[10] six months later he made little attempt to veil his resentment against the Bewick Company and expressed the hope, possibly not altogether sincere, that the difficulties confronting the publication might not be insuperable.

Hawthorne by no means had a free rein as editor. In the some eighteen numbers issued before he took charge, as well as in three distinct editorial pronouncements in the earlier pages of the magazine,[11] the nature of the publication and also the policies and editorial methods had been established. Furthermore, the engravings for each issue were chosen by the publishers. Not only was Hawthorne denied the right to reject even the worst of the illustrations, for all of which he was obliged to supply accompanying written matter, but it seems to have been the habit of the publishers to give him far from adequate notice of what embellishments they planned to use in each issue. Thus he was at times forced to provide, al-

[9] Both notes are reprinted in the text.

[10] In the introductory note Bradford published in the first number after he reassumed the editorial duties (III [October, 1836], 1), he acknowledged the compliments Hawthorne had paid him and added in a footnote, surely with more show of resentment than of gratitude and esteem: "Having been particularly engaged in preparing a Volume for publication, the present Editor has not had opportunity to examine the late numbers of the Magazine; but he feels it due to the Editor of those numbers to say, that, as far as he has looked into them, he has seen enough to prove, that there was a desire to preserve the character of the work, according to its original design."

[11] I (Sept., 1834), 1; I (Aug., 1835), 336; II (Sept., 1835), 1–2. The magazine was avowedly in imitation of *The Penny Magazine of the Society for the Diffusion of Useful Knowledge* (London, 1831 ff.); its contents not only were to be informational and practical, but also were to be largely American in nature.

most literally overnight, commentaries on topics he knew nothing about—a threshing-machine, for example, or the armor of Louis XIV's soldiers. Less than a month after he had begun compiling his first issue, Hawthorne wrote to Elizabeth in regard to a life of Hamilton she was preparing, "Perhaps I will get the infernal people to take his head off for the next number." And he added, "Their pen-and-ink sketch can't possibly be worse than their wood scratching. I am ashamed of the whole concern." [12] He did succeed in postponing the engraving and the life of Hamilton until the May issue, but was forced ultimately to complete Elizabeth's article because he had only sudden notice that the engraving was to be included. In explanation to his sister he remarked, "I seldom have more than a day or two's notice." [13] At another time he was faced with the problem of providing a biographical account to accompany a portrait of Jefferson and wrote to ask Elizabeth to provide it, adding, "If you don't, I must; and it is not a subject that suits me." [14]

Little wonder then that, when Hawthorne came to take his farewell of the magazine in his note at the end of the August number, he lamented openly that he had not been allowed full control over the contents and commented in particular that he had not been able to veto objectionable embellishments.

For the most part, Hawthorne's editorial duties entailed the most depressing hackwork. Following the policy already established, he filled each issue with quotations from books and periodicals, with paraphrases or summaries of materials published elsewhere, with combinations of facts and statistics accumulated from various sources, with comments on the illustrations, the quotations, or the paraphrases; but occasionally he supplied accounts of his own observations and original essays.

His methods and his attitude toward his work are clearly enough indicated in his letters to Elizabeth, in which he usually begged for more contributions and explained how she should go about pre-

[12] To Elizabeth, Feb. 5. In a similar vein he once wrote to Louisa (n.d.), "Read this infernal magazine and send your criticisms. To me it appears very dull and respectable—almost worthy of Mr. Bradford himself."

[13] To Elizabeth, March 22.

[14] To Elizabeth, Feb. 10.

paring them. Often his request was urgent. In one letter he asked for her "concoctions, prose and poetical," and concluded, as he did in at least two other letters, with "Concoct—concoct—concoct." [15] To encourage her, he once wrote, "I make nothing of writing a history or biography before dinner. Do you the same." [16] On another occasion he urged her to hurry along her life of Hamilton, saying that she could consult "some biographical dictionary—Allen's, for instance." [17] Again, "In regard to ordinary biographical subjects, my way is to take some old magazine and make an abstract —you can't think how easy it is." [18] Late in March, after having to make changes in one of her contributions, he cautioned, "You should not make quotations; but put other people's thoughts into your own words, and amalgamate the whole into a mass." [19]

But as to the extent and nature of Elizabeth's help no conclusive answer seems possible. Yet there is considerable evidence to indicate that her original contributions were almost negligible and that she busied herself chiefly in making excerpts from books and magazines. Hawthorne seems to have expected her to compose a good many original sketches. In the middle of February he asked her to write a life of Jefferson, comparable to the sketch of Hamilton she was then working on; [20] and a little later he wrote, "Ebe should have sent me some original poetry—and other original concoctions." [21] Regarding a completed number of the magazine, he remarked, "I have written all but about half a page with my own pen; except what Ebe wrote. Let her send more; for I have worked my brain hard enough for this month." [22] Again, "Send back the

[15] To Elizabeth, Jan. 25. Two weeks later he wrote: "You may extract everything good that you come across—provided always it be not too good; and even if it should be, perhaps it will not quite ruin the Magazine; my own selections being bad enough to satisfy anybody. I can't help it" (to Elizabeth, Feb. 10).

[16] *Ibid.*   [17] To [Louisa], Feb. 5.   [18] To Elizabeth, Feb. 10.

[19] To Elizabeth, March 22.

[20] To Elizabeth, Feb. 10; to [Louisa], Feb. 17. A book on Jefferson and Adams was charged against Hawthorne's card at the Salem Athenaeum Library on February 20 ("Books Read by Nathaniel Hawthorne, 1828–1850," *Essex Institute Historical Collections,* LXVIII [Jan., 1932], 65–87).

[21] To [Louisa], March 3.   [22] To [Louisa], n.d.

valise as soon as possible for I am horribly in want of new extracts. Send all you can." [23]

Elizabeth seems to have sent no original poetry, however; Hawthorne was obliged to complete the sketch of Hamilton nearly two months after his sister had begun it; and the life of Jefferson, if ever finished, did not find its way into the magazine. It is worth noting, too, that in the dozen or so letters I have seen, Hawthorne does not imply that his sister wrote any original pieces besides the sketch of Hamilton or that she undertook any others except the life of Jefferson. Furthermore, his repeated instructions as to how she should write and his comment, some two months after they had begun work, that her method in writing the article on Hamilton was wrong, suggest that for the first three issues, at least, she had not done more than one original article of any length.

Two dozen or more books and periodicals from which material was taken for use in the magazine during Hawthorne's editorship were drawn against his card at the Salem Athenaeum Library.[24] They were doubtless borrowed and used by Elizabeth. A check on the references in the magazine to these books shows that almost without exception they were used to supply only direct quotations. These quotations are rather numerous, many of them long, and it is quite probable that they represent the bulk of Elizabeth's assistance in the editorial venture. Thus, without reference to internal evidence,[25] it seems safe to conclude that Hawthorne himself wrote most of the original compositions and also, of course, made many of the abstracts from books.

Hawthorne's remarks in his letters and his instructions to Elizabeth doubtless indicate his method of compiling a good part of the contents of each issue, but even such matter displays his customary mastery of prose style and is enlivened by frequent touches of his own personality. And in the heap of chaff there are several longer

[23] To [Elizabeth], n.d.

[24] Cf. "Books Read by Nathaniel Hawthorne" and the list of Books and Authors at the end of this volume.

[25] For remarks on the style and method of Elizabeth in comparison with Hawthorne's, see n. 20 in the text.

sketches and a good number of brief notes which bear the recognizable stamp of the author's genius and may well be included in the Hawthorne canon. Some of the essays, among them "An Ontario Steamboat" and "The Duston Family," had in all likelihood been composed earlier; but others, such as "April Fools," were probably turned out for the magazine itself.

Approximately a fourth of the contents of each issue came as direct quotation from books or periodicals, for the most part current or of recent date; and some ten or twelve articles were translated from the French. Hawthorne dealt freely with what he quoted from the pages of books, rarely reproducing the matter exactly. More often he adapted the punctuation and phrasing to fit his own style, and not infrequently he spliced excerpts together with transitions of his own making. Avowed paraphrases or summaries of published matter make up another fourth of the contents; and into still another one-fourth went material brought together from sundry sources and fused into pieces of general information, together with Hawthorne's comments on the engravings and on quoted or paraphrased items. Many of these articles were composed of quotations or summaries followed by the editor's comments. The remaining fourth include Hawthorne's own compositions in the nature of essays or brief notes and represent matter gathered from his own experiences or from sundry unidentified sources. Three or four pieces signed by initials appear to have been supplied by outside contributors. During his six months as editor Hawthorne printed a dozen or more poems, some by contemporary American authors and others by Bunyan, Lamb, and Coleridge; and three of the issues followed the precedent set under Bradford's editorship and carried a sheet of music on the back page.

That Hawthorne soon lost any enthusiasm he may have had at the outset and that he found the task too deadening and too exacting may be inferred from the increasingly greater bulk of quoted excerpts with each succeeding issue. After the first two months his long essays and his sketches of a biographical or historical nature became less numerous, and he filled the pages with more passages from books and magazines and with brief notes which required a

minimum of effort. His resentment can be read unmistakably between the lines in several of the articles he found himself compelled to write. In the sketches printed in the April issue along with
the numerous engravings of soldiers and the paraphernalia of war,
for example, the style is plodding and forced; but there are several
Hawthornesque thrusts of facetiousness and mock-seriousness. Even
in writing these obvious space-fillers, he was·able to introduce something of his own moral slant in his general remarks on war. Here
was Hawthorne most conspicuously smarting under the unenlight-
ened dictatorship of his employers; here was the same revulsion
from the material world and its demands that later on he was to feel
as customs officer and as consul, even as Brook Farmer. It is not
surprising, then, that his interest in the editorial venture cooled
early and soon turned to bitter protest. He was able a few years later
to measure coal in Boston and Salem and to interview stranded
Americans in Liverpool. In such work he was unhappy, to be sure,
but he held his rebellion in check. His work for the Bewick Company, though, was a different matter. It meant an infringement on
the realm of his art. Every day brought more painful compromises
with his ideals. The young man who had recalled *Fanshawe* and
destroyed every copy he could lay hands on, who had burned the
"Seven Tales of My Native Land," and who had spent the twelve
lonely years of apprenticeship "under the eaves"—this man could
not reconcile himself long to compiling a monthly hodge-podge of
"useful and entertaining knowledge."

A good proportion of the selections in the present volume can
stand on their own merits. Others of them, we can be sure, Hawthorne would never have given a place among his acknowledged
writings. Yet even these, along with the notebooks and the letters,
have a contribution to make toward an understanding of Hawthorne, man and artist. They indicate what he was reading, what in
his reading attracted him most, and his own estimates of what he
read. True, the realm which he might include was circumscribed by
the editorial policy and methods handed on to him, by the engravings chosen by the publishers, by the words "useful and entertaining knowledge" in the title of the magazine, and by the inter-

ests of his reading public; but there remained some opportunity for him to follow his own inclinations. In truth, on page after page Hawthorne's peculiar characteristics come to light: his interest in early American history, his predilection for moralizing, his comparisons of America with Europe, his concern with such timely matters as the current reform movements, and his interest in the supernatural and in a wide variety of curious information. In the magazine there are short forestudies of some of his later writings, of "Main Street" and "A Bell's Biography," [26] for instance, and also many details that went into the formation of his imaginative works. Here, too, is adequate refutation of the large group of critics who have framed neatly turned statements to the effect that Hawthorne was unaware of the world about him and remained oblivious to the movements that were stirring his contemporaries.[27] When there was occasion, as in the magazine—and Hawthorne did not believe there was occasion in his tales and romances—he spoke with a note of assurance about reform movements, scientific developments, and political questions.

The materials which Hawthorne included in the *American Magazine* fall roughly into five divisions: (1) biographical sketches; (2) accounts of history and geography; (3) information on nature, science, industry, and architecture; (4) literary criticism; and (5) miscellaneous items of curious, paradoxical, or provocative information.[28]

In biography and history Hawthorne evidenced his customary partiality for America of the Colonial and Revolutionary periods, and so included a preponderance of notes on figures, events, and monuments related to early New England. In the biographies his

[26] See text, pp. 159, 185.

[27] See Louis Bromfield, "Hawthorne," *American Writers on American Literature,* ed. John Macy, New York, 1931, p. 98; Francis Gribble, "Hawthorne from an English Point of View," *The Critic,* XLV (July, 1904), 65; Theodore T. Munger, "Notes on *The Scarlet Letter,*" *The Atlantic Monthly,* XCIII (April, 1904), 523; Hattie Tyng Griswold, *Home Life of Great Authors,* Chicago, 1913, p. 211; W. C. Brownell, *American Prose Masters,* New York, 1925, p. 102.

[28] This division has been followed for the arrangement of the material in this volume. Within each section the selections appear in the same order as in the pages of the magazine.

method was much the same as in the sketches that make up *Grand-father's Chair:* his custom was to choose one episode from the life of his subject and to elaborate on it, passing briefly over the remaining incidents.[29] The biography of John Adams is a good example. Hawthorne's sense for the symbolic and the ironic was so pricked by Adams's interview with King George soon after the Revolution had ended that he dwelt at length on that interview, interpolating a wealth of concrete and dramatic detail. In a few instances he dealt with contemporary figures and events. The May number contains, for example, a sketch of the life of John C. Calhoun. But here Hawthorne was careful to avoid the dangerous issues of the Bank and the tariff and nullification and slavery. "But our narrative," he wrote when his account had reached the struggle between Jackson and Calhoun, "has now brought us to forbidden ground, where the embers of faction are still smouldering, and may scorch our feet, if we venture farther." On another occasion he wrote with reference to a volume of Thomas Green Fessenden's poems he was reviewing: "Some of these passages it would violate the neutrality of our Magazine to extract." More than once he alluded to the threatened war with France in 1835 and 1836. Other historical material includes a few notes on the Cromwellian era in England and some passing items about the American Indians, as well as a number of minor notes on world history unusual or exotic enough to catch his attention. The same interests, all of these, that Hawthorne evidenced in his tales and romances.

The nature and purpose of the *American Magazine* demanded that Hawthorne include a generous amount of "useful" information, but the issues which he compiled contain a smaller proportion of articles on such practical subjects as the cultivation of flowers and potatoes and strawberries, the production of sugar, and the mining of salt than had appeared before he became editor. Pursuing his interests, Hawthorne selected sundry unusual items from the realms of nature, science, and industry—frequently items that he might

---

[29] Cf. the account of Governor Phipps in *Grandfather's Chair, The Writings of Nathaniel Hawthorne,* Old Manse ed., Boston, 1900, XII, 69–78. Unless stated otherwise, all subsequent references to Hawthorne's works are to this edition.

have embodied in stories as striking manifestations of abstract ideas. He wrote a note, for example, on a gas spring, another on the discovery of fossils in England, and yet a third on the unearthing of ruins in Mexico. Furthermore, he showed a marked fondness for the phases of medical science bordering on the miraculous—for instance, the length of the life-span in various regions of the globe and the possibilities of lengthening man's life on earth. There is also ample evidence in the magazine to prove that Hawthorne was cognizant of the practical world about him. The innovations in military science, the advancements made by the railroads, the current explorations, the interest in phrenology, the developments in practical architecture—all come in for comment. And there is an abundance of notes on queer scientific facts and novelties of invention. It is not difficult to catch in these items gleams of the mind that produced "The Birthmark," "Rappaccini's Daughter," "Dr. Heidegger's Experiment," "A Virtuoso's Collection," and *Septimius Felton*.

Criticism of art and literature in the magazine is not bulky. There are a few comments on the better known painters and sculptors and a dozen or more literary pronouncements—two or three in the nature of full book reviews or critical estimates, but some of them no more than casual remarks by way of introducing books from which quotations have been taken. Bunyan's *The Life and Death of Mr. Badman* is discussed at some length, and Thomas Green Fessenden's poems are appraised in several complimentary paragraphs.[30] In the sketch of John C. Calhoun, Hawthorne takes occasion to set down some of his views on the writing of biography.

Among the pieces most characteristic of Hawthorne, as he has revealed himself elsewhere in his writings, are the sketches involving his remarks on crime and sin, his attitude toward the past, his fondness for moralizing, and his interest in the efforts at reform. From the *State Trials* and other sources he gathered a number of accounts of crimes and court trials—suitable and essential materials for

---

[30] Hawthorne was doubtless prompted to review Fessenden's poems because he was staying with the Fessendens at the time (see *Hawthorne's Writings*, XVII, 53). Some two years later he wrote a sketch of Fessenden's life for *The American Monthly Magazine* (V [Jan., 1838], 30–40).

his preoccupation with sin. In one sketch he developed the idea that guilt is contagious, and that hence the crimes of the past should not be handed down in records—a thesis later presented fully and forcefully through the mouth of Holgrave in *The House of the Seven Gables*.

The plea for reform was sounded far less frequently and less vigorously by Hawthorne than by his predecessors in the editorial chair,[31] but in his half a dozen issues he found room for at least a score of comments on the questions of woman's rights, capital punishment, and temperance; and he called attention again and again to the evils of war. His protests against dueling assume added significance when we recall that within two years he was to stop barely short of a duel himself and his friend Jonathan Cilley was to lose his life in a duel.[32]

Hawthorne's moralizing tone and outlook are much in evidence in the *American Magazine*. Here, as was habitual with him, he was able to see in every significant happening or character an outward manifestation of some abstract idea, and he was ever free in pointing a meaning for any factual information he set down. The morals, often paradoxical in nature, which he frequently drew at the conclusion of quotations or paraphrases are much like the morals pointed in the concluding paragraphs of his tales and sketches. For example, after relating that in Mexico it was the custom in a certain religious ceremony to deify a slave for forty days and then sacrifice him, Hawthorne remarked that so it is with man: he is often nearest to destruction when he appears to be highest. There are numerous other notes to indicate that Hawthorne saw some moral or symbolic significance in virtually every item from history or nature: He remarked that there is a pleasant smell at the foot of the rainbow. If there is truth in the legend that the grass is paler in a martyr's path, he asserted, New England, and Salem in particular, should have much bleached grass. A quotation in which Pepys tells of kissing the lips of a dead queen suggested the question of

[31] The pages of the magazine before Hawthorne's time inveighed vigorously and repeatedly against capital punishment, slavery, tobacco, intoxicants, and all varieties of intemperance.

[32] See Woodberry, pp. 78, 79.

whether the putrefying body of a queen would smell better than "meaner clay." And again he declared that the magnificence of the church has nothing to do with the righteousness of the congregation. There is one ironic observation, especially typical of Hawthorne, that, whereas certain Spanish priests blessed and then shot their besiegers, the New England clergymen shot the Indians without blessing them.

Hawthorne the editor and drudging compiler had in common with Hawthorne the writer of tales and romances much of the same ironic and satiric approach, but in the *American Magazine* he evidenced more of lightness and humor than was his custom. Here are a few jokes included for their own sake, as well as a few puns. Some of the longer sketches show a humor of plan and method of development paralleled perhaps only in "The Celestial Railroad" among his other writings. "April Fools" is possibly the best example in the magazine of his restrained, ironic humor; but others make use of a freer and more robust humor, as in the description of the armor worn by medieval knights.

In these selections, then, we have an abundance of hackwork, it is true. Here, to be sure, we find the romancer engaged in downright journalistic drudgery, turning out summaries and paraphrases. But Hawthorne could touch nothing without leaving his stamp on it—his peculiar moral and allegorical slant, his own turn of thought and phrase, in short, the stamp of his own individuality. These writings, therefore, have a place, alongside the notebooks and the lesser tales and sketches, in explaining Hawthorne the man and the genius.

BIOGRAPHY

Washington

What American has not beheld the majestic features of WASH-
INGTON!—A generation has been born, and arrived at middle
age, since he departed. Yet, were it possible that his illustrious shade
should return, to mark the mighty growth of the country which he
made a nation—were he to walk, in visible shape, the streets of our
cities, not one among the crowd but would know Washington; were
he to enter the most solitary farm-house, its inmates would at once
recognise their awful guest; were he to visit that far western region,
which he left a wilderness, the population of its busy towns would
bow before him; or were he to pause near a New England school-
house, the group of children round the door would gaze at him,
and whisper—'It is Washington, our Father!'

In some of its innumerable representations, his face must have
met every eye. His figure in Italian marble, wrought with the
noblest sculpture, looks down from its pedestal upon the delibera-
tions of our legislative halls. His bust is seen in the niches of our
galleries, and his picture, with the calm dignity which every painter
of Washington has thrown over the canvass, meets our gaze upon
the walls. His statue, indeed, has not yet taken its destined place,
beneath the dome of the Capitol. But the chisel of an American sculptor [1] is even now re-creating the form, from which the nation, and

[1] Through the efforts of James Fenimore Cooper, Horatio Greenough (1805–52)
was chosen by Congress to execute a statue of Washington for the National Capitol.
Greenough's conception was grand, and he worked almost eight years on the statue.
But when it was completed (1843), it became the butt of numerous journalistic thrusts,
especially after it proved to be too heavy for the floor of the Capitol and was placed
outside the building. In view of Hawthorne's dislike for nude statues (see text, p. 138

posterity, shall receive its idea of the living presence of Washington. The successful accomplishment of this most honourable task is worth the toil of a life-time, and will satisfy the loftiest aspirations of the artist, by indissolubly connecting his fame with the immortality of his subject. Yet, were the mein [*sic*] and aspect of Washington preserved only in the statues, busts, and pictures, which adorn our halls of state, our galleries of art, and the mansions of the wealthy, such honours alone would not distinguish him from the vulgar crowd of heroes, who have grown illustrious by the ruin of their country, and to the sorrow of the world. It is a far surer token of the universal reverence which hallows his memory, that his waxen image keeps its place among those of the great men of the day, who figure at a country show—that the village painter tries his skill upon that noble face, and hangs the unworthy effigy before the tavern-door—that the silver medal,[2] which was struck after his death, bearing his urn and profile, is treasured by the poor—and, more than all, that prints of Washington, dark with smoke, are pasted over the hearths of so many American homes. And long may he be there! No cottage should be without his likeness, no mansion without his picture, no legislative hall without his statue, that rich and poor, the highest statesman and the humblest citizen, may have him always before their eyes, and copy, each according to his station, the public and private virtues of Washington.

We here present a portrait of the Father of our Country,[3] as the first of a series of vignettes of the successive Presidents of the

---

and n. 144) there is something of irony in his high expectations of this statue—it shows Washington nude above the waist.

[2] Hawthorne's allusion here is to the medal struck in 1800 and described as follows (James Ross Snowden, *A Description of the Medals of Washington*, Philadelphia, 1861, p. 31):

Obverse. Bust of Washington, in civil dress, facing the right. *Legend.* GEORGE WASHINGTON, OB: 14 DEC[R]. 1799. AE: 68. *Reverse.* Branches of oak and laurel inclosing the inscription. THE HERO OF FREEDOM, THE PRIDE OF HIS COUNTRY AND ORNAMENT OF HUMAN NATURE. 1800. Above is a bundle of arrows. *Legend.* LATE PRESIDENT OF THE UNITED STATES OF AMERICA. *Size* 23.

[3] This portrait, signed by Alonzo Hartwell, one of the engravers forming the Boston Bewick Company, fills four-fifths of the first page of the March issue.

United States. The bust of Washington is represented on a pedestal, amid the battle-smoke and lowering clouds, but with a radiance brightening about his head, prophetic of the peaceful prosperity which his skill and valour won for us. Military emblems are displayed around him; there are the stars and stripes, which he reared so high among the banners of the nations, and there the cap which he placed on the triumphant head of Liberty; while the cannon, the musket and bayonet, the war-like drum, the pyramid of balls, and other martial insignia, are strewn at the base of the pedestal. In the back-ground, is seen the famous Passage of the Delaware. On the right, the chief figure among a group of officers, sits Washington on horseback, and downward to the bank of the river goes the ponderous artillery and all the military array. On the left, the troops are embarking, some already in the midst of the river, and others just pushing from the strand. This scene has been worthily selected to adorn the vignette of Washington; for it was one of the hero's greatest military exploits, by which, at the darkest period of the Revolution, he not only escaped a superiour enemy, but surprised and captured a large body of Hessian troops, at Trenton; and thus gave another aspect to the war.

These emblems refer exclusively to Washington's military deeds. —But it should never be forgotten, that it is not merely in the character of a hero, that his fame shines resplendent, and will remain undimmed by the gathering mist of ages. It is true, that no other man possessed the peculiar military talent, the caution mingled with boldness, the judgment, the equanimity which never sank too low nor rose too high, that were requisite to carry us triumphantly through the Revolutionary contest. Yet it may be justly said, that, even while the war was raging, his civil virtues and abilities held no inferiour place to those which marked him as a soldier. It was his moral strength of character that gave firmness to a tottering cause. Other great generals have been idolized by their armies, because victory was sure to follow where they led; their fame has been won by triumphant marches, and conquest on every field. Fortune has been the better half of all their deeds. But his defeats never snatched one laurel from the brow of Washington. In him, his

soldiers recognised qualities far superiour to those of the mere
military chieftain, and gave him their confidence as unreservedly
at Long Island, as at Yorktown. And, in the troubled times that succeeded the Revolution, no influence but Washington's could have
harmonized the discordant elements of our country; no other arm
could have upheld the State.

If, therefore, they could have been visible amid the war-smoke
and the thunder-cloud, the artist would have mingled tokens of the
peaceful virtues, and the statesman's calmer wisdom, with those
heroic emblems. A canopy of state, to represent his civil sway—a
horn of plenty, scattering its abundance on the soil—a written scroll,
to denote the power of his pen—a Bible, to point out his trust, in
doubt and danger—a bounteous harvest-field, instead of warriors
and steeds, and a wintry river—all these might have been fitly seen
around the bust of Washington. In our pride of country, let it be
the proudest thought, that America, in the very struggle that
brought her into existence as a nation, gave to history the purest and
loftiest name that ever shone among its pages.

(March, pp. 265-66)

Major General Lincoln [4]

General Lincoln was a Massachusetts man, and born of reputable
parentage, in the year 1733, at Hingham, a town long famous for
wooden ware. He received a common school education, and spent
the early part of his life in the homely New England way, toiling
on his hereditary farm, and performing the duties of town-clerk,
representative, and other honourable offices, both civil and military.
At the breaking out of the Revolution, he was more than forty
years old, and like a thousand other gentleman farmers in the
province, had cherished his wife, ruled his household, and plowed
his own furrow, ever since the age of manhood. On the day of
Lexington battle, being the Colonel of the second regiment of Suffolk militia, he mustered his men for the field, but was prevented

---

[4] This sketch is accompanied by a small woodcut of the bust of Lincoln.

from marching by the news of the flight of the British forces back to Boston. In February, 1776, he was made a Brigadier, and in May of the same year, a Major General of the State militia, and received the latter rank in the Continental army, early in 1777.

Being stationed at Bound Brook, on the Raritan, he had an extent of five or six miles to guard, with a force of less than five hundred men, fit for duty. On the thirteenth of April, owing to the negligence of his patroles, he was surprised by a large party of the enemy, under Cornwallis [5] and Grant,[6] who came upon him so suddenly, that the General and one of his aids had barely time to get on horseback. The other aid was taken, as were also a few pieces of artillery. On account of his popularity with the New England militia, Lincoln was now sent to join the northern army, under Schuyler,[7] and afterwards under Gates,[8] to whose success at Saratoga he materially contributed. But, in one of the conflicts that preceded Burgoyne's [9] surrender, Lincoln, as he passed with his aids from one part of the line to another, perceived a small body of troops in the German uniform, near the point whither he was riding. As many of the American soldiers wore captured uniforms, the General conceived that this party was of the number, and was galloping up to take the command, when the Germans let fly a volley and hit him in the leg. The wound was very severe, compelling him to retire from the seat of war, first to Albany, and afterwards to Hingham; nor (though he resumed his duties in the course of the following Summer,) did he entirely recover his health for several years.

At the request of the delegates from South Carolina, General Lincoln was next placed in command of the Southern Department. In December, 1778, he arrived at Charleston, having fallen from his

[5] Charles Cornwallis (1737–1805), general in the British army.

[6] James Grant (1720–1806) served in the British army in the French and Indian Wars and through the Revolution.

[7] Philip John Schuyler (1733–1804) saw service with the British forces in the French and Indian Wars and then with the American army during the Revolution.

[8] Horatio Gates (c. 1728–1806), an officer in the American Revolutionary army, was in command at Saratoga.

[9] John Burgoyne (1722–92), general in the British army.

carriage on the way thither, and grievously injured his knee. The difficulties of his present command were such as to preclude any very brilliant exploit; and some of the southern people expressed their discontent, in such a manner that it reached the General's ear, and, with other reasons, induced him to solicit a recall. But the Governour and Council of South Carolina, with General Moultrie [10] and the principal inhabitants, persuaded him to continue at the head of the department. In the winter of 1779 and 1780, Sir Henry Clinton [11] having set on foot an expedition against South Carolina, the General resolved to defend Charleston; and accordingly sustained a siege from the thirtieth of March till the eleventh of the following May. Then, the principal inhabitants and county militia having petitioned for a surrender, and the militia of the town having thrown down their arms; the troops being worn down with fatigue, and nothing to eat but rice, nor half enough of that; there being nine thousand men of the flower of the British army, within twenty yards of the American lines, besides their naval force and a great number of blacks; his own troops amounting to but two thousand five hundred, part of whom had refused to act; the cannon being dismounted, or silenced for want of ammunition; the citizens discontented; and affairs generally in a hopeless state; Lincoln found it necessary to ask terms of capitulation. The country did him justice. He continued to enjoy the respect and confidence of Congress and the Commander in Chief; and by his long defence, the plans of the British were frustrated, and North Carolina saved from their dominion, during the remainder of the.year.

General Lincoln returned to Hingham on parole, and was exchanged in the November following. At Yorktown, he commanded a central division with great credit, and was deputed by General Washington to receive the sword of the vanquished commander, as a requital for the misfortune of giving up his own, at Charleston. In October, 1781, without losing his rank in the army, he was appointed

[10] William Moultrie (c. 1730–1805) was a general in the Revolutionary War and was later a prominent statesman in South Carolina, serving the state as governor for two terms, 1785–87 and 1793–95.

[11] Sir Henry Clinton (c. 1738–95) was a British general who saw service in Boston, New York, Philadelphia, and South Carolina.

Secretary of War, and retained that office for the next two years; when he resigned it with a high eulogium from Congress. He now betook himself to his farm again, till, during Shay's [*sic*] War,[12] he was put at the head of the militia of Massachusetts, and gained an almost bloodless victory over the insurgents, at Petersham. He was afterwards elected Lieutenant Governour. In 1789, he was appointed Collector of Boston, and, in the Autumn of the same year, while proceeding to the South, as a Commissioner to treat with the Creek Indians, he visited Mount Vernon, and enjoyed another meeting with his old Commander in Chief. After these good services, and in the enjoyment of his well-won honours, General Lincoln died of natural decay, on the 9th of May, 1810, in the seventy-seventh year of his age.

General Henry Lee, of Virginia, in his Memoirs of the War,[13] has said that 'Lincoln was a good, but not a consummate soldier.' The judgment is a fair one. In our view, it would have detracted from the character in which we would hold him up to the observation of our readers, had his soldiership been perfect. Few men have a better claim to be remembered by posterity, than General Lincoln, but not on the score of splendid achievements, or deep knowledge of the military art, or a natural genius for war. He is an admirable example of what the New England soldier generally has been, and always ought to be—a man of plain good sense and respectable abilities, which he exercised in peaceful pursuits, till the situation of his country made him leave the ploughshare for the sword. He then set his mind to work, with its native force, upon the new business of warfare, and accomplished it well.[14]

Trained soldiers could find little to criticise in his management of

[12] Shays's Rebellion, led by Daniel Shays (1747–1825), was an insurrection in Massachusetts at the end of 1786 and the beginning of 1787.

[13] *Memoirs of the War in the Southern Department of the United States,* Philadelphia, 1812, I, 75: "Upright, mild, and amiable, he was universally respected and beloved; a truly good man, and a brave and prudent, but not consummate, soldier." General Henry Lee (1756–1818), known as "Light-Horse Harry" Lee, served during the Revolution and later was in charge of the forces to suppress the Whisky Rebellion. He was elected to Congress in 1785 and was governor of Virginia, 1792–95.

[14] For other comments of Hawthorne's on the character of the American soldier, see text, pp. 77, 87–88, 153–55.

a battle or a siege. He might be pretty confidently relied upon, to do all that ought to be done, whether in attack or defence, with the means committed to his charge. With such leaders—and there will be enough of them in every contest—we need never fear that an enemy should step far within our borders, or remain there long.

(March, pp. 267–68)

Commodore Dale [15]

Richard Dale, a distinguished naval officer of the Revolution, was a native of Virginia, and born in Norfolk county, in the year 1756. He early showed that strong predilection for the sea, which appears to be an innate propensity in most of those who are destined to signalize themselves by maritime exploits, whether of battle or discovery. At the age of twelve, he made a voyage to Liverpool, and from that period, till the war opened a more congenial field for his activity, he continued in the merchant service. In 1776, he was appointed lieutenant of an armed ship which had been fitted out by the state of Virginia. While cruising in James river, in one of the boats of this vessel, he was captured by a tender of the Liverpool frigate, and put on board a British prison-ship, at Norfolk.

Dale was at this time but twenty years old, and having spent his youth and part of his boyhood on the ocean, can scarcely be supposed to have studied the great principles of the Revolution with that reflective spirit, which influenced the conduct of elder patriots. He had drawn his sword for liberty in the heat of an ardent and adventurous temperament, that made him rush into the conflict, without much caring on which side he fought. It is not therefore a matter of surprise, that, under great temptations, he should, for a brief period, have wavered in his fidelity to the righteous cause. While imprisoned at Norfolk, he was visited by Bridges Gutteridge, an old schoolmate, who, like himself, had followed the sea, and now commanded a tender in the British service. Gutteridge found little difficulty in persuading his friend to make a cruise with him

---

[15] A small woodcut of Dale precedes this sketch.

up the Rappahannock. But Dale was soon punished for his inconstancy. In an engagement with a fleet of pilot-boats, several of Gutteridge's men were killed, and our hero was severely wounded by a musket-ball, which hit him in a part where wounds and death are generally synonymous—the head. Dale seems to have taken this rap on the cranium as a strong hint to reflect seriously on his past conduct: which he accordingly did, and resolved never again, as he expressed it, to 'put himself in the way of the balls of his country.'

After his recovery, being doubtful of his reception among the friends of liberty, he sailed for Bermuda, but was captured on his passage by Commodore John Barry,[16] of whom we gave a notice in the last number of the Magazine. After an explanation with the Commodore, Dale reentered the American service as a midshipman. Not long afterwards, he was taken by the British frigate Liverpool, and having been exchanged, was appointed to the United States ship Lexington. The latter vessel, on her passage from Morlaix in France to America, fell in with an English ten-gun cutter, which, though inferiour in size, proved an over-match for the Yankee ship. Such was the criminal and almost incredible lack of preparation on board the Lexington, that, while traversing a sea that was thronged with the enemy, her cannon were not in a state to be fired; nor, in the beginning of the engagement, could they be discharged, except by the flash of a musket. These difficulties were so far remedied during the battle, as to enable the crew to fire away all their shot, besides a large quantity of old iron; when, the slaughter having been great, especially of officers, the Americans were compelled to strike their flag. They were carried to England and confined in the Mill Prison at Plymouth, where all, officers and crew together, were implicated in a charge of high treason. So severe was the treatment to which they were subjected, in common with the other American prisoners, that a general sympathy was excited; and sixteen or seventeen thousand pounds were subscribed, to supply them with some of the comforts of life.

[16] Commodore John Barry (1745–1803) of the American navy. The March issue of the magazine (pp. 285–86) contains a sketch of Barry's life, which Hawthorne doubtless wrote but which has been omitted from this volume.

After a confinement of considerable length, Dale, in company with Captain Johnson,[17] his former commander, contrived to escape, and travelled from Plymouth to London. They there took passage on board a trading vessel, bound to Dunkirk, and were proceeding down the Thames, when their progress was stopped by a press-gang, who had been sent expressly in pursuit of the fugitives. Dale and Johnson were now carried back to the Mill Prison and thrown into the Black Hole; a noisome dungeon, well worthy of its name. After a durance of forty days, they were restored to the same footing with the rest of the prisoners; but Dale, whose spirit nothing could break or depress, was sentenced to another term in the Black Hole, for the crime of singing 'rebellious songs.' Finally, in 1779, the bold mariner again made his escape, and, by dexterous management, procured a passport for his passage to France. On arriving at the port of L'Orient, he became acquainted with the famous John Paul Jones, who, recognising Dale as a kindred spirit, immediately received him as master's mate, and soon after appointed him his first lieutenant in the Bon Homme Richard. This was an old East Indiaman, unfit for a fighting vessel in her best days, and now almost unseaworthy; but any ship would have been a ship of war, while John Paul Jones walked her quarter-deck. If she possessed no fighting properties, that valiant adventurer could create them.

The Bon Homme Richard sailed from L'Orient, in the Summer of 1779, and cruised in the North Sea, spreading alarm along the western coast of Scotland, where Paul Jones had been born and spent his youth. In company with Jones were the Alliance, the Pallas, and the Revenge; but the squadron appears not to have acted in concert, or, at least, to have acknowledged neither of the captains as its commodore. On the nineteenth of September, off Flamborough Head, on the northeast coast of England, they discovered a fleet of several hundred sail, homeward bound from the Baltic, under convoy of the frigate Serapis, and the Countess of Scarborough,

[17] Captain Henry Johnson had been in command of the *Lexington*. See Gardner W. Allen, *A Naval History of the American Revolution*, Boston, 1913, I, 152, 267–76.

a sloop of war. On perceiving the enemy, the frigate made signals to the merchant vessels, which immediately scudded for the neighbouring coast, leaving the Serapis and her consort to fight it out with Paul Jones and his companions. Captain Cottineau,[18] of the Pallas, engaged the Countess of Scarborough; but the Alliance kept aloof during the greater part of the conflict which ensued; and when she did interfere, it was so clumsily, that her shot struck the Bon Homme Richard quite as often as the Serapis. Paul Jones was therefore matched single-handed with the Serapis, a superiour ship in weight of metal, and manned with a first-rate crew; while the Bon Homme Richard's having been recruited in a French port, were a rabble of all nations, many of whom could not understand each other's language.

The battle began at dark, and was more full of strange and impressive incidents, of sudden changes of fortune, and acts of desperate valour, than any other engagement between two single ships, that is recorded in naval annals. The vessels were lashed so close together, that, in loading the cannon, the rammers of each protruded through the port-holes of the other; and thus they discharged their shot against an enemy who stood almost within arm's length. Several times, the vessels were set on fire by the wads of the guns, and threw up sheets of flame, which, ascending above the smoke that enveloped their hulls, seemed about to involve both parties in one destruction. The gun-deck of the Bon Homme Richard was blown up by the bursting of some of her cannon; an accident which cost many of her crew their lives. The Serapis was equally unfortunate, in the explosion of a large quantity of powder on her deck. At one period, the Bon Homme Richard being reported as sinking, the master-at-arms let loose all the prisoners from the hold, who accordingly broke forth among the crew, some half-dead with fear, others ready to bear a hand in the battle, and all contributing their share to the terrours of the scene. On both sides, the boarders made des-

[18] Denis Nicholas Cottineau (1746–1808), a native of France, had served formerly in the French navy. He commanded the *Pallas* in Paul Jones's engagement, described here by Hawthorne, with the British squadron under Pearson.

perate assaults, and were as desperately repelled. This terrible business went on till midnight, when the Serapis struck the flag which she had so gallantly defended; and the American crew being removed on board the conquered ship, the Bon Homme Richard soon after sunk, going down victorious to the depths of ocean, which alone could cleanse her blood-stained deck. Each ship had lost forty-seven men killed and sixty-four wounded. Whatever glory may be won in naval war, should crown the victors in this battle; and even the vanquished should wear a greener laurel than the conquerors in most other fights.

Lieutenant Dale distinguished himself, and received a wound, which he scarcely felt till the excitement of the contest was over. He next served under Captain Nicholson,[19] on board the Trumbull of thirty-two guns, which vessel was soon captured by a British frigate and sloop of war. Dale was again wounded, and found himself for the fifth time a prisoner. Being exchanged, he sailed as chief officer, and afterwards as captain of the Queen of France, an armed merchantman; and continued in the command of her till the close of the Revolution. In 1794, he was one of the six captains who were appointed from the merchant service to the navy of the United States. In 1801, he had command of the Mediterranean squadron, in which capacity he protected the American commerce from the meditated depredations of the Barbary corsairs. Having returned to the United States in 1802, he was again appointed to the Mediterranean station, but under circumstances which, he conceived, would have rendered it injurious to his honour to accept the command. He therefore retired from the navy.

The active, bold, and enterprising character of Commodore Dale may be estimated from the numerous incidents, which we have been compelled to crowd into the foregoing hasty narrative. The decline of his life was as peaceful as his youth had been stirring and adventurous, and he died in 1826, at the age of seventy years.

(*April, pp. 320–21*)

[19] Captain James Nicholson (*c.* 1737–1804), with the assistance of Dale and a small crew, was able to hold the *Trumbull* for a time against overwhelming odds (1781).

Alexander Hamilton [20]

To none of the eminent men of the Revolution are we more indebted than to Hamilton, both for his services in the course of that memorable contest, and for the sagacity with which, at its close, he discerned the political necessities of the country, and assisted in laying the foundations of our present prosperity. He saw, perhaps, more clearly than most other statesmen of that period, how greatly the future welfare of the people depended upon the developement of those resources which could only be drawn forth by the pervading influence of an energetic government. Nor be it imputed

[20] A major portion of the life of Hamilton was written by Elizabeth. She evidently made a beginning by the first of February, building her sketch largely out of excerpts and abstracts from the first volume of John Church Hamilton's *The Life of Alexander Hamilton* (New York, 1834). Her article grew to the requisite length but did not complete the span of Hamilton's life, and she seems to have been very hesitant about bringing it to a close. Early in February Hawthorne suggested that she could· "finish her life of Hamilton by consulting some biographical dictionary—Allen's, for instance" (letter to [Louisa], Feb. 5); and during the following month and a half before Elizabeth sent her MS. to him, he wrote at least three requests (Feb. 10 and 17 and March 17) that she finish her article. Then on March 22 he wrote, "You need proceed no further with Hamilton. As the press was in want of him, I have been compelled to finish his life myself, this forenoon. . . . I approve of your life; but have been obliged to correct some of your naughty notions about arbitrary government. You should not make quotations; but put other people's thought into your own words, and amalgamate the whole into a mass" (to Elizabeth, March 22).

In the light of these remarks it is not difficult to determine Elizabeth's part and Hawthorne's part in the sketch of Hamilton, and internal evidence alone would be conclusive enough. The first paragraph was doubtless from Hawthorne's pen, included to correct her "naughty notions about arbitrary government." Then follow his sister's abstracts from the full-length life in her hands, and the last four paragraphs are Hawthorne's. The differences in style and method are readily apparent. Elizabeth's passages proceed with mincing steps, never getting far from her original, and she gets no farther than the year 1777. When Hawthorne takes over, he disposes of the rest of the war period in one short paragraph, apparently keeping in it something from Elizabeth's manuscript, and continues to traverse the remaining years of Hamilton's life with long swinging strides that allow him to touch only the high points and at the same time to offer some apology for Hamilton's leanings toward a strong federal government.

This biographical essay follows a full-page woodcut of the figure of Hamilton (see the final paragraph of the sketch), which introduces the May number.

to him as a crime, if his opinions on this subject went to an extent, which, by the light of subsequent experience, we are now wise enough to shun. Even the errour of those opinions probably contributed to our welfare; and his fame is destined to 'grow with the growth, and strengthen with the strength' [21] of that Union, which it was his warmest wish to render indissoluble.

Alexander Hamilton was born in the island of Nevis, in January, 1757. On the maternal side, he was of French extraction; his father was a descendant of the noble Scottish family of Hamilton. His childhood afforded many indications of talent, and at the age of thirteen, his ambition seems to have been as intense as at any subsequent period of his life. He was then in the counting-house of an opulent merchant of Santa Cruz; and, in a letter to a school-fellow, he 'confesses that his ambition is prevalent, so that he contemns the grovelling condition of a clerk, or the like, to which his fortune condemns him, and would willingly risk his life, though not his character, to exalt his station. He wishes there was a war.' Yet he was exceedingly assiduous in the duties of his situation, and evinced such a capacity for business, that before he attained his fourteenth year, Mr. Cruger,[22] his employer, confided to him the conduct of his extensive establishment, during his absence on a visit to the American continent. He afterwards frequently adverted to this occupation as the most useful part of his education; he acquired in its details a method and facility peculiarly advantageous to the future Financier. Its teachings were practical, and therefore well suited to the practical character of his mind.

Shortly after this time, some of the West Indian islands were desolated by a hurricane, of which Hamilton wrote, and published in a newspaper, a description which attracted much notice, and induced his friends to yield to his wishes for a more liberal education

[21] Pope's *Essay on Man*, Epistle II, l. 136: "Grows with his growth, and strengthens with his strength."

[22] Nicholas Cruger, a wealthy merchant at Santa Cruz. These paragraphs track very closely J. C. Hamilton's life of his father, from which the quotations are drawn; and the awkward turning here of direct into indirect discourse, with the quotation marks retained, shows the work of Elizabeth's unskilled hand (cf. *The Life of Alexander Hamilton*, I, 4–5).

than his native island could afford. Accordingly, at the age of fifteen, he took passage for New York, and soon after became a student of King's College, then under the Presidency of the Rev. Dr. Cooper.[23] His acquaintance with miscellaneous literature was at this time extensive; he had made some progress in the study of mathematics, and of chemistry, which he afterwards recommended as a science, 'well adapted to excite curiosity, and create new combinations of thoughts.' Some of his early compositions in verse have been preserved, displaying much poetical talent. His favourite authors were Pope and Plutarch; but he also perused, with great interest, works of controversial divinity. 'While a student at King's College,' says his friend, Col. Troup,[24] 'he was attentive to public worship, and in the habit of praying on his knees night and morning. I lived in the same room with him for some time, and have often been powerfully affected by the fervour and eloquence of his prayers. He had read many of the polemical writers on religious subjects, and was a zealous believer in the fundamental doctrines of Christianity. I confess, that the arguments with which he was accustomed to justify his belief, have tended in no small degree to confirm my own faith in revealed religion.'

But the whole intensity of Hamilton's character was soon to be elicited by that Revolution, whose perils placed him in his appropriate sphere of action, and in which no other man, so young as himself, was so enviably distinguished. His earliest impressions were favourable to the rights of the crown; but these were speedily effaced, and feelings more befitting his future career awakened, by a visit to Boston, soon after the destruction of the tea. Massachusetts was, from the beginning, in Hamilton's own words, 'the pivot on which the Revolution turned,' and the excitement of the public mind was never greater than at that time. Hamilton returned to

---

[23] Dr. Myles Cooper (1735–85) came to America in 1762 and in the following year became president of King's College. He was a violent Tory, and because of Loyalist pamphlets which he wrote during the Revolution he was mobbed and had to flee to England.

[24] Colonel Robert Troup (1757–1832), Hamilton's most intimate friend during his days at King's College, served in the Revolutionary War and was subsequently a prominent lawyer. This quotation comes from a letter written by Troup (*ibid.*, I, 10).

New York, strong in zeal and in argument, and on the sixth of July, 1774, at the age of seventeen, made his first essay as an Orator, and publicly pledged his devotion to the cause of liberty. It was at a large assemblage of the citizens, long remembered as 'the great meeting in the fields.' He had previously been in the habit of 'walking several hours each day under the shade of some large trees in Batteau, now Dey street, talking to himself in an under tone of voice, apparently engaged in deep thought; a practice which he continued through life. This circumstance attracted the attention of his neighbours, to whom he was known as the Young West Indian, and led them to engage in conversation with him. One of them, re-marking the vigour and maturity of his thoughts, urged him to ad-dress this meeting to which all the patriots were looking with the greatest interest. From this seeming intrusion he at first recoiled; but, after listening attentively to the respective speakers, and finding several points untouched, he presented himself to the assembled mul-titude. The novelty of the attempt, his youthful countenance, his slender and diminutive form, awakened curiosity and attracted at-tention. Overawed by the scene, before him, he at first hesitated and faltered; but, as he proceeded almost unconsciously to utter his accustomed reflections, his mind warmed with the theme, his en-ergies were recovered, and after a discussion, clear, cogent and novel, of the great principles involved in the controversy, he depicted in glowing colours the long continued and long endured oppressions of the mother country, he insisted on the duty of resistance, pointed to the means and certainty of success, and described the waves of rebellion sparkling with fire, and washing back on the shores of England the wrecks of her power, her wealth, and her glory. The breathless silence ceased as he closed, and the whispered murmur, 'it is a Collegian! it is a Collegian!' was lost in loud expressions of wonder and applause, at the extraordinary eloquence of the young stranger.' * From this time, the studies of Hamilton were chiefly

---

* Life of Hamilton, by his Son.[25]

[25] The quotations here come from J. C. Hamilton, I, 22–66. This book was drawn from the Salem Athenaeum Library on January 4, 1836, presumably for Elizabeth's use ("Books Read by Nathaniel Hawthorne").

directed to politics and the art of war. He acquainted himself, as much as possible, with the details of military discipline, and with statesmanlike ability, inquired into the resources of the country; and the disposition of her inhabitants for vigorous and united efforts. He repeatedly took a part in the public discussions, and engaged in a controversy with the Rev. Dr. Cooper; the Episcopal clergymen of New York and Connecticut, having zealously espoused the ministerial side in the contest. He also wrote several political pamphlets which were attributed to Gov. Livingston [26] and to Mr. Jay,[27] and which were esteemed to confer additional celebrity upon these eminent men; but when, on the inquiry to which of them the honour belonged, the author was ascertained to be a youth of eighteen, but recently admitted to college, and new to the country, admiration of the works was lost in surprise at the discovery. 'I remember,' says Col. Troup, 'that in a conversation I once had with Dr. Cooper, about these pamphlets, he insisted that Mr. Jay must be the author, it being impossible to suppose that so young a man as Hamilton could have written them.' On the part of the British government, liberal offers were made him, which, it is scarcely necessary to say, he declined without hesitation.

The adherents of the crown were, from various causes, numerous in New York. There was little unity of feeling among the inhabitants, who were dissimilar in origin and in creed, and among whom property was more unequally distributed than in some of the other colonies. Landed estates were held by a peculiar tenure; education was not generally diffused; the patronage and expenditure of the government was also large; and all these circumstances combined to render the popular party less prompt to resist, and far more cautious in deliberation and resolution than might have been expected. Still, revolutionary sentiments and feelings were strong, and strengthening, among the people; and in the discussion of the momentous questions of the day, Hamilton continued to participate

[26] William Livingston (1723–90) was an able lawyer, controversial writer, soldier, and statesman. He was a member of the Continental Congress and served as governor of New Jersey.

[27] John Jay (1745–1829), statesman, diplomat, and Chief Justice of the Supreme Court.

with his pen and with his voice, till the course of events summoned him to render services of a different nature. In March, 1776, he was appointed by the Convention of New York, 'Captain of the Provincial Company of Artillery,' one of the first companies raised by that province. He 'recruited his men, and, with the remnant of his second and last remittance from Santa Cruz, equipped them: He attended to their drill and his other duties with a zeal and diligence which soon made his company conspicuous for their appearance, and the regularity of their movements.'

Immediately after the Declaration of Independence, he was ordered upon active service. He was very soon fortunate enough 'to attract the observant eye of Washington, who, on the inspection of some works which Hamilton was engaged in throwing up, entered into conversation with him, invited him to his marquee, and formed a high estimate of his capacity.'

He distinguished himself at the battle of White Plains, and through the whole of that arduous campaign, one of the most disheartening of the whole war. 'Well do I remember the day,' said a friend, 'when Hamilton's company marched into Princeton. It was a model of discipline; at its head was a boy, and I wondered at his youth; but what was my surprise, when struck with his diminutive figure, he was pointed out to me as that Hamilton of whom we had already heard so much.' At the close of the season, his company, from exposure in battle and from the severity of the weather, was reduced to twenty-five men. On the first of March, 1777, he was appointed Aid-de-camp to General Washington, with the rank of Lieutenant Colonel. He was then twenty years of age.

Adverting to the selection of the members of his staff, Gen. Washington says, in a letter to Col. Harrison,[28] of January 9th, 1777:— 'As to military knowledge, I do not expect to find gentlemen much skilled in it; if they can write a good letter, write quick, are methodical and diligent, it is all I expect to find in my aids.' And, in a subsequent letter to Congress, requesting additional assistance, he remarks: 'the business which has given constant exercise to the pen of

---

[28] Colonel Robert H. Harrison (1745–90) was a distinguished lawyer who served as a member of Washington's staff from 1775 to 1781.

my secretary, and not only frequently, but always, to those of my aids, has rendered it impracticable for the former to register the copies of my letters, instructions, &c. in books, and thus valuable documents which may be of equal public utility and private satisfaction, remain in loose sheets and in the rough manner in which they were drawn.' Washington's principal Secretary was Col. Robert H. Harrison, of Maryland, and upon him the labour of the correspondence chiefly devolved; but such of the more elaborate and important communications, as were not written by the Commander in Chief himself, were the productions of Hamilton's pen. 'This larger and more appropriate sphere of action, gave to his mind not only a wider, but a loftier range. He was called, not merely to execute subordinate parts, but to assist in planning campaigns, in devising means to support them, in corresponding with the different members of this extensive empire, and in introducing order and harmony into the general system.' [29]

From this period till the close of the war, his conduct displayed the utmost zeal, assiduity and valour; he acquired the most brilliant distinction at the siege of Yorktown, as well as on several previous occasions. He early perceived the incompetency of a 'merely federative and advisory' system of government, like the old Confederacy, to a vigorous prosecution of the war; and saw, in the financial embarrassments of the country, greater cause of alarm, than in the temporary successes of the British arms. 'He looked, with intense anxiety, to the adoption of some effectual means by which the distresses of the country might be reached at their source;' and endeavoured, in various ways, to urge upon the people, the necessity of confiding to Congress an authority adequate to the emergencies of the times.

At the close of the Revolution, Hamilton, then scarcely twenty-five years of age, had already gained a high and secure place in American history. Our limits will allow us merely to glance at the career of his manhood, which, in point of ability and distinction, fulfilled the promise of his youth. When his military services were

[29] To this point Elizabeth had covered only seventy pages of the life she was following. Hawthorne's hand is in evidence from here to the end of the sketch.

no longer required, he had commenced the study of the law, and speedily became eminent in the profession. In political life, he was one of the strongest champions of the party which had Washington at its head. He assisted in framing the Constitution of the United States, and greatly contributed to prepare the popular mind for its reception, by the admirable series of articles, entitled the Federalist.[30] Of this work, as profound as any, and more generally intelligible than most, that have been written on the science of government, the larger portion proceeded from the pen of Hamilton. In recommending the present Constitution, he considered it not the most perfect that might have been framed, but better than the old Confederation, and the best that the people of America would consent to impose upon themselves. Hamilton had not sufficient faith in the capacity of the people for self-government; and while it was yet a matter of theory, we cannot wonder that his severe and practical mind should have distrusted the result. Had there been the same hesitation in America, at that period, between a monarchy and a republic, that there was in France, at her late Revolution, Hamilton, with pure but mistaken patriotism, would probably have given his voice for the former; or, at least, his nominal republic would have been very like a monarchy in its institutions. Fortunately, the bare proposal would have been met by an outcry of abhorrence; and Hamilton lent his great powers to the formation of a government, republican both in name and spirit, but endowed with all the energy that was needful to its own support.

Washington, on his installation as our first President, named Hamilton Secretary of the Treasury, the duties of which office he discharged with his usual ability. During the insurrection in Pennsylvania,[31] when the people of the western counties took arms against the general government, Hamilton was placed at the head of the force destined to act against them. The disturbances being quelled without bloodshed, he resigned his post. His last appearance in a military character was again by the side of Washington, in 1798, as second in command of the army, which was to be called into

---

[30] Other contributors to the eighty-five *Federalist* articles were Madison and Jay.

[31] This insurrection, 1794, is generally known as the Whisky Rebellion.

service in case of hostilities with France. When the cloud of war had blown over, General Hamilton resumed the practice of the law, in the city of New York. He never again held any public office, but was considered the leader of the Federal party, which was then, and ever afterwards, in the minority, on all points of national dispute. The life of this eminent man was now drawing to a bloody close. In 1804, Aaron Burr, then Vice-President of the United States, peremptorily demanded an explanation from General Hamilton, in regard to some aspersions which the latter was supposed to have cast on his integrity. This demand was rejected. The consequence was a meeting at Hoboken, where Hamilton fell at the first fire, pouring out his lifeblood on the same sod, which had before been wet by that of his son.[32] He may thus far be absolved from the guilt of duelling, that he had no wish to take the life of Colonel Burr, and had resolved not to return his fire.

The vignette of the present number of our Magazine is from the Statue of Hamilton, which, by the liberality of the merchants of New York, was placed in the Exchange of that city. The material was the purest Italian marble, and was sculptured by Mr. Hughes,[33] at an expense of several thousand dollars. This noble Statue had occupied its pedestal but a few months, when it was involved in the wide destruction, caused by the Great Fire of last December.

(May, pp. 354–56)

John C. Calhoun [34]

On the father's side, Mr. Calhoun is of Irish descent. His grandfather came to America in 1733, and settled first in Pennsylvania, whence he afterwards removed to the backwoods of Virginia, and

[32] Philip Hamilton was killed by George I. Eacker in November, 1801, in a duel growing out of a speech by Eacker praising Aaron Burr at the expense of Alexander Hamilton.

[33] Ball Hughes (1806–68) had received considerable recognition as a sculptor in England before coming to America to continue his work. One of his statues was the first to be cast in bronze in America.

[34] This sketch accompanies a small wood engraving of the bust of Calhoun.

finally to South Carolina. In this latter migration, he seems to have been accompanied, like an ancient patriarch, by his married children and their offspring. The family planted itself on the borders of the Cherokee country, and soon underwent a bloody attack from the Indians, in which the eldest son, with half the males of 'Calhoun's settlement,' were slain. The mother of the family, and several other women, besides a number of children, were massacred. During the hostilities that ensued, Mr. Calhoun's father, Patrick Calhoun, was appointed captain of a body of rangers, in which office he displayed great courage and ability. These events occurred long prior to the birth of John Caldwell Calhoun, which took place on the eighteenth of March, 1782.

His early education was irregular and imperfect. When thirteen years old, he was placed at an academy, where he had free access to a circulating library, with liberty of choice between the light and fanciful, and the more solid literature, which it contained. He at once rejected the trash, and devoted himself to the perusal of history and metaphysics, with such an intensity of application that, in a few months, he had nearly ruined his health. In consequence, he was withdrawn from the academy, and became engrossed with rural sports and occupations, till the age of eighteen. He appears to have looked forward to a life spent in similar pursuits; nor was he easily persuaded by his brother, who saw his great natural abilities, to resume the studies which had been so long broken off. It is not probable that Mr. Calhoun, whatever might have been his pursuit or profession, would have lived without distinction of one sort or other, or have died without leaving some mark of his existence. Yet, however high may be a young man's talent, a classical education and a learned profession are desirable, not so much because they add to his natural gifts, as because they put him in the most direct road to his proper sphere of action. A farmer may have the intellect of a statesman; but it depends upon contingencies whether it will ever be brought into play; whereas a lawyer reaches, as a matter of course, that rank in public life to which his talents may entitle him. Certainly, if Mr. Calhoun had not yielded to his brother's advice, his distinction would have come later, and the country would have lacked the many services which he rendered her, while yet in his early manhood.

In two years from the time of his return to the academy, he was admitted to the Junior Class of Yale College, and was graduated, in two years more, with the highest honours of that institution. He received, also, a part of his legal education in New England, at the Litchfield law-school. Here, in the discussions of a debating society, he showed those powers of argument and eloquence, which were very soon to place him in the highest rank of public men. Although, in after life, he has stood forth the champion of a party, which appeared ready to withdraw the hand of union from New England, there must be many kindly feelings in his heart, towards that portion of his native country. Returning to the South, he was admitted to the bar in 1807, and at once assumed his place among the ablest members of the profession. His first step in public life was the delivery of an address, during the excitement arising from the attack on the frigate Chesapeake.[35] After serving two sessions in the legislature of South Carolina, he was sent, in 1811, at the age of twenty-nine, to Congress; whither his fame had preceded him, and immediately obtained him a most important part in the conduct of national affairs. He was appointed to the committee on foreign relations, and in the course of the same session, on the withdrawal of General Porter,[36] became chairman of that committee. Thus, in seven years from the period of his leaving college, had Mr. Calhoun reached a station, which made him a leader of the administration party, a chief advocate of hostile measures against Great Britain, and one of the strongest supporters of the war, when it commenced.

[35] The attack on the United States frigate *Chesapeake* occurred in the spring of 1807. Among the crew of the *Chesapeake* were four deserters from the British navy. When Commodore Barrow refused to return the deserters, because two of them were American citizens, the British ship *Leonard* fired on the *Chesapeake,* which was not prepared to return the fire and was forced to strike its colors. The deserters were seized. At Washington a storm of protest resulted, but the affair was settled peaceably, and Barrow was suspended for five years because he had not kept the *Chesapeake* in fighting condition.

[36] Peter Buell Porter (1773–1844), Senator from Connecticut, did not seek re-election in 1812, and Calhoun became chairman of the Committee on Foreign Affairs in the Twelfth Congress.

The life of a leading statesman is so mixed up with the annals of his country, that, in regard to him, there is scarcely any distinction between biography and history. Great national events compose the incidents of such a life. The narrative should not flow on in the narrow line, which suffices to represent the course of private men, but, if it aim to give any tolerable idea of its subject, must be allowed a latitude as wide as the land itself. Other characters, also—those of the statesman's friends or opponents—should be developed, in order to throw light upon his own. And as, in one sense, the most important part of the life of such a man, consists in his principles and opinions, these should be deduced from his actions, or gathered, where it is possible, from the records of his pen or the words of his own mouth. The speeches, by which he influenced with his breath the destinies of his country, are not mere words, but mighty deeds, and should be preserved as such in his biography, not only as incidents of his life, but as interpreters of other incidents. His nominal rank—the public stations which he may have filled—are comparatively of no moment. External greatness is not a guarantee for greatness of soul and intellect; nor, where the latter exists, does the former effect any thing towards a portraiture of it. Yet, in a brief sketch like this, all that we can do is to trace Mr. Calhoun from one station or office to another, and leave almost the whole of his real biography untold.[37]

At the close of the war, as chairman of the committee on currency, Mr. Calhoun was the chief instrument in establishing the bank of the United States. Whatever may be the ultimate tendency of such an institution, it had undoubtedly the immediate effect of regulating the currency of the country, which was then in a state of unprecedented disorder. On the accession of Mr. Monroe to the Presidency, Mr. Calhoun became Secretary of War, which office he continued to hold for the next eight years. Under his charge, the department was relieved from nearly all its immense burden of

[37] This exposition of Hawthorne's views on biography may well be considered among his pronouncements in literary criticism, especially in connection with his comments on the novel and the romance in the prefaces to *The House of the Seven Gables* (*Writings,* VII, xxi–xxii) and *The Blithedale Romance* (*ibid.,* VIII, xxix–xxxi).

debt, and the expenses of the army were reduced more than one third. In the mean time, at an earlier age than usual, his name had been brought forward, among the most prominent candidates for the Presidency of the United States. As there was not, however, a probability of his being elected by the people, he withdrew his pretensions to the higher dignity, and became, by the suffrages of a large majority, Vice-President. We need hardly remind the reader, that there was no election of President by the people, and that Mr. Adams, without a plurality of the people's votes, was the choice of the House of Representatives. As Mr. Calhoun objected, on principle, to this mode of election, and held the opinion, that, when the choice did devolve upon the Representatives, they should be guided by the popular will, he now ranked with the opposition. On the accession of General Jackson to the Presidency, Mr. Calhoun began his second term of office, as a supporter of the Chief Magistrate.

The strong character of the new President, his tenacious grasp of his own opinions, and energetic action upon them, made it difficult for a man, himself of so decided principles as Mr. Calhoun, to remain in perfect harmony with him. Differences soon arose between the two highest officers of the nation, so important in their nature as wholly to alienate them from each other, both in their political and private relations. This hostility was embittered, when Mr. Calhoun took his stand as the champion of Nullification, and the President gave the whole strength of his arm to the support of the Union. But our narrative has now brought us to forbidden ground, where the embers of faction are still smouldering, and may scorch our feet, if we venture farther.[38] In reference to Mr. Calhoun's public life, we will merely add, that he left the office of Vice-President for a seat in the Senate, where he fought the battles of South Carolina with the great statesman of the North. But we must not conclude without a tribute to his political integrity, which—whether his judgment may have been right or wrong—is as unquestionable as his private honour.

(*May, pp. 359–60*)

[38] See text, p. 217, for another statement of Hawthorne's on the neutral position which the magazine assumed on all controversial matters.

John Adams [39]

John Adams was lineally descended from an old Puritan patriarch, who fled, as his tombstone expresses it, from the 'Dragon Persecution,' and came to New England with seven married children. He had also the blood of the Plymouth pilgrims in his veins, derived from the marriage of John Alden, one of the May-Flower's passengers, with a lady whom he had wooed as proxy for the valiant Captain Standish. From 1630, when the patriarch Adams crossed the Atlantic, down till 1735, when John Adams was born, the successive generations of the family continued on the same farm, which he himself has transmitted to his son. The descendant of so honorable a lineage was bound, by peculiar obligations, to uphold those civil and religious principles for which his ancestors had become exiles. Accordingly, he may be taken as an example of the primitive New-England character, modified by the change of time and circumstances, yet the same in its oaken substance as of old.

He was educated at Harvard College, and took his first degree in 1755. While pursuing the study of the law, he had charge of the grammar school in Worcester, and during his residence there, attracted the notice and favour of Mr. Gridley,[40] the Attorney General of the Province. That his abilities were early developed is remarkably proved by the existence of a letter, written at the age of twenty, in which he infers the future greatness of America, from causes which had not yet even begun to operate. Such prophecies have sometimes flowed from the consummate wisdom of experienced statesmen, but never before from the natural sagacity of a stripling, inspired by youthful imagination. It is probable that the author himself had hardly a suspicion of the mighty truths which he was uttering; he followed his own fancy, and wandered into prophecy. But, in regard to his own career, the farthest flight of fancy could not have reached that eminence, whither the rising fortunes of his coun-

[39] This article introduces the August number and has as illustration a half-page woodcut of a bust of Adams.

[40] Jeremiah Gridley (1702–67) was a noted teacher and lawyer of Massachusetts, serving as attorney-general, colonel of the militia and president of the Marine Society.

try were to bear him up. There were many young Americans, at that day, who never dreamed of any thing so strange as their own destiny—to ascend, from the middle ranks of colonial life, into the sphere of rulers, legislators, generals, and ambassadors. Such promotion is now in the ordinary course of things. Then, it was impossible, save by the overturn of a government which seemed to stand on the same basis as the constitution and throne of England.

John Adams commenced the practice of the law in his native town of Quincy, which was then a part of ancient Braintree. In 1763, he was married to Abigail Smith, a country clergyman's daughter, and an excellent woman, with whom, though she died some years before him, he lived in wedlock more than half a century. He published, in 1765, a dissertation on the Canon and Feudal Law,[41] in which he explained the Puritan principles of religion and government, and brought them to bear upon the disputes between Great Britain and the colonies. A year afterwards, he removed to Boston. His professional standing was now so high, that, in 1768, Governor Bernard [42] offered him the post of Advocate General of the court of Admiralty. But Mr. Adams had ranked himself decisively with the friends of the people; and had he accepted a lucrative office under the crown, although no conditions were annexed, his course could not have been the same as heretofore. In truth, the offer must have been intended quite as much to silence his political opposition, as to secure his legal services. He therefore declined it, but gave a noble evidence, not long afterwards, that no base subserviency to the people, any more than to the government, could make him swerve from his own ideas of right. This truth was shown in 1770, by his conduct in reference to the Boston Massacre. Few men have had such an opportunity of proving their rectitude and independence, and fewer

[41] *A Dissertation on the Canon and the Feudal Law,* published first in four installments without title in *The Boston Gazette,* Aug., 1765. It was printed immediately in *The London Chronicle* and was reprinted at London in 1768 (see Charles Francis Adams, ed., *The Works of John Adams,* Boston, 1850–56, II, 150; III, 447–64).

[42] Sir Francis Bernard (*c.* 1714–79) was governor of New Jersey, 1758–60, and of Massachusetts, 1760–69. He had become thoroughly unpopular with the people before he was succeeded by Thomas Hutchinson. Bernard's term of office and his ultimate removal are narrated in *Grandfather's Chair (Writings,* XII, 163 ff., 197–98).

still have possessed the strength of character to take advantage of it.

The scene of bloodshed in King Street was a natural consequence of the relative positions of the soldiery and the people. No good feeling could possibly exist between them. On the part of the troops, the haughty consciousness that Britain had made them the keepers of the province, together with a sense of the odium in which they were held, produced a contemptuous antipathy towards the colonists. The latter saw themselves treated like subjugated rebels, with a court-of-guard in the centre of their metropolis, and cannon pointed against the town-house. Their continual bickerings with the individual soldiers galled them, as the captive is galled by each separate link of his chain. They bestowed on these instruments of despotism the hatred which was rightfully due to those who sent them. In such cases, when the malevolence between the citizen and armed soldier has reached its height, the immediate provocation is generally given by the oppressed party, and bloodily resented by the oppressors. This was the almost inevitable result in Boston. At the sight of their own blood, the ferment of the people became terrible, and was shared for a time, by the calmest patriots in New England. A multitude, computed at ten or twelve thousand, assembled at Faneuil Hall, and adjourned thence to the Old South church. There went a rumour, that the tragedy in King Street had been premeditated, and was but the prelude to a general massacre. For defence against this exaggerated, yet not altogether shadowy danger, a military guard was enrolled, and the town put itself under martial law. No British officer or soldier could have walked the streets with safety to his life; a parade would have been the signal for a battle. Samuel Adams and other leading patriots were sent as a committee to the Lieutenant Governor and Council, to demand the removal of the troops, as the only method of preventing an appeal to arms. Hutchinson [43] felt the necessity of the measure; the two British regiments were ordered to Castle William; and their commander, Colonel

---

[43] Thomas Hutchinson (1711–80) was the last royal governor of Massachusetts, holding office as acting-governor, 1769–71, and as governor, 1771–74. He wrote *The History of the Colony of Massachusetts Bay,* Boston, 1764–67, 1828 (see n. 91).

Dalrymple,[44] was compelled to seek the protection of a popular leader, on his way to the waterside.

Such was the state of affairs, when John Adams, himself a leading patriot, and a member of the military guard, was solicited to undertake the defence of Captain Preston,[45] and the soldiers who had fired the fatal volley. It was a singular compliment to his integrity, that the prisoners should have sought the aid of a man so situated. Not one man in a thousand could have so freed himself from party excitement, as to do justice to the cause; not one in a million, taking all circumstances into consideration, would have made the attempt. But Mr. Adams did it; he exerted his whole strength, for that single time, in a cause which the king and ministry approved—and won the blood-stained regulars their lives. Undoubtedly, he considered them guiltless of murder; yet, had they suffered the penalty of that crime, posterity, after the coolest reconsideration of the trial could not absolutely have called the sentence an unjust one.

It does not appear that the confidence of his countrymen was shaken; or if so, it was only for the moment. In 1773, he was chosen a member of the provincial Council, but was rejected by Governor Hutchinson, and afterwards by General Gage.[46]

In the year 1775, John Adams, as a delegate in Congress, nominated George Washington to the post of Commander in Chief of the American armies. The glory of the choice appears to belong principally to Mr. Adams, and, did he need a secondary reputation, this would have been claim enough to his country's gratitude. The service cannot be too highly estimated. Washington's character was of such a nature, that, if some sagacious individual had not pointed him out, he probably would not have been the foremost figure in

[44] Colonel John Dalrymple, sixth Earl of Stair (1749–1821), fought in the British army during the Revolutionary War and served in various diplomatic capacities after 1782.

[45] Captain Charles Preston was in command of the British soldiers who fired on the colonists at the Boston Massacre. He was acquitted in the trial which followed.

[46] General Thomas Gage (1721–87) was a popular officer of the British army in America until he was made governor-in-chief of Massachusetts in 1774. Thenceforward he was unpopular with both the colonists and the home government.

the public eye. And had another been raised, in the first instance, to the military supremacy, there is no reason to suppose that a second opportunity would have offered for the elevation of the only man who could have saved us from Britain, without consigning us to anarchy or native despotism. Setting him aside, inefficiency on the one hand, or talent combined with dangerous ambition on the other, must have been the sole alternative. It is true, that, had there been no Washington, the country would still have wrought out its freedom in the end; but after a far longer term of blood and tumult.

Mr. Adams was one of the committee who drafted the Declaration of Independence; and the calm, yet high enthusiasm of the letter in which he announced that event to a friend, and prophesied that its anniversary would become a national festival, must be recollected by every American. He had a share in all the weightiest business of Congress, and bore the burden of much that was less important; being a member of no less than ninety committees, and chairmen of twenty five. In 1777, he was appointed Commissioner to France, in the room of Silas Deane.[47] Returning home in 1779, he was again sent out, in the Autumn of the same year, with powers to conclude a treaty of peace and commerce.

Mr. Adams in 1785, was appointed the first minister to the court of St. James. If in his early youth, the whole progress of his high destiny could have been foreshown to him, this event would probably have excited the most of wonder and anticipation. That he should approach the throne of his hereditary sovereign, as ambassador from an independent nation! In a letter to the American Secretary of State,[48] Mr. Adams has fully narrated the circumstances of

[47] Silas Deane (1737–89), as a secret agent to France, secured the services of Lafayette and others for the American cause. He was a member of both Continental Congresses, and was subsequently disgraced, not to be vindicated until after his death.

Hawthorne's method in the remainder of this sketch—expanding one striking situation and elaborating on the various psychological implications—was followed both in his imaginative writings and in such biographical and historical sketches as comprise Grandfather's Chair.

[48] Hawthorne here drew on letters from Adams to John Jay dated May 30, June 1 and 2, 1785 (The Works of John Adams, VIII, 252–59). The letter of June 2 carries a full account of the interview with King George. A comparison of Hawthorne's sketch

his interview with King George. Sir Clement Dormer, Master of Ceremonies, had hinted to him that a complimentary address was expected from foreign ministers, on their presentation; and the Dutch and Swedish envoys, probably at the instance of the English court, had advised him to the same effect. It may well be supposed that something of the kind was desirable, to sooth the mortified feelings of the King. But of all the duties that could have been imposed on Mr. Adams, that of paying a set compliment to any man, was the one least suited to his character and turn of mind; and of all complimentary addresses, one of which George the Third should be the object, and the relations of England with America the subject, was the most difficult to frame. It required, among other things, a tact, an adroitness, and a refinement of taste, which John Adams does not seem to have possessed. Accordingly, in our judgment, this was the scene of his public life, in which he made the least advantageous figure. The very tone, in which he describes the interview, is

with the text of this letter, quoted in part below, will indicate the extent of his interpolations and the facts underlying his analysis:

Bath Hotel, Westminster, 2 June, 1785

Dear Sir,—During my interview with the Marquis of Carmarthen, he told me that it was customary for every foreign minister, at his first presentation to the King, to make his Majesty some compliments conformable to the spirit of his letter of credence; and when Sir Clement Cottrell Dormer, the master of the ceremonies, came to inform me that he should accompany me to the secretary of state and to Court, he said that every foreign minister whom he had attended to the Queen had always made a harangue to her Majesty, and he understood, though he had not been present, that they always harangued the King.

. . . All this was conformable to the advice lately given by the Count de Vergennes to Mr. Jefferson; so that, finding it was a custom established at both these great Courts, and that this Court and the foreign ministers expected it, I thought I could not avoid it, although my first thought and inclination had been to deliver my credentials silently and retire.

. . . When we arrived in the antechamber, the *oeil de boeuf* of St. James's, the master of the ceremonies met me and attended me, while the secretary of state went to take the commands of the King. While I stood in this place, where it seems all ministers stand upon such occasions, always attended by the master of ceremonies, the room very full of ministers of state, lords, and bishops, and all sorts of courtiers, as well as the next room, which is the King's bedchamber, you may well suppose I was the focus of all eyes. I was relieved, however, from the embarrassment of it by the Swedish and Dutch ministers, who came to me, and entertained me in a very

not quite such as we could have desired him to use. On arriving at the palace, Mr. Adams was ushered into the ante-chamber, which was then thronged with noble lords and right reverend bishops, generals, officers of state, and courtiers of every degree, among whose embroidered and magnificent array, the unpretending figure of the American minister attracted the eyes of all. He speaks gratefully of the Dutch and Swedish envoys, who relieved the awkwardness of his situation by giving him the favour of their countenance. After an interval of some length, the Master of the Ceremonies appeared, and ushered Mr. Adams into the presence-chamber.

We may pardon the minister of our proud Democracy, if he felt, at that moment, that he had not always been a Republican; if his thoughts went back, as they doubtless did, to the old times, when the people were wont to pray for their gracious monarch in the meeting-house of Braintree, and his own gray-headed sire had prayed for him at his hearth—if, in short, the impressions of infancy and youth were not utterly subdued by the settled principles of manhood. Mr. Adams advanced, making an obeisance at the threshold, a second in the centre of the chamber, and a third in the immediate presence of

---

agreeable conversation during the whole time. Some other gentlemen, whom I had seen before, came to make their compliments too, until the Marquis of Carmarthen returned and desired me to go with him to his Majesty. I went with his Lordship through the levee room into the King's closet. The door was shut, and I was left with his Majesty and the secretary of state alone. I made the three reverences,—one at the door, another about half way, and a third before the presence,—according to the usage established at this and all the northern Courts of Europe, and then addressed myself to his Majesty in the following words:—

"Sir,—The United States of America have appointed me their minister plenipotentiary to your Majesty, and have directed me to deliver to your Majesty this letter which contains the evidence of it. It is in obedience to their express commands, that I have the honor to assure your Majesty of their unanimous disposition and desire to cultivate the most friendly and liberal intercourse between your Majesty's subjects and their citizens, and of their best wishes for your Majesty's health and happiness, and for that of your royal family. The appointment of a minister from the United States to your Majesty's Court will form an epoch in the history of England and of America. I think myself more fortunate than all my fellow-citizens, in having the distinguished honor to be the first to stand in your Majesty's royal presence in a diplomatic character; and I shall esteem myself the happiest of men, if I can be instrumental in recommending my country more and more to your Majesty's royal benevolence, and of restoring an entire esteem, confidence, and affection, or, in better words, the old good nature and the old good humor between people, who, though separated by an

the King, who stood with the prime minister to receive him. He then proceeded to deliver his complimentary address. It was short and simple, presenting not many particular points that are tangible by criticism, and containing one or two sentences that could hardly have been better thought or better said. He hoped that the 'old good nature and the old good humour' would be revived between England and America. The chief specific fault that can be pointed out, was the recommendation of our country to his majesty's 'Royal Benevolence,' when she had already proved that the royal anger was not very terrible. But the general tone of the address need not have been greatly changed, had its purport been to thank the sovereign for his clemency in receiving the rebellious colonies to favour, on the terms of mutual concession which, in the latter part of the contest, Great Britain desired to substitute for independence. Mr. Adams took a decidedly lower stand than the position of the United States entitled him to take.

---

ocean, and under different governments, have the same language, a similar religion, and kindred blood.

"I beg your Majesty's permission to add, that, although I have some time before been intrusted by my country, it was never in my whole life in a manner so agreeable to myself."

The King listened to every word I said, with dignity, but with an apparent emotion. Whether it was the nature of the interview, or whether it was my visible agitation, for I felt more than I did or could express, that touched him, I cannot say. But he was much affected, and answered me with more tremor than I had spoken with, and said:—

"Sir,—The circumstances of this audience are so extraordinary, the language you have now held is so extremely proper, and the feelings you have discovered so justly adapted to the occasion, that I must say that I not only receive with pleasure the assurance of the friendly dispositions of the United States, but that I am very glad the choice has fallen upon you to be their minister. I wish you, sir, to believe, and that it may be understood in America, that I have done nothing in the late contest but what I thought myself indispensably bound to do, by the duty which I owed to my people. I will be very frank with you. I was the last to consent to the separation; but the separation having been made, and having become inevitable, I have always said, as I say now, that I would be the first to meet the friendship of the United States as an independent power. The moment I see such sentiments and language as yours prevail, and a disposition to give to this country the preference, that moment I shall say, let the circumstances of language, religion, and blood have their natural and full effect."

I dare not say that these were the King's precise words, and, it is even possible, that I may have in some particular mistaken his meaning; for, although his pronunciation

The King, on the other hand, if the report of Mr. Adams have not done him more than justice, appeared to greater advantage than in any previous or subsequent moment of his reign. The address appears to have been of a more agreeable tenor than he had anticipated. Of the many humiliations which befel that unhappy monarch, perhaps few were felt so bitterly as this almost compulsory interview with the representative of a people, once his subjects, afterwards rebels, and now free. To George the Third, however profound might be the ambassador's three obeisances, the mere entrance of an American into the presence chamber, unless to crave the honour of kissing his liege's royal hand, was the last token of a realm dismembered. Yet his deportment was dignified, though not unmarked by natural emotion; his reply to the address was apt, and full of good feeling and just sentiments; and with an air of easy condescension, he took the ascendency which Mr. Adams had yielded to him. There was a kingly spirit in what he said. Though

---

is as distinct as I ever heard, he hesitated some time between his periods, and between the members of the same period. He was indeed much affected, and I confess I was not less so, and, therefore I cannot be certain that I was so cool and attentive, heard so clearly, and understood so perfectly, as to be confident of all his words or sense; and, I think, that all which he said to me should at present be kept secret in America, unless his Majesty or his secretary of state, who alone was present, should judge proper to report it. This I do say, that the foregoing is his Majesty's meaning as I then understood it, and his own words as nearly as I can recollect them.

The King then asked me whether I came last from France, and upon my answering in the affirmative, he put on an air of familiarity, and, smiling, or rather laughing, said, "there is an opinion among some people that you are not the most attached of all your countrymen to the manners of France." I was surprised at this, because I thought it an indiscretion and a departure from the dignity. I was a little embarrassed, but determined not to deny the truth on one hand, nor leave him to infer from it any attachment to England on the other. I threw off as much gravity as I could, and assumed an air of gayety and a tone of decision as far as was decent, and said, "that opinion, sir, is not mistaken; I must avow to your Majesty, I have no attachment but to my own country." The King replied, as quick as lightning, "an honest man will never have any other."

The King then said a word or two to the secretary of state, which, being between them, I did not hear, and then turned round and bowed to me, as is customary with all kings and princes when they give the signal to retire. I retreated, stepping backward, as is the etiquette, and, making my last reverence at the door of the chamber, I went my way. . . .

With great respect, &c.

JOHN ADAMS

he spoke of America as free, yet his speech conveys the impression that he still felt himself a sovereign by Divine-Right, as much on one side of the Atlantic as the other. Well might he think so, when he perceived that neither the war of tongue and pen, nor of the sword, nor triumph itself, had extinguished the sentiment of loyalty in the breast of this sturdy commonwealth's man. To the formal address and reply succeeded a brief and good humoured conversation; after which the King bowed, as a signal that the audience was at an end; and Mr. Adams retired, highly gratified with the gracious deportment of his Majesty.

If, as we have hinted our opinion, Mr. Adams did bend somewhat lower than befitted the representative of a victorious people, the sacrifice of dignity was recompensed by no solid profit. George the Third, whatever good qualities he might possess, was as obstinate a man as ever lived.—Pig-headed is just the phrase to express his temper, which is, in some degree, the temper of John Bull himself. England was in the sulks, and would not shake hands cordially with America. In the course of the three years that Mr. Adams continued in London, he was not favoured, we believe, with another private audience; nor did Great Britain send an ambassador to our own government. Mr. Adams at length solicited his recall, and returned home in 1788. His life, for some years afterwards, was not such as to supply many events for our narrative. He assisted in forming the Constitution of his native state. During the presidency of Washington, he was Vice-President, and when the former retired from office, John Adams, after a hard contest with Jefferson, became President of the United States.

Mr. Adams was not the choice of the people. The House of Representatives made him President. The country was at that period infected with the contagion of French anarchy; and as Mr. Adams was supposed to give the preference to England, he had to contend with a strong and violent opposition, throughout his term of office. He was even accused of holding monarchical principles.

His administration, beginning under no favourable auspices, went on through a continual storm, and terminated in a cloud. At the end of the first four years, Mr. Jefferson came in by a triumphant majority, and President Adams retired to domestic life.

This was in 1801, when he had reached the age of sixty-six. His long course of public services was now closed. At the period of his retirement, he did not enjoy the unreserved, and cordial approbation of any party. Some of his measures had gone far towards alienating the Federalists, although, as the least evil in their choice, they gave him a general vote for the second term of office. Mr. Adams was a man of warm passions, and liable, it is said, to a certain wrong-headedness, which sometimes caused him to assume rather an unamiable attitude, in regard to men with whom it is a pity that he should have differed. He had bitter enemies, who have left proofs of their hostility in newspapers, pamphlets, and volumes, the virulence of which now makes us smile, when we light upon them in some obscure corner of a library. On his part, Mr. Adams was not · slow to resent, nor cautious to hide his resentment. He once observed, pointing to his own portrait,—'That fellow could never keep his mouth shut!' Certainly, this was a great fault in a statesman, but a fault which oftenest marks integrity. Thomas Jefferson, his successful rival, but never his personal foe, has borne the strongest testimony that John Adams was an honest man. His whole life confirms the fact.

In his old age, the world acknowledged it. As the Ex-President went farther and farther down into the vale of years, his path became still greener and more peaceful. The young, to whom he was a man of History, did reverence to the hoary sage, now long emerged from the dust of contending parties, and drawing cheerfully towards his sepulchre. He loved to linger by the wayside, and tell of the great deeds of the past, and the great men of whom he was a brother. At length, when the full Jubilee was finished, since that band of mighty brethren signed the deed of freedom, the survivor mingled his expiring breath with the swell of consummated triumph. INDEPENDENCE FOREVER!—were the last words that John Adams uttered. Such a death, had there been no other evidence, was proof unanswerable of a patriotic life.

(*August, pp. 481–84*)

HISTORY AND GEOGRAPHY

Jerusalem [49]

Jerusalem was first called Salem, and Solyma, and is supposed to have been founded by Melchizedek. It was built upon Mount Sion, and gradually spread over other hills in the vicinity, with deep vales sinking down between. The Jebusites, a people of Canaan, conquered it from its original founders, and were themselves driven out by Joshua, who, in his division of the Land of Promise, assigned this, afterward sacred city, to the tribe of Benjamin. A strong hold, however, remained in the possession of the Jebusites, till the days of the warriour-psalmist, by whom they were utterly expelled. Jerusalem was thence called the city of David.

No other city in the world presents such a dismal history of siege, storm, intestine commotion, captivity, famine, pestilence, and every sort of ruin, continued and repeated through a course of ages, as Jerusalem. In the year 3046 before Christ, it was taken by Shishak, who is supposed to have been Sesostris, king of Egypt. It was afterwards destroyed by Nabuzaradan, general under Nebuchadnezzar; 'the walls,' as Nehemiah says, 'were broken down, and the gates were burned with fire;' [50] and in this desolation it remained, a hundred and fifty years. Many centuries after it had been rebuilt, Alexander 'the Great,' being refused assistance by the Jews in his warfare, determined again to destroy the city. But as he drew near, at the head of his triumphant army, a procession came forth from the gate—where now we may see yonder train of camels entering—and advanced to meet him, with the wild clangour of the Jewish music. First marched the people, all in white, followed by the Levites in

[49] This article is illustrated by a half-page engraving, "The Walls of Jerusalem."
[50] Nehemiah 1: 3.

their robes, all preceding the High Priest, who had put on his garments of purple and gold and wore a tiara on his head, whereon was a golden plate, inscribed with the name of the Lord. Overawed by the magnificence of the array, the Conquerour of the World bowed himself before the Priest, and offered his worship to that God whose holy city he had threatened to cast down. But Jerusalem was seldom so fortunate in its victors, as in the case of the mighty Macedonian. The eastern monarchs made war upon it, time after time, slaughtered its inhabitants, by hundreds of thousands, or made slaves of them, and defiled the temple with the statues of Heathen deities.

In the year 66 of the Christian era, the Jews attempted to throw off the Roman yoke, which had long before been imposed upon them by Pompey. The Emperour Nero sent Vespasian to quell them, who, being subsequently called to the imperial purple, deputed his son Titus to carry on the war. Titus accordingly laid siege to Jerusalem, which was almost torn asunder by the factions of its inhabitants; so that the civil war within the walls was even more frightful than the war of invasion at the gates; and to increase the horrors of the period to the utmost, a famine raged within the city. In Scripture there is a prophecy, that Jerusalem being reduced to the extremity of want, a tender and delicate woman should devour her own child; and, in the course of the siege, the terrible words of the prophet were literally fulfilled; and she, on whom was laid the doom of the ancient prophecy, was named Mary, a lady of one of the noblest families in the city. Titus was so shocked by this horrible fact, that he swore to bury the remembrance of it under the ruins of the city. He had intended, however, to preserve the temple; but after Jerusalem was taken, a soldier flung a blazing torch within the holy edifice, which burst into sudden flames, and was consumed to ashes. A small number of Jews were suffered to continue in their native city, and paid tribute to the Romans. But, about half a century afterwards, the inhabitants of Jerusalem having become numerous and again stirring up a rebellion, the Emperour Adrian made war upon them, slaughtered five hundred thousand men, razed the city to its foundation, and sowed the hills, where it had stood, with salt. Thus the words of its terrible prophets were made good, by Jerusalem's complete destruction.[51]

The Christian Emperour, Constantine the Great, afterwards partially rebuilt the city, and protected the Christians who had settled there in considerable numbers. In the year of Christ 363, the Emperour Julian, the Apostate, scorning the prophecies of Scripture, attempted to renew the temple; not one stone of which had lain upon another, since the time of Titus. But no sooner was the work commenced, than earthquakes shook down the rising structure; fire burst from the earth and consumed the materials that had been collected; and other awful wonders so affrighted the workmen, that, although Pagans, they no longer dared to set their feet on the site of the Jewish Temple.

Many noble and sanctified persons now came on pilgrimage to Jerusalem, and monks took up their residence there. In 614, when the city was taken by the Persians, nine thousand Christians were made slaves. Heraclius afterwards gained possession of it, and forbade any Jew to come within three miles of its walls. The next conquerour of Jerusalem was the Caliph Omar, from whose reign it continued several centuries under the dominion of the Saracens. In 1076, it was taken by the Turks. A few years subsequently, Peter the Hermit preached the Crusades among the princes and nobles of Europe, and persuaded many of them to lead their vassals to the Holy Land, which they wrested from the Pagans, and made Godfrey of Bouillon, king of Jerusalem. Five monarchs of Gothic origin succeeded each other in a dominion that was little more than nominal; the Pagans again established themselves in the city, and could not be driven out by the valour of subsequent Crusaders.

In after ages, though the Turks still governed Jerusalem, Christians were permitted to settle there, and almost every nation in Europe was represented by a small community of stationary monks. A church was built upon Mount Calvary, which, though less than a hundred paces long and fifty wide, contained under its roof twelve or thirteen holy places, where some incident, relative to the death

---

[51] Hawthorne used a number of these details in much the same fashion in *Peter Parley's Universal History on the Basis of Geography* (New York, 1837, I, 90–91).

or resurrection of our Saviour, was supposed to have occurred. There was the very spot on which the Cross had stood; there was the Holy Sepulchre, around which the rock had been hewn away, so that it was now a grotto above the earth, instead of a cave beneath it; there, too, was the cleft, which the earthquake rent asunder at the time of the crucifixion. It was held as faith by the Greeks and Arminians, that, every Easter eve, a flame descended into the Holy Sepulchre, and kindled all the lamps and candles which were there. The pilgrims, who visited Jerusalem, lighted tapers at this sacred flame, and daubed the melting wax upon pieces of linen, which they intended as their shrouds. The monks of the Greek Church were accustomed to contend with those of the Church of Rome, for the privilege of celebrating Mass in the Holy Sepulchre; and it is a curious and rather melancholy fact, that these Christians have shed blood in such a quarrel, in that place of awful sanctity —and the unbelieving Turks have interfered to keep the peace! [52]

(*March, pp. 269–70*)

An Ontario Steam-Boat [53]

The Steam-boats on the Canadian lakes, afford opportunities for a varied observation of society. In the spacious one, on board which I had embarked at Ogdensburgh, and was voyaging westward, to the other extremity of Lake Ontario, there were three different orders of passengers;—an aristocracy, in the grand cabin and ladies' saloon; a commonalty in the forward cabin; and, lastly, a male and female multitude on the forward deck, constituting as veritable a Mob, as could be found in any country. These latter did not belong to that proud and independent class, among our native citizens, who chance, in the present generation, to be at the bottom of the body politic; they were the exiles of another clime—the scum which every wind blows off the Irish shores—the pauper-dregs which England

[52] For a similar comparison of Hawthorne's between Christians and Turks, at the expense of the Christians, see "The Gentle Boy" (*Writings*, I, 94, 112).

[53] Reprinted in *Writings*, XVII, 209–18. Hawthorne appears to have taken this trip in the summer of 1830 or 1831 (see Woodberry, pp. 40–41).

flings out upon America. Thus, within the precincts of our Steam-boat—which indeed was ample enough, being about two hundred feet from stem to stern—there were materials for studying the characteristics of different nations, and the peculiarities of different castes. And the study was simplified, in comparison to what it might have been in a wider sphere, by the strongly marked distinctions of rank that were constituted by the regulations of the vessel. In our country at large, the different ranks melt and mingle into one another, so that it is as impossible to draw a decided line between any two contiguous classes, as to divide a rainbow accurately into its various hues. But here, the high, the middling, and the low, had classified themselves, and the laws of the vessel rigidly kept each inferiour from stepping beyond his proper limits. The mob of the deck would have infringed these immutable laws, had they ventured abaft the wheels, or into the forward cabin; while the honest yeomen, or other thrifty citizens, who were the rightful occupants of that portion of the boat, would have incurred both the rebuke of the captain and the haughty stare of the gentry, had they thrust themselves into the department of the latter. Here, therefore, was something analogous to that picturesque state of society, in other countries and earlier times, when each upper class excluded every lower one from its privileges, and when each individual was content with his allotted position, because there was no possibility of bettering it.

I, by paying ten dollars instead of six or four, had entitled myself to the aristocratic privileges of our floating community. But, to confess the truth, I would as willingly have been any where else, as in the grand cabin. There was good company, assuredly;—among others, a Canadian judge, with his two daughters, whose stately beauty and bright complexions made me proud to feel that they were my countrywomen; though I doubt whether these lovely girls would have acknowledged that their country was the same as mine. The inhabitants of the British provinces have not yet acquired the sentiment of brotherhood or sisterhood, towards their neighbours of the States. Besides these, there was a Scotch gentleman, the agent of some land company in England; a Frenchman, attached to the embassy at Washington; a major in the British army; and some dozen or two of our own fashionables, running their annual round of Quebec, Montreal, the Lakes and Springs.—All were very gentlemanly and ladylike people, but too much alike to be made portraits of, and affording few strong points for a general picture. Much of their time was spent at cards and backgammon, or in promenading from end to end of the cabin, numbering the burnished mahogany panels as they passed, and viewing their own figures in one or other of the tall mirrors, which, at each end of the long apartment, appeared to lengthen out the scene. Then came the dinner, with its successive courses, soup, fish, meat, pastry, and a dessert, all attended with a somewhat affected punctuality of ceremonies. Lastly, the slow sipping of their wine kept them at the table, till it was well nigh time to spread it again for supper. On the whole, the time passed wearily, and left little but a blank behind it.

What was the state of affairs in the forward cabin, I cannot positively say. There the passengers of the second class feasted on the relics of the original banquet, in company with the steward, waiters, and ladies' maids. A pleasant sketch, I think, might be made of the permanent household of a steam-boat, from the captain downward; though it is observable, that people in this and similar situations have little variety of character, and seldom much depth of intelligence. Their ideas and sentiments are confined within a narrow sphere; so far as that extends, they are sufficiently acute, but not a step beyond it. They see, it is true, many different figures of men and women, but scarcely any thing of human nature; for the continually varying crowd, which is brought into temporary connexion with them, always turns the same surface to their view, and shows nothing beneath that surface. And the circumstances of their daily life, in spite of much seeming variety, are nevertheless arranged in so strict a routine, that their minds and characters are moulded by it. But this is not what I particularly meant to write about.

The scene on the forward deck interested my mind more than any thing else that was connected with our voyage. On this occasion, it chanced that an unusual number of passengers were congregated there.—All were expected to find their own provisions; several, of a somewhat more respectable rank in life, had brought their beds and bedding, all the way from England or Ireland; and for the rest, as night came on, some sort of litter was supplied by the officers of the boat. The decks, where they were to sleep, was not, it must be understood, open to the sky, but was sufficiently roofed over by the promenade-deck. On each side of the vessel was a pair of folding doors, extending between the wheels and the ladies' saloon; and when these were shut, the deck became in reality a cabin. I shall not soon forget the view which I took of it, after it had been arranged as a sleeping apartment for at least, fifty people, male and female.

A single lamp shed a dim ray over the scene, and there was also a dusky light from the boat's furnaces, which enabled me to distinguish quite as much as it was allowable to look upon, and a good deal more than it would be decorous to describe. In one corner, a bed was spread out on the deck, and a family had already taken up their night's quarters; the father and mother, with their faces turned towards each other on the pillow, were talking of their private affairs; while three or four children, whose heads protruded from the foot of the bed, were already asleep. Others, both men and women, were putting on their night-caps, or enveloping their heads in handkerchiefs, and laying aside their upper garments. Some were strewn at random about the deck, as if they had dropped down, just where they had happened to be standing. Two men, seeing nothing softer than the oak-plank to stretch themselves upon, had sat down back to back, and thus mutually supporting each other, were beginning to nod. Slender girls were preparing to repose their maiden-like forms on the wide, promiscuous couch of the deck. A young woman, who had a babe at her bosom, but whose husband was nowhere to be seen, was wrangling with the steward for some better accommodation than the rug which he had assigned her. In short, to dwell no longer upon the particulars of the scene, it was, to my unaccustomed eye, a strange and sad one—and so much the more sad, because it seemed entirely a matter of course, and a thing of established custom, to men, women, and children. I know not what their habits might have been, in their native land; but since they quitted it, these poor people had led such a life in the steerages of the vessels, that brought them across the Atlantic, that they probably stept ashore, far ruder and wilder beings than they had embarked; and afterwards, thrown homeless upon the wharves of Quebec and Montreal, and left to wander whither they might, and subsist how they could, it was impossible for their moral natures not to have become wofully deranged and debased. I was grieved, also, to discern a want of fellow-feeling among them. They appeared, it is true, to form one community, but connected by no other bond than that which pervades a flock of wild geese in the sky, or a herd of wild horses in the desert. They were all going the same way, by a sort of instinct—some laws of mutual aid and fellowship had necessarily been established—yet each individual was lonely and selfish. Even domestic ties did not invariably retain their hallowed strength.

But there was one group, that had attracted my notice several times, in the course of the day; and it did me good to look at them. They were a father and mother, and two or three children, evidently in very straightened circumstances, yet preserving a decency of aspect, that told of better days gone by, and was also a sure prophecy of better days to come. It was a token of moral strength, that would assuredly bear them through all their troubles, and bring them at length to a good end. This family now sat together near one of the furnaces, the light of which was thrown upon their sober, yet not uncheerful faces, so that they looked precisely like the members of a comfortable household, sitting in the glow of their own fireside. And so it was their own fireside. In one sense, they were homeless, but in another, they were always at home; for domestic love, the remembrance of joys and sorrows shared together, the mutual anxieties and hopes, the united trust in Heaven, these gave them a home in one another's hearts; and whatever sky might be above them, that sky was the roof of their home.

Still, the general impression that I had received from the scene, here so slightly sketched, was a very painful one. Turning away, I ascended to the promenade deck, and there paced to and fro, in the solitude of wild Ontario at nightfall. The steersman sat in a small square apartment, at the forward extremity of the deck; but I soon forgot his presence, and ceased to hear the voices of two or three Canadian boatmen, who were chatting French in the forecastle. The stars were now brightening, as the twilight withdrew. The breeze had been strong throughout the day, and was still rising; while the billows whitened around us, and rolled short and sharp, so as to give the vessel a most uneasy motion; indeed, the peculiar tossing of the waves, on the lakes, often turns the stomachs of old seamen. No land was visible; for a head-wind had compelled us to keep farther seaward than in the ordinary passage. Far astern of us, I saw the faint gleam of a white sail, which we were fast leaving; and it was singular, how much the sight of that distant sail increased my sense of the loneliness of our situation.

For an hour or more, I paced the promenade, meditating on the varied congregation of human life that was beneath me. I was troubled on account of the poor vagabonds of the deck. It seemed as if a particular Providence were more necessary, for the guidance of this mob of desperate individuals, than for people of better regulated lives; yet it was difficult to conceive how they were not lost from that guidance, drifting at large along the stream of existence. What was to become of them all, when not a single one had the certainty of food or shelter, from one day to the next? And the women! Had they been guarded by fond fathers, counselled by watchful mothers, and wooed with chaste and honourable love? And if so, must not all these good influences have been done away, by the disordered habits of their more recent life? Amid such reflections, I found no better comfort than in the hope and trust, that it might be with these homeless exiles, in their passage through the world, as it was with them and all of us, in the voyage on which we had embarked together. As we had all our destined port, and the skill of the steersman would suffice to bring us thither, so had each of these poor wanderers a home in futurity—and the God above them knew where to find it.

It was cheering, also, to reflect, that nothing short of settled depravity could resist the strength of moral influences, diffused throughout our native land;—that the stock of home-bred virtue is large enough to absorb and neutralize so much of foreign vice;—and that the outcasts of Europe, if not by their own choice, yet by an almost inevitable necessity, promote the welfare of the country that receives them to its bosom.

(March, pp. 270–72)

Old Pirates

Among the British State Trials,[54] are recorded the trials of several pirates, who infested the coast of South Carolina, about the year 1718.[55] The name of one of them was Thatch. He had a ship of forty guns, and one hundred and forty men, with a fleet of smaller vessels, over which he exercised the authority of Commodore. Such was the force of his armament, that he lay at the bar of Charleston, in full sight of the town, and seized and rifled several ships, bound inward and outward. He levied contributions on the government, and took prisoner a member of the Colonial Council. Notwithstanding these outrages, some of his men were allowed to land, and walk openly about the streets of Charleston. One Vaughan afterwards acted in a similar way.[56] The feats of these bold rovers sound

[54] *A Complete Collection of State Trials, 1163–1820,* London, 1816–20. The first twenty-one volumes, compiled by T. B. Howell and published in 1816, include trials "from the earliest period to the year 1783" and incorporate the contents of F. Hargrave's *A Complete Collection of State Trials,* London, 1742; 1776–81, fourth ed. Thomas Jones Howell continued the compilation to the year 1820 in twelve additional volumes, 1817–20. Volume thirty-four is an index. Hawthorne borrowed the *State Trials* from the Salem Athenaeum Library several times in February, March, and April, 1832 ("Books Read by Nathaniel Hawthorne"). He also had access to the work in the Boston Athenaeum; see *Catalogue of the Library of the Boston Athenaeum, 1807–71,* Boston, 1874–82.

[55] "The Trials of Major Stede Bonnet and Thirty-Three Others, at the Court of Vice-Admiralty, at Charles-Town, in South-Carolina, for Piracy: 5 George I. A. D. 1718" (*State Trials,* XV, 1231–1302).

[56] The source of this passage is the following (*ibid.,* XV, 1244):

. . . Thatch, the pirate, came and lay off this harbour with a ship of 40 guns mounted, and 140 men, and as well fitted with warlike stores of all sorts as any fifth rate ship in the navy, with three or four pirate sloops under his command. And after having taken Mr. Samuel Wragg, one of the council of the province, bound out from this place to London, as also Mr. Marks, and several other vessels going out and coming into this harbour, they plundered those vessels going home to England from hence of about 1,500 £ sterling, in gold and pieces of eight. And after that, they had the almost unheard of impudence to send up one Richards, and two or three

strangely, when we reflect that they took place on the North American sea-coast, now so secure; although a century later, the pirates
of the West Indies have displayed almost equal effrontery.

But the most noted hero of the black flag—the 'Archipirate, or
Chief of Pirates,' as the prosecuting officer calls him—was Major
Stede Bonnet.[57] The Attorney General of South Carolina complained,
that some persons had expressed themselves favourably towards
Bonnet, as being a 'gentleman, a man of honour, a man of fortune,
and one that had received a liberal education.' [58] All the government witnesses appear to have felt a high respect for this accomplished and excellent person. Pell,[59] the boatswain of his vessel, who
had turned King's evidence, was almost willing to relinquish his
own pardon, rather than testify against Major Bonnet. The Admiralty Judge seems to have partaken of the general sympathy; he
passed sentence with singular courtesy, and expressions of high consideration towards the criminal; [60] and the hangman did his office
with as much politeness as the circumstances would permit.[61]

---

more of the pirates with the said Mr. Marks, with a message to the government, to
demand a chest of medicines of the value of 400 £, and to send them back with
the medicines, without offering any violence to them or otherwise they would send
in the heads of Mr. Wragg and all those prisoners they had on board; and Richards,
and two or three more of the pirates, walked upon the bay, and in our public streets,
to and fro in the face of all the people, waiting for the governor's answer. And the
government, for the preservation of the lives of the gentlemen they had taken, were
forced to yield to their demands. . . . Afterwards one Vaughan, another noted pirate,
came and lay at our bar, and sent in another insolent message.

[57] The prosecuting officer was Richard Allen, the Attorney General of South
Carolina, who said of Bonnet, "Nay, he was the Archipirata, as it is now taken in
the worst sense, or the chief pirate" (*ibid.,* XV, 1246).

[58] Allen remarked early in the trial, "I am sorry to hear some expressions drop
from private persons . . . in favour of the pirates, and particularly of Bonnet; that
he is a gentleman, a man of honour, a man of fortune, and one that has had a liberal
education" (*ibid.,* XV, 1246).

[59] Ignatius Pell was the first witness questioned (*ibid.,* XV, 1250).

[60] In passing sentence on Bonnet, Nicholas Trott, "Judge of the Vice-Admiralty and
Chief-Justice of the said Province of South Carolina," made a most courteous speech
(*ibid.,* XV, 1298–1302). Among other things he said, "You being a gentleman that
have had the advantage of a liberal education, and being generally esteemed a man
of letters, I believe it will be needless for me to explain to you the nature of repentance
and faith in Christ" (*ibid.,* XV, 1299).

[61] Bonnet was hanged at White-Point, near Charleston, on December 10, 1718.

This Major Bonnet, and his associates, appear to have been partisans of the Stuart family, which was then in exile, and whose hopes of returning to the British throne, had recently been frustrated by the accession of the House of Hanover. It is noticed that the Pretender's health had been drunk by the pirates, aboard one of their prizes.[62] As the exiled monarch might be considered as always at war with his rebellious kingdom, so his adherents might consider themselves justified in carrying on actual hostilities;—at least, such an argument might satisfy the consciences of desperate men, and throw a specious veil over their crimes. Hence, perhaps, the sympathy which they received from the South Carolinians, who probably were not such devoted Whigs as the people of New England. But, in truth, the days of the Buccaneers were then so recent, that the public feeling was every where very lenient towards pirates; although the laws against them were as severe, and as rigidly executed, as at present. The famous Captain Kidd was suffered to go at large, several days, in Boston, and it was even whispered that the British ministry, and the king himself, were concerned in his depredations.

(*March, pp. 272–73*)

New York [63]

The first European discoverer of the island, on which New York is situated, was Henry Hudson, an Englishman in the service of the Dutch East India Company. In 1609, when he visited the site which is now covered with the innumerable edifices and thronged with the population of this great city, it was wild, rough, and desolate. The island, which is about fourteen miles long, and less than a mile in average breadth, was overshadowed by a thick forest, wherever the soil was fruitful enough to supply nourishment. The

---

[62] One of the witnesses, James Killing, testified, "So they made bowls of punch, and went to drinking the Pretender's health, and hoped to see him king of the English nation: they sung a song or two" (*ibid.*, XV, 1252–53).

[63] Opposite this article is a full-page embellishment, a "View of the City of New York."

beach was sandy, but broken by ledges of rock, and interrupted by numerous inlets; the surface of the interiour was diversified with sandy hills, masses of rock, ponds, swamps, and marshes. Such, when the old Dutch vessel anchored off Manhattan island, was the aspect of the spot, which the engraving now represents as a mass of contiguous roofs, with steeples pointing to the clouds, and the ships of every nation thronging at its wharves. Old Henry Hudson would have been even more wonderstruck at the steam-boats which we see in the river, than the red men were at his big canoe.

The Dutch early planted a garrison upon the island; but the city appears not to have been laid out till 1656, forty-five years after the first discovery. It was originally called New Amsterdam, deriving its name from the capital of Holland, whose daughter it might be considered. But the Dutch government was not long to retain its sway over the infant city. In the year 1664, it was claimed by Colonel Robert [sic] Nicolls,[64] under the authority of king Charles the Second, as being within the English jurisdiction, which, on very doubtful grounds, was said to cover the whole space between Virginia and New England. The right of the strongest, however, was indisputably on the English side; and Peter Stuyvesant, the Dutch Governour, a stout old soldier with a wooden leg, was reluctantly compelled to surrender New Amsterdam—which misfortune, according to Knickerbocker,[65] a highly esteemed historian, went near to break his heart. At the period when Colonel Nicolls took possession of the city, it consisted of several small streets, with houses in the Dutch fashion, presenting their gable-ends in front. Nine years afterwards, during a war between Great Britain and Holland, New York again came into possession of its original founders, being taken by a Dutch fleet; but was restored to the English authorities at the peace of 1674.

In 1689, when the Stuarts were driven from the throne of England by the Prince of Orange, the Dutch inhabitants of New York

[64] Colonel Richard Nicolls (1624–72) was the officer in command of the troops which took possession of New Amsterdam for England. He served as the first English governor of the colony, 1664–68.

[65] In the concluding pages of Washington Irving's *A History of New York, by Diedrich Knickerbocker* (1809).

eagerly seized the opportunity to place the city under the dominion of a monarch of their own blood. The English rulers, and principal gentlemen, were favourers of the Stuarts; but Jacob Leisler,[66] a Dutchman, took military possession of the town with a force of forty-nine men, and sent a written message to the Prince of Orange, informing him of this important accession to his party. Leisler doubtless anticipated some distinguished mark of favour from the Prince, who had now become King William the Third. But the unfortunate Dutch captain had made many enemies during his short period of power in New York, and by their machinations, he was condemned to death for high treason, and underwent his sentence soon after the arrival of Colonel Sloughter,[67] the English Governour, whom King William had sent over. The troubles, arising from this dark and complicated affair, continued to disturb the city and province for several years afterwards.

In the year 1708, the original Dutch settlers of New York had become intermingled with many new emigrants from other countries; there were then in the city a great majority of Dutch Calvinists, whose mode of worship was on the plan of the church of Holland— a considerable number of French refugees, who had been exiled by Louis XIV, for their adherence to the faith of Geneva—a few English Episcopalians, and a yet smaller proportion of English and Irish Presbyterians. Notwithstanding these amalgamations of various stocks, the city continued to be Dutch in its aspect and general character, for many succeeding years. The language, however, went gradually into disuse, and in 1756, there were but two churches wherein religious services were performed in Dutch, and their congregations continually diminished. It is a proof, indeed, that the national character of Holland is strongly marked and deeply ingrained, that so small a community as that of New Amsterdam, passing under a foreign government, should so long have retained the characteristics of the country whence it sprung.

[66] Jacob Leisler (1640–91) was executed for having seized the government, although he had surrendered the rule to the first properly appointed governor, Sloughter.

[67] Colonel Henry Sloughter died in 1691. See Mrs. Schuyler van Rensselaer, *History of the City of New York in the Seventeenth Century*, New York, 1909, II, 444 ff.

No historical sketch of New York, however brief and rapid, should omit to notice the Negro Plot, which seems to partake somewhat of the character of the Catholic and innumerable other plots, that threw England into such confusion, and cost so many men their lives, in Charles the Second's days. This mysterious business took place in 1741, at which period there were eighteen thousand inhabitants in the city, one-sixth of whom were slaves. Several incendiary attempts having been made, it was rumoured that the slaves, in conjunction with a few white men, had laid a conspiracy to burn the whole city to ashes, and murder the inhabitants. On this suspicion, one hundred and fifty-four negroes were imprisoned, fourteen of whom were subsequently burnt to death at the stake, eighteen hanged, and seventy-one transported. Twenty whites were also committed to prison, of whom two were executed. This horrible severity, which would hardly have been justifiable, even had the slaves fully succeeded in their alleged plot, makes us shudder when we read the doubts of the historian, whether any such design had ever had existence. There was probably a panic and excitement; the inhabitants were at once terror-struck and blood-thirsty; and if ever New York should reproach New England with the martyrdom of the witches, it will be fair to ask, where they have hidden the ashes of their negroes who perished at the stake.

In 1776, after the battle of Long Island, the city was taken by the British; and a few days subsequent to that event, a fire broke out which consumed one thousand houses. New York continued the head-quarters of the hostile army, the capital of the English government in America, and the metropolis of its affairs, till the peace of 1783; when the last roll of the British drum was heard along its streets, as the troops marched to the point of embarkation. Since that period, the events which would chiefly be touched upon, in a sketch like this, are the prevalence of Yellow Fever, at some seasons, the ravages of the Cholera in 1832, and the Great Fire of December, 1835; which latter calamity will doubtless be an epoch in the history of New York, and never, we trust, be outshone by any future conflagration. We cannot give a better idea of the rapid growth of the city, since the peace of Independence, than by stating the number of its inhabitants, at successive periods. In 1785, there were 35,-000; in 1800, they had nearly doubled, being 60,000; in 1810, they had become 95,000; in 1825, they amounted to 165,000, and in 1830, to 200,000; and the increase of every year would be sufficient, were they to take up their residence in a desert, to form a very considerable city. Besides the permanent population, from ten to twenty thousand strangers are usually there.

The geographical position of New York will secure it against any of those reverses, which have sometimes caused grass to grow in the streets of cities, once as busy and populous as this. It is happily situated on the central portion of the sea-board, the most convenient for intercourse with the American ports, for regular communication with France and England, and for commerce with all the maritime countries of the world. Canada and all the West send their produce thither, by the Erie and Champlain canals, and down the Hudson river. It is already a great city, and can hardly fail to increase, and cover the whole island on which it stands. Broadway, which runs through it like a back-bone, while the cross streets form the ribs, is about three miles long, and eighty feet in width. Here the jewellers have their shops, with the dealers in silks, and all sorts of showy commodities, making it the most splendid promenade on our side of the Atlantic. South street is where the wholesale merchants most do congregate; at least, they did so, before the recent conflagration. In Pearl street, the chief business is the retailing of dry goods. Wall street is the haunt of the stock-brokers, and of all who buy money or sell it; and the effect of the transactions there is felt at the Bourse in Paris, and on the Exchange in London. The Battery is a beautiful walk, whither the citizens may escape from the dust and din, and enjoy the fresh sea-breeze. It would require a volume to describe the public buildings, the institutions of learning and science, the hundred churches, the theatres, the great hotels, which have clustered on the spot where the Dutchmen traced their muddy streets; and where still a few of their antique houses, with high-peaked roofs, remain among the edifices of brick, stone, and marble, with which their successors have burdened the narrow island.

The site of New York, as will be seen by the engraving which we present of it, has none of those inequalities which give a picturesque aspect to a city. In this particular, Boston far exceeds it. But the land and water scenery, of which New York forms a component part, is said to be excelled by no prospect in the world.

(*March, pp. 275-76*)

Captain Franklin's Expedition [68]

In May, 1819, Captain Franklin [69] left England for America, to the northern regions of which country he was bound, on a land expedition of discovery and research. His companions, besides two sailors, were Midshipmen Hood [70] and Back [71] of the British navy, and Dr. Richardson, [72] a learned naturalist. Toward the last of August the party arrived at York, a principal depot of the Hudson's Bay Company, where they received the instructions necessary to the further prosecution of their enterprise. It was past the middle of October, when they reached the station called the Cumberland House, after a journey of nearly seven hundred miles, since leaving York. In that high latitude, of sixty-four degrees, the autumnal weather was as severe as that of midwinter, in a more southern clime; and Captain Franklin felt the necessity of awaiting the return of Spring, before venturing further towards the inclement region of the Arctic Circle. But, as he had been advised to visit the district of Athabusca, in order to obtain guides and interpreters, as well as information respecting the country which stretches north of Slave Lake, he started

[68] With this sketch appears a half-page engraving, "Col. Franklin's Encampment, sketched by himself."

[69] Sir John Franklin (1786-1847) commanded an expedition, 1819-22, to establish the geography of the northern coast of North America. In 1823 he published at London his *Narrative of a Journey to the Shores of the Polar Sea in the Years 1819-22.*

[70] Robert Hood. For the account of Hood's death, see *ibid.,* II, 337-44.

[71] Sir George Back (1796-1878) served in the British navy during the Napoleonic War and later became an admiral. After the Arctic expedition of 1819-22 he had a part in several similar ventures. He recorded his experiences in published narratives.

[72] Sir John Richardson (1787-1865), an arctic explorer and naturalist and a surgeon in the British navy from 1807 to 1855, accompanied Sir John Franklin on two expeditions.

for Fort Chippewayan, accompanied by Mr. Back and one of the sailors. Mr. Hood and Dr. Richardson remained at Cumberland House.

Captain Franklin and his companions were two months in reaching Fort Chippewayan, which is little short of a thousand miles from Cumberland. The country through which they passed was thinly inhabited, and seldom afforded them any shelter from the inclement sky, during the long and dreary nights of a northern winter.—The engraving is from a design sketched by Captain Franklin, and represents one of their encampments. The dogs are unharnessed from the sledges, and may be seen trotting about in the open space, or reposing themselves after their fatigues. The fire is kindled, and sends its smoke up among the wintry pines, while its blaze glows upon their huge trunks and snow-covered branches, and gleams far into the wild avenues of the forest, till its light is lost in their lonesome obscurity. Supported by three stakes over the fire, hangs the kettle, wherein the adventurers are cooking a rich stew, composed of birds, rabbits, and other delectable ingredients, which will soon be set smoking upon the ground, and make them an excellent supper. The dogs also will partake, and then lie down comfortably at the feet of their masters, who, when their hunger is satisfied, will seat themselves round their fireside in the forest, and talk of the beloved ones whom they have left at the hearths of distant England. Then, their hearts yearning with the remembrances that have been roused, they will stretch themselves on the frozen earth, whence the snow has been shovelled away, and strive to sleep that they may be ready for the toils of the morrow. The deep, broad tones of the wind will sigh through the overarching branches—the trunks of the pines will creak, and cause the dogs to awake, with a sharp and sudden bark—sometimes, too, it will be needful to throw a fresh heap of wood upon the fire, and kindle up the wintry wilderness with a more cheerful light. But, after awhile, the twinkling stars, in the cold blue firmament, will cease to glimmer upon the travellers' eyes; they will sleep, and dream of home. May they awake with their toes unharmed by frost, and spend the next winter with their sweethearts and wives, by a good coal fire in England!

We must not forget to notice the marks on the trunk of the large tree, on the right, by which, when they resume their journey in the morning, the travellers will direct their course.

In the Spring, after Captain Franklin's visit to Fort Chippewayan, he and his companions set out northward, to accomplish the objects of their expedition. They were accompanied by about a score of Canadians and Indians, who were to serve as guides and interpreters. Their course lay north and west, and carried them as high as the sixty-eighth degree of latitude, when it was deemed necessary to retrace their steps. It was now the Autumn of 1821. Their journey back towards the civilized world, through a dreary waste, where the winter had set in at the beginning of September, was one of extreme hardship, and attended with many misfortunes. Sometimes, indeed, they were fortunate enough to kill a musk-ox; in which case, they immediately devoured the intestines raw, and even made a meal of the contents of the stomach, which had already satisfied the appetite of the poor ox. Occasionally, they caught a few fish, or shot a bear, which, from the nature of his food, tasted as much like fish as flesh. One or two reindeer, also, afforded them a providential supply. But owing to the number of mouths to be fed, and partly to the improvidence of the Canadians, they were almost continually in want of food, and often compelled to gnaw the bones of deer or musk-oxen, the flesh of which had been long ago devoured by the wolves. A certain unpalatable herb, which they found among the snow, was also made use of, to allay their hunger, although it caused a terrible commotion of their inward regions. Some sat down, in starvation of body and anguish of spirit, and ate up their old shoes— a portion of their apparel which, one would think, they could least dispense with, being to travel through the snow.

Some of the party were so worn out by these hardships, that it was deemed expedient for Captain Franklin to hasten onward, with those who were in a condition to accompany him, and seek assistance for their more exhausted companions. Dr. Richardson and Mr. Hood were among those who remained behind; and the latter, happening to be left alone with an Iroquois Indian, who belonged to the party, was shot by him through the head. The murderer and the survivors travelled on together for a considerable time; but, as the Iroquois appeared to meditate further bloodshed, Dr. Richardson tried the case in his own mind, and felt it his duty to take this Indian's life. Accordingly, he shot him dead with a pistol. It was the act of a determined man, yet a conscientious one; and we know of few more striking incidents than this, when a gentleman of education and sensibility found himself compelled to act as judge, jury, and executioner, on a fellow creature, and put him to death in cold blood.

It would require too large a portion of our pages, to trace all the weary and painful steps of the travellers, and tell how one sank down and died in the snow, and was frozen like a block of ice, before his companions found him—and how all were pined away to skin and bone; so that they looked like a party of skeletons, straggling back to repose their fleshless joints in the grave yards of their native country. They at length encountered some Indians, with whom they had formed an acquaintance on their outward journey, and who were under the influence of the North-West Company. These wild people, when Captain Franklin first came to their regions, had heard that a great chief was about to visit them, and likewise a great medicine chief, whose skill could not only cure the sick, but raise dead corpses and clothe skeletons with flesh. And now they beheld the great chief, a half-starved man, so weak that one of their children might have overcome him; and Dr. Richardson, the great Medicine Chief, himself a skeleton, and far more likely to die than raise the dead. However, they treated the poor strangers kindly, and gave them so much food that they had nearly split asunder—the Doctor, as well as the rest; for while exhorting his companions to abstain, he kept eating at an enormous rate.

When the party had recovered sufficient strength to pursue their journey, the Indians put their baggage into canoes, to which they harnessed their dogs, and set forth across the frozen and snow-covered surface of Slave-Lake. This is the scene to which our cut refers. The dogs, as the reader will perceive, are stout animals, and go at a pretty brisk trot, with their tails curled over their backs, in token of good spirits. They are an excellent substitute for horses, except in the trifling particular, that a man must walk by their side, instead of riding comfortably in the vehicle behind them.

(*March, pp. 281–83*)

Mexican Custom

Forty days before the feast of one of their gods, the ancient Mexicans used to purchase a slave of very fine shape, who, during that time, represented the deity to whom he was to be sacrificed on the day of festival. They arrayed and ornamented him like a god, and he spent all the forty days of his deification, in dancing and rejoicing, and all sorts of pleasures. The Mexicans were attendant on his festivities. They paid him divine worship; but lest he should forget his inevitable fate, two ancient ministers of the idol refreshed his memory, by saying, whenever he appeared to enjoy himself best,— 'Lord, thy pleasures will end a few days hence.' The deified slave was obliged to answer, with a cheerful air—'Be it so'—and continued his mirth. When the forty days were past, they sacrificed their mock deity, at midnight, offered his heart to the moon, threw it afterwards before the idol, cast his body from the top of the temple, and concluded the whole with a dance.

What the Mexicans meant by this singular custom, or whether it had any meaning, we cannot say. Yet all, who are surrounded with pomp and festivities, might not be the worse for such monitors as the Mexican priests, to remind them how soon their pleasures are to end. Another sort of moral, however, might be extracted, and applied very patly to what has been the usual fate of men idolized by the people, in countries where the people are a mob. While they appear most great and powerful, they are but slaves to their own idolaters, who, in a little time, are likely enough to sacrifice them to a new idol, or cast them down from their high places, and dance and make merry at their ruin. But, though the public favour, in all countries, is subject to ebb and flow, yet such tremendous vicissitudes of popular adoration and hatred can never occur among a truly enlightened people. The more a people thinks, and the more it learns, the less will it be acted upon by frenzied impulses; as knowledge is diffused, popularity will become more a matter of judgment than of feeling; and the great men of futurity will seldom rise so high, or fall so low, as the great men of the past. On this principle we trust and believe that American history will tell of fewer great men—great by their actions, their fortunes, and their influence, and signalized by their fate—than have appeared in any other country. Perhaps it is a sign of the healthy condition of a people and a government, when the latter is administered by men of not extraordinary character, with abilities sufficient for the perfect discharge of their duties, and nothing more.

(March, p. 295)

Soldiers

De Boufflers,[73] an old French Marshal, was of opinion, that 'No man was fit for a dragoon, who, in time of war, outlived two campaigns, or in peace, did not, once at least in fifteen days, get his head broken in a private quarrel.' This gives us a strong idea of the wild, reckless, ruffian-like fellows, who then composed the mercenary armies of Europe; and probably there has been little improvement since. On the evidence of our military annals, we are entitled to claim for the American soldiery a far different character. They have individually a higher rank as moral beings;—they cannot be drilled into machines, nor maddened into wild beasts. The citizen, with his recollections of domestic life and civil government, is never entirely lost in the soldier, with no home but his tent, and no law but his leader's word. American troops would never, we think, be guilty of such enormities as disgraced the British army, after the storm of Badajoz; for each man would be restrained by a law within himself, though, as far as external circumstances were concerned, he might be left lawless. Nor would the disorganization of the army, drive the individual soldiers to despair; as was the case

---

[73] Louis François, Duc de Boufflers (1644–1711), was marshal of France and served in every important French military campaign from 1663 until his death.

with the French, on their retreat from Moscow. Perhaps it is not too much to say, that no American ever was a thorough soldier, and nothing but a soldier. Long and frequent warfare, and the necessity of standing armies, might create thousands of such military monsters; but they would be too severe a curse upon our native land, except as a punishment to the guilt and madness, which would have given them existence.

(*March, p. 296*)

Death of Hindoos on the Ganges [74]

The Ganges, which flows through Hindostan, is considered a sacred river, by the natives of that region, and is supposed to possess properties even more miraculous than those of the river Jordan, in which Naaman, the Syrian, washed away his leprosy. Whatever diseases afflict the Hindoos, their universal remedy is sought in its waters; which, therefore, to these poor heathen, supply the place of our panaceas and patent medicines—and, certainly, at a much more reasonable rate. It might be termed, indeed, an immense stream of doctor's stuff, flowing through the whole country, and offering its virtues to all who need them, without money and without price. Such is their faith in its efficacy, that, if the sick can but drag themselves to the banks of the Ganges, or be borne thither by their friends, they often neglect all remedies, except to bathe in its waters, and drink them. In many cases, perhaps, this simple treatment is the best that could be adopted for their diseases; and it is probable that numerous cures are wrought by the imagination of the patient, which it is well known, can convert water into a really powerful medicine. But, undoubtedly, thousands die upon the banks of the river for want of proper care. This, however, can hardly be considered a misfortune by the Hindoos, many of whom, while in perfect health, drown themselves in the Ganges, and expect thus to be cleansed from all their earthly pollutions, and be received into the regions of bliss, because they died in the holy river.

[74] Accompanying this note is a quarter-page woodcut, "A Hindoo Temple, and an invalid on the Banks of the Ganges."

The principal figure in the plate represents a dying man, to whom the Brahmin, or Hindoo priest, is administering a draught of the sacred water. Should this fail of performing the cure, as seems most likely from the desperate condition of the patient, the Brahmin will proceed to fill his mouth and eyes with mud from the banks, and thus hasten the termination of the poor man's misery. The women, shrouded in their robes, one of whom is kneeling at the feet of the expiring Hindoo, while the other stands somewhat apart with her son, are his two wives. The kneeling wife clasps his hand, and appears in great affliction; the other, having a son to comfort her, is less overcome by the expected loss of his father. But Hindoo wives, it must be recollected, have often cause to lament their husbands with much sincerer grief than widows in more civilized countries, from a dread of being immolated on their funeral piles.

Several persons are seen bathing in the Ganges, and others are bearing away its waters, to serve for medicinal purposes, or to purify their souls by washing their face and hands. On the right is the temple of a Hindoo god, at the threshold of which we observe a dying man, with his head turned towards the door, so that his last breath will be offered at the shrine of a senseless idol. Happy are they, to whom has been revealed a surer trust for their dying moments.

(*March, p. 297*)

The French Soldiery [75]

France, under Napoleon, seems to have been set up by Providence for the instruction of the world, as an example of the misery that must inevitably be diffused through the whole body of a nation, which makes war and conquest a part of its settled policy. The in-

---

[75] This article was doubtless one of those Hawthorne had in mind in writing the protest of his valedictory note (see text, pp. 224–25). The tone of the entire sketch shows that he was writing on the subject only because the Bewick Company had chosen the cuts, seven of them, and he had no choice but to supply the copy. But even here, and especially in the first paragraph and occasional asides, we have some of Hawthorne's most delightful irony and light satire.

terruption of peaceful pursuits—the ruin of commerce—the waste of so large a portion of her products to be burnt as gun-powder, or otherwise thrown away in munitions of war—the conversion of the chief strength of her population into unproductive soldiers, whom her worn-out labourers were to feed, and who, for her own good, had far better have been kept in one great alms-house, than sent forth to ravage the world—the dreadful slaughter of her sons, so that, in the burning deserts of Africa, on the frozen plains of Russia, all over Europe, and in three quarters of the earth, a ghastly army of the slain would have arisen, had any trumpet-call been loud enough to rally them—the demoralization of those who escaped the bullet and the sword, and brought their ruffian habits back to their native soil—the broken constitutions and lingering deaths of hundreds of thousands, in succeeding years—the tears of parents, the blasted prospects of affection, the domestic grief in every shape— the deep taint of the national character, which has been left by her drunkenness of blood, and which is visible in every rank of society and department of morals—such were some of the consequences, to France herself, of twenty years of war and glory. While ravaging the other nations of the earth, she avenged them in the very act. Her bonfires of victory cost her as dear, as if her own dwellings had been torn down to kindle them. The annals of her brilliant achievements were written in the best blood of her veins. And this incalculable amount of misery would have been the same, even had her conquests been followed by none of the reverses that snatched them all away; nor would she have derived any more solid benefit, than a gallery of pictures and statues, plundered from vanquished nations, in her capital; and a few triumphal arches, and proud monuments, inscribed with the great N of Napoleon le Grand. But even these poor rewards were torn from her grasp; and Europe trampled on her, and left her in the dust—a signal instance of what must be the inevitable doom, sooner or later, of every people that pursues military glory for its own sake, and without a superlative regard to the cause in which they fight.

The process by which Napoleon brought into the line of his army almost every young Frenchman, who had strength to march, was called the Conscription. In each municipality throughout France, the male inhabitants, between the ages of twenty and twenty-five, were summoned, at stated intervals, to register their names at the town-house. If any person, liable to the Conscription, failed to give in his name, not only he, but his whole family, were subject to a criminal prosecution. Whenever the carnage of one of the Emperour's great victories had made a fresh supply of soldiers necessary, the Minister at War gave notice of the numbers of thousands that would be required, and a portion of the names of the persons, who were registered in the several municipalities, were immediately drawn, as in a lottery. As many of the first drawn numbers, as made up the amount which the War Minister had demanded, were marched off at a moment's warning; while the others were to follow, at the next summons. The most ignominious punishments were inflicted on those conscripts who did not immediately obey the call. Incurable asthma, confirmed spitting of blood, and the early stages of consumption, did not absolutely free the patient from his liability to the Conscription; if the summons were urgent, he might still be made to march, though it were only to die in the bivouac. On arriving at the depôts, the recruits were distributed among the various corps of artillery, cuirassiers, dragoons and infantry, or sappers and miners, according to their strength and stature. In this way, the whole youth of France, as they reached the age of manhood, were enrolled as soldiers, and remained such, during the pleasure of government. It is said that the average height of the present generation of Frenchmen, who were born under the rule of Napoleon, is considerably less than in former times; owing to the strongest and tallest young men having been slain, or otherwise restrained from marriage; while the business of keeping up the population was left to an inferiour class. And yet, so deeply seated was her warlike frenzy, that, when the Great Captain fell, poor battered France deemed it her chief misfortune, that she must now cease to fight for glory!

These remarks have been suggested by the examination of some cuts of the different corps of the French army, part of which were given in the last Magazine, and a few more are added in the present number. It will perhaps be interesting to the American people, just at the present crisis, to receive what little information we can bestow as to the men, who may possibly, before another year, attempt to find room for a bivouac on our own seaboard.[76] The first figure shows the ancient garb and weapons of a grenadier, in the reign of Louis XIV, another glorious Despot; of whom, however, France had grown so intolerably weary, that, when his funeral pomp was passing from the palace of his ancestors to their tomb, the people hooted and reviled their dead monarch, till his attendants were glad to hide him in the dust and darkness. The first grenadiers carried an axe, a sabre, and a leathern bag, containing twelve or fifteen hand-grenades—a murderous little globe of iron, stuffed with gunpowder, which, being thrown among a group of soldiers, was likely enough to kill or mangle half a dozen of them. The grenadier in the cut holds his burning match in one hand, and in the other his lighted grenade, wherewith he appears to be meditating slaughter.

The next figure is a grenadier of Napoleon's famous Old Guard, a body of the most gallant and perfect soldiers that ever followed, like slaves, at any conquerour's heels. Their life, like that of the soldiers of Wallenstein,

> Was but a Battle and a March;
> And like the wind's course, never-ceasing, restless,
> They stormed across the war-convulsed earth.[77]

Men, armed and accoutred like this figure, strode victorious in their day, through the streets of every capital on the continent of

---

[76] The threatened war with France in 1835 and 1836 (see also the last paragraph of this article) arose from misunderstandings growing out of President Jackson's seventh annual message to Congress, into which the French read an impeachment of the good faith of their government and a threat of reprisals if the installments due the United States were not paid promptly. The French government at first refused to make any payments until an official explanation should be made, but Jackson insisted that no insult had been intended and refused to make any explanations. He asked Congress to exclude French ships from American ports and to make preparations for war. The crisis was averted, however, at the intervention of the British government.

[77] Schiller's *The Death of Wallenstein*, II, iii. Hawthorne has quoted here, with slight inaccuracy, lines from Carlyle's *The Life of Friedrich Schiller* (1825); see p. 157 of the edition published at Philadelphia in 1859.

Europe. Wherever their Emperour fought a battle, there they lay in heaps; they would have rushed to certain death, at the motion of his finger. They did so rush, at Waterloo, and made such an Aceldama of that dreadful field, that the English farmers imported their bones by the ship-loads, to manure their crops. Such was the final destiny of the Old Guard—to nourish, with the marrow of their bones, the wheat that was to feed Napoleon's bitterest enemies!

The third figure is the Grenadier of the present day, the very man whose bayonet may shortly be levelled at our own breasts. He is evidently the true son of his father, fonder of the drum than of the fiddle—these two ridiculous instruments being able, at any time, to set a Frenchman mad with fun or fury. His moustaches and bent brows give the fellow a most grim aspect, and to do him justice, he has already proved, at Antwerp and Algiers, that he possesses the whole stock of military virtues proper to his nation.

The French *Cuirassiêrs* are a body of cavalry, who have retained, in part, the ancient custom of defensive armour, which has been generally laid aside, from the time that gunpowder created a very important change in the science of war. A few hundred years ago, the knights and men-at-arms were iron from head to foot; their caps were of cast-iron, somewhat like a porridge-pot; their coats and breeches of iron plates, which had to be riveted together by a blacksmith, before the warriour was ready for the field; their boots were also of iron, and their gloves, or gauntlets, were covered with iron scales. In the iron plate that covered the face, there was a cross-slit over the mouth and nose, and two holes for the eyes, through which the knight peeped, like a prisoner out of his dungeon. In fact, he was one of the most miserable of prisoners; for, after he was once hammered into his iron panoply, he could not possibly get out, without assistance; and unlike all other captives, except a snail, he was compelled to carry his dungeon on his back. These men of iron —they may well be called so, since their hearts were iron, as well as their garments—mounted on horses that wore iron breast-plates, rode boldly into the battle and laid about them on all sides, conscious that neither sword, spear, arrow, nor club, would inflict the least damage on such a mass of rusty metal as they presented. Sometimes they tumbled from their horses, and lay like land-tortoises in their shells, unhurt by the trampling of contending armies over them. The only death in battle, to which they were liable, was by smothering.

After the invention of fire-arms, this heavy defensive armour became, in many cases, worse than useless. A cannon-ball would, of course, smash it all to pieces, and even a musket-bullet, fired point-blank, would generally pierce the breast-plate, and sometimes carry fragments of the iron into the wound. The whole system of defensive armour had been calculated for wars in which the only artillery was the bow-and-arrow, and where the fortune of a battle was to be decided by hand-to-hand conflicts, with sword and spear. This state of things being done away, the heavy-armed gentry found it convenient to come out of their shells. But a regiment, or more, of cuirassiers, have always been retained in France; rather, perhaps, under the old Bourbon monarchy, as contributing to the splendour of the royal household, than as an important portion of the army. They did, however, distinguish themselves, during the wars of Louis XIV, and his successor. Under the consulate of Bonaparte, three new regiments of cuirassiers were added to the one that had previously existed, and soon after his coronation as Emperour, these were increased to twelve. At the present day, there are ten regiments. Their defensive armour is a polished steel breast-plate and helmet, the latter on the ancient Roman pattern; their principal offensive weapon, a sabre; for though they carry pistols at their saddle-bow, it is not with these that they ever do any important execution. Their mode of fighting is to charge in line, with the point of the sabre advanced, as is seen in the first cut, representing a cuirassier under Napoleon.

These regiments are composed of the largest and strongest men in the service, and when mounted on horses of corresponding size and vigour, (which, however, are seldom found in France,) their onset must be tremendous. One would suppose, that, by the mere weight and momentum of steeds and men, even without the use of the sabre, the steel-breasted line would trample down and annihilate a body of ordinary cavalry. Napoleon specially intended them to break the squares or masses, into which infantry throw themselves to repel a charge of horse. They failed to do this at Waterloo; and great credit has been claimed for the British infantry, on account of their gallant defence with the bayonet; but a writer in the United Service Journal states, that no real contact took place, on that occasion, between the French horse and the masses of infantry. The French would come on at the gallop, as if they intended to plunge headlong into the midst of the foe, but, when within a few yards, would discharge their pistols, and ride round the masses, seeking, it seems, for some point that was not bristling with bayonets. The English writer, a military man, gives it as his opinion, that a square of infantry could not, with merely the musket and bayonet, defend itself against a resolute charge of heavy horse. These cuirassiers, it is said, were more than a match for the light cavalry of the British, but were mastered, in their turn, by the heavy dragoons, who rode over the French, like a troop of monkeys mounted on goats. The cuirassier of 1834, of whom we subjoin a cut, differs little from his predecessor.

The next corps, whom we shall pass in review, are the *Lancers*. These were created by Napoleon, as opponents to the Hulans and Cossacks, a sort of light cavalry in the service of the Emperour of Russia. Napoleon's first regiment was formed at Warsaw, in 1807, and composed of Poles, who were afterwards incorporated into the Imperial Guard, still retaining the lance.

A second and third regiment were afterwards added. Their lances were poles, ten or twelve feet long, made of black ash, and terminating in a steel blade with three sides. A small flag was also attached to the lance, not as an ornament, but to affright the enemy's horses. Besides this weapon, they had a fusil and bayonet, an hussar-sabre, and pistols. They were doubtless well calculated to oppose the wild Cossacks, who likewise carried lances, and never charged in line, but came on tumultuously, each warriour trusting to his own skill in the management of his horse and weapon. We have seen different opinions expressed, as to the efficiency of the lancers, when opposed to cavalry armed merely with the sabre.—Some of the Eng-

lish officers affirm, that, as the steel points of the French lances
stuck out two or three yards beyond the horses' heads, their own
dragoons lost a third more men than the enemy, in every charge;
the steel was in their breasts, before they could come within sword's
length. Others ridicule the accoutrements of the lancer, and say,
that, by bending forward on his horse's neck, at the same time ward-
ing the lance upward with his sabre, the dragoon had the gentleman
of the long pole at his mercy. We have read, that the French lancers
did little service at Waterloo, except to ride over those parts of the
field whence the fury of the conflict had eddied away, and thrust
their lances down the throats of the wounded British soldiers.
'What!'—they would cry, as the prostrate foe turned himself in his
blood, at the sound of their horses' tramp—'You are not dead yet!'
And before the word was out of the ruffian's mouth, the steel head
of his lance had saved the surgeon a labour. We may reasonably
conclude, that, if Napoleon had judged this corps fit for any better
service against regular troops, than to kill dead or disabled men, he
would have armed a more considerable portion of his cavalry with
the lance. Since 1831, there have been six lancer regiments in the
French army.

The discipline of the French soldiers is perfect in its way, but
differs from that of the troops of any other nation. In this particular,
they form a singular contrast to the Prussians, whose army is an immense machine, composed of a hundred thousand, or more, of
individual machines, none of which are good for any thing in their
separate capacities. The same remark may be applied to the British,
though not in an equal degree. The drill of the Prussians has always
been unmercifully severe; and Dr. Moore,[78] father of Sir John

[78] Dr. John Moore (1729–1802) was a Scottish physician and author. For the
characterization here of the French and the German soldiers Hawthorne leaned
heavily on Moore's *A View of Society and Manners in France, Switzerland, and Germany,* London, 1779; see the second edition, 1800, I, 337–41; II, 138–61. The following (*ibid.,* II, 154) is the passage Hawthorne alludes to specifically: "I then mentioned
a fact which appeared to me still more extraordinary. A hussar, at the last review, had
fallen from his horse at full gallop, and was so much bruised, that it was found necessary to carry him to the hospital; and I had been assured, that as soon as the man
should be perfectly recovered, he would certainly be punished for having fallen."

Moore,[79] relates, that, whenever a dragoon chanced to fall from his horse, though every bone in his body might be broken, yet, if he escaped with his neck, he was sure to be flogged, the moment that he came out of the hospital. Such a system was suited to the heavy and sluggish character of the German soldiery, who needed a set-tled rule for every movement; they could not march, but at a measured step, nor discharge their muskets, except in the regular routine; and if any thing deranged their clock-work, the battle was irretrievably lost. But a Frenchman is as different from a German, as quicksilver from lead. It is impossible to make a machine of him. To a certain extent, he must be allowed the liberty of indi-vidual action, and be free to fume, and fret, and dance, and work off his superfluous vivacity, while other troops stand as motionless as the leaden soldiers of a toy-shop. Gentlemen, who have seen their infantry regiments, say, that they form hardly so straight a line as our militia at a brigade-muster, even when the latter have neither a stone-wall nor a plough-furrow to dress by. But it must not hence be concluded, that our militia could stand a moment, in the open field, before the charge of these most gallant troops; or that the soldiership of the French has not been pushed to the highest per-fection of which it is susceptible. The French discipline seems to hang loose about the soldier, but, to all desirable purposes, it is as strong as iron; it resembles an ancient shirt of chain-mail, flexible to all the motions of the body, yet woven with the links of steel. Their system cherishes a martial enthusiasm, and makes victory depend upon it; the soldier's spirit is not broken by rigid forms, nor are his violations of duty punished by aught of ignomiy; if he have committed a military crime, a platoon of his comrades are drawn out, and he dies a military death. Owing to these causes, and also to their natural character, the French soldiery must be acknowl-edged a gallant and chivalrous set of men. In good spirits, and under a leader whom they idolize, (for if they do not idolize, they despise him,) they are a terrible foe. They pour their irregular masses down upon the hostile ranks with the shock of a tornado;

[79] Sir John Moore (1761–1809), a British general, served in America during the Revolution and in the Napoleonic War.

and firm must be the embattled line that can resist it. Yet, if resisted, the conflict is half won. The first shock is the fiercest, and every succeeding wave breaks more feebly against the rocky barrier which it cannot overthrow.

It is now twenty years, since France's broken sword was wrested from her by the strength of Europe. During all that period, she may be said to have been at peace; for, though, here and there, her trumpet has sounded, yet no event has occurred that could fully rouse up the martial spirit of the people. In this long interval, there is reason to believe, that she has learnt a wiser interpretation of that pernicious phrase, 'La Gloire,' and has discovered that her true glory consists in the welfare of her children; and that even the laurel is a plant of peaceful growth, and withers when the soil is kept continually wet with blood. We would fain hope so. And if France has ceased to be a warlike power, and to dream of victory on foreign fields, and of captive kings paying court to their conquerour in her capital, then, indeed, the millenium is at hand, and the nations may beat their swords into ploughshares and their spears into pruning-hooks, and cast their cannon into church-bells, and ring an exulting peal throughout the earth. This, perhaps, is too great a miracle for prudent men to count upon. Her martial fire still lives, under the ashes that have been heaped upon it. Even now there needs but a strong breath, to blow it into a flame, which should leap across the Atlantic, and set all the world a-blaze. Her young men were nurslings of War. From earliest childhood, they have stood at the knees of Napoleon's grim veterans, and heard them tell of those hundred victories, the least of which would have immortalized the Man of Destiny, who won them all. And as they listened, their hearts have burned. It irks them, that they walk so peacefully through life, and have never felt the battle-frenzy, nor seen the cannon-smoke sweep heavily away, and disclose the spectacle of a hard-fought field.

A few weeks since, it was far within the limits of allowable speculation, that such a field might be fought, where we should hear the booming of the artillery. Heaven has averted the calamity from our Land of Peace. But had it come—doubt it not, my countrymen!

—posterity would have seen no tokens of the French Invasion, save when the plough should pass over some ancient battle-ground, and turn up the rusted steel of a lance, a battered helmet, or a ball-pierced cuirass.

(March, pp. 305-9)

Preservation of the Dead

The last American Journal of Science [80] gives an account of the invention (by Segato,[81] an Italian) of a new method of preserving the bodies of the dead. The facts are drawn from a pamphlet, published at Florence. Segato has visited Africa, for the purpose of constructing a map of its northern regions. Among the sands of the desert, he discovered a carbonized substance, which, on close examination, proved to be animal matter. He afterwards found the entire body of a man, about a third smaller than the size of life; it had been carbonized by the heat of the sand, and was partly black, and partly of the colour of soot. It occurred to Segato, that it might be possible to imitate this natural process, by means of art; and on his return to Italy, he began the necessary experiments, and appears to have been completely successful in converting animal substances to stone. His method of operation is not given; but the following are some of the results.

Entire animal bodies may be as readily subjected to the process as small portions. They become hard, and acquire properties precisely similar to those of stone. The skin, muscles, nerves, veins, and blood, all undergo the same change; nor need the viscera be removed. The colour, form, and general appearance, remain unchanged. Offensive substances lose their smell. Putrefaction is checked at once. If the process be carried only to a given degree, the joints are perfectly

[80] Henry N. Day, "Notice of a New Mode of Preserving Animal Bodies," *The American Journal of Science and Arts,* XXIX (1836), 359–62.

[81] Jerome Segato (1792–1836), an Italian traveler and naturalist, conducted an expedition to Egypt in 1827 and 1828. The result was a report, with maps, published at Florence in 1835. A pamphlet was published by Joseph Pellegrini at Florence in 1835, relating Segato's discovery of a method of preserving animal bodies.

flexible. The bones of skeletons, which have undergone this operation, remain united by their natural ligaments, which, though pli-
able, are solid and stony. Moisture and insects can do no injury to
animals thus preserved. The hair does not fall off, but retains a
natural appearance. The size of the body, after the process, is a little
less than in its natural state; but no alteration takes place in the
weight. The eyes, in most of the animals that have been thus em-
balmed, sparkle, and lack only the power of motion, to appear just
like life.

As proofs of the efficacy of his invention, Segato shows a canary-
bird, which was preserved ten years ago, and has not undergone the
slightest change; also, the eggs of the land-turtle, water-snakes,
toads, fishes, snails, and insects. It has likewise been successfully
tried on various portions of the human body. The inventor possesses
the emaciated hand of a lady who died of consumption; a foot,
retaining the nails; the liver of an intemperate man, as hard and
lustrous as ebony; an entire human brain, with all its convolutions;
a girl's scalp, with the hair hanging in ringlets; and the head of an
infant, partly destroyed and discoloured by putrefaction, which had
begun its work before the experiment was made. But Segato's
greatest curiosity is a table, inlaid with two hundred and fourteen
pieces of stone, (or what appears such,) of splendid and variegated
hues, admirably polished, and so intensely hard, that a file can
scarcely make the slightest scratch upon them. These stones, which
would be mistaken for specimens of the most precious marbles, are
different portions of the human body—the heart, liver, pancreas,
spleen, tongue, brain, and arteries. Thus a multitude of men and
women, once alive, have contributed fragments of their vital organs
to form Segato's inlaid table; a poet, perhaps, has given his brain, an
orator his tongue, a hypochondriac his spleen, and a love-sick girl
her heart—for even so tender a thing as a young girl's heart can
now be changed to stone. In her lifetime, it may be all softness; but
after death, if it pass through Segato's hands, a file can make no
impression on it.[82]

[82] In this connection see the various items mentioned in "A Virtuoso's Collection,"
among them the heart of Bloody Mary (*Writings,* V, 340–41).

The limited means of the inventor have not hitherto permitted him to try the process on an entire human body; although the expense would be only one-tenth as great as that of embalming in the ordinary way. It is confidently believed, that dead persons may thus be preserved for ages, with precisely the aspect that they wore, when Death laid his hand upon them. We can perceive no reason why these stony figures, which once were mortal, should not last as long as a marble statue. Instead of seeking the sculptor's aid to perpetuate the form and features of distinguished men, the public may henceforth possess their very shapes and substance, when the aspiring souls have left them. The statesman may stand in the legislative hall, where he once led the debate, as indestructible as the marble pillars which support the roof. He might be literally a pillar of the state. Daniel Webster's form might help to uphold the Capitol, assisted by the great of all parties, each lending a stony arm to the good cause. The warriour—our own old General [83]—might stand forever on the summit of a battle-monument, overlooking his field of victory at New Orleans. Nay, every mortal, when the heart has ceased to beat, may be straightway transformed into a tombstone, and our cemeteries be thronged with the people of past generations, fixing their frozen stare upon the living world.[84]

But never may we—the writer—stand amid that marble crowd! In God's own time, we would fain be buried as our father's [sic] were. We desire to give mortality its own. Our clay must not be baulked of its repose. We are willing to let it moulder beneath the little hillock, and that the sods should gradually settle down, and leave no traces of our grave. We have no yearnings for the grossness of this earthly immortality.[85] If somewhat of our soul and intellect might live in the memory of men, we should be glad. It would be an image of the ethereal and indestructible. But what belongs to earth, let the earth take it.

(*April, pp. 314-15*)

[83] Andrew Jackson.

[84] The substance of this sketch possibly had some part in the formulation of the basic idea underlying "The Man of Adamant" (1837).

[85] These remarks on the possibility of an "earthly immortality" for the human body suggest Hawthorne's treatment of the idea of an eternal life on earth in "Dr. Heidegger's Experiment," *Doctor Grimshawe's Secret,* and *Septimius Felton.*

The Boston Tea Party * [86]

In the year 1773, the British government, after a long series of efforts to establish the principle of taxation in the American Provinces, attempted to secure its object through the medium of the East India Company. There were then in the warehouses of that body upwards of seventeen millions pounds of tea, in addition to which quantity, the importations of the current year were expected to be larger than usual. By an act of Parliament, which had been framed with a view to the circumstances of the period, the East India Company, on exportation of their superfluous teas to America, were to be allowed a drawback to the full amount of the English duties. The Company bound itself to pay the duty of three-pence per pound, which Parliament had laid on teas imported into the Colonies. In accordance with the act of Parliament, the Lords Commissioners of the Treasury gave license for the exportation of six hundred thousand pounds of tea; which quantity was to be distributed to various ports along the American coast. So soon as the project became known, applications were made to the directors of the East India Company, by a number of merchants in the colonial trade, soliciting a share of what they conceived would be a very profitable business. Some recommended the establishment of a branch of the East India House in a central port of America, whence minor ramifications might be extended all over the continent. The plan finally adopted was, to bestow the agency on merchants of good

---

* The writer of this sketch has not had the pleasure of hearing Mr. Tha[t]cher's lecture [87] on the same subject; nor would he have felt himself at liberty to take an easy advantage of that gentleman's original research, until its results were given to the public, through the press.

[86] See text, p. 119. A narrative of the story of the Boston Tea Party forms a part of *Grandfather's Chair* (*Writings*, XII, 220–22). On the page opposite the account in the magazine is an engraving with the caption "Destruction of Tea, in Boston Harbour, in 1773."

[87] Benjamin Bussey Thatcher (1809–40) was a prominent Boston editor, lawyer, lecturer, and philanthropist. He published a book entitled *Traits of the Tea Party* in 1835.

repute in the Colonies, who could give satisfactory security, or obtain the guaranty of London houses. Among these, Richard Clarke [88] and sons, Benjamin Faneuil, and Joshua Winslow, were appointed agents for the disposal of the tea in Boston.*

The East India Company, and those who solicited or accepted an agency in this affair, considered it merely in a commercial light. They appear not to have understood or felt, that the Americans would object to the proposed measure, on the ground of abstract principle. Whatever doubt was entertained, respecting the profitable nature of the concern, arose from the fact, that large quantities of tea were smuggled from Holland, and might possibly be bought lower than the Company could afford to put their own, when burdened with the colonial duty. It was hoped, however, that the English exporters might be able to undersell the Dutch, even with the duties annexed, or at least to come so near their prices, that the difference would not compensate the risk of smuggling. But no sooner did the news reach the Colonies, than an opposition sprung up, on grounds which had nothing to do with the high or low price of the commodity. The people at once penetrated the design of the British ministry, and saw that, if successful, it would leave them without a plea against any extent of taxation that Parliament might choose to inflict. In anticipation of the arrival of the tea-ships, public meetings were called at several sea-ports, resolutions were passed to prevent the landing of the cargoes, and the Consignees were enjoined to refuse their agency in the disposal of them.

Boston, especially, which had always led their colonial defence against the ministerial aggressions, here again took a prominent part. Soon after the names of the agents were made known, Mr.

---

* The quantity of tea consumed in Massachusetts was estimated at 2400 chests per annum; and in all America at 19,400 chests; or upwards of six millions of pounds. It was supposed, that, of three millions of inhabitants, one third were in the habit of drinking tea twice a day.—Bohea was the kind principally used.

[88] Richard Clarke (1711–95). Because of the disfavor in which the colonists held Clarke after the Boston Tea Party, he moved to England in 1775 to live with his daughter and her husband, John Singleton Copley, the artist.

Richard Clarke and his son were roused from sleep, in the dead of night, by a knocking at their door. Looking forth from the window, they saw in the courtyard, where the moon shone very bright, the figures of two men, one of whom told the Consignees that he had brought them a letter from the country. A servant received it from these midnight messengers. It proved to be a formal summons, in the name of the Freemen of Massachusetts, commanding Richard Clarke and son to appear at Liberty Tree, at high noon on the ensuing Wednesday, then and there to make a public surrender of their trust, as agents for the disposal of the tea. A letter in the same terms was likewise delivered to each of the other Consignees. The next morning, printed notifications were seen at all the corners and public places, calling on the Freemen of the Province to assemble at Liberty Tree, and witness the public resignation of the agents. At eleven o'clock in the forenoon of the appointed day, the bells of all the churches began to ring, and continued their peal for a full hour; while the town-crier went from street to street, summoning the people to the place of meeting. A multitude accordingly assembled, among whom were the selectmen of the town. The Consignees, however, shut themselves into one of their warehouses, and would neither obey the summons, nor give any satisfactory reply to a committee, who were sent to them from the Freemen at Liberty Tree. Various other meetings were held, and such a spirit manifested, as convinced the agents, that the patronage of the powerful East India Company ought by no means to have been solicited as a favour, but rather deprecated as a calamity. They now wrote to London, expressing their doubts whether the commission could be executed.*

---

* The Consignees appear subsequently to have crept out of the business, by refusing to receive the teas of the owner and masters of the vessels. The latter made them a formal offer of the cargoes, and drew up a protest, on their declining to meddle with them. The people then considered Mr. Rotch,[89] the ship-owner, as responsible for the disposal of the teas.

Griffin's Wharf, mentioned in the next paragraph, is now called Liverpool Wharf.

[89] William Rotch (1734–1828) was a Nantucket whaling merchant, and the founder of a successful business in France.

All these proceedings were anteriour to the arrival of the tea. The first of the vessels entered the harbour of Boston on Sunday, the twenty-eighth of November, and was followed, in the course of the same week, by two others. On the twenty-ninth, a meeting was convoked at Faneuil Hall, and adjourned, on account of the over-flowing multitude, to the Old South Church, where the Consignees were required to appear, and pledge themselves to send back the ships, without payment of the duties which had accrued by their entry at the port. These demands were not complied with. A committee, appointed by the meeting, took possession of the ships and moored them at Griffin's wharf, in charge of a volunteer watch, consisting of a captain and twenty-five men. If molested in the day-time, they were to give notice by ringing the bells; if at night, by tolling them. Six persons were appointed to raise the surrounding country, in case the government should seek assistance from the troops at Castle William, or the vessels of war which lay in the harbour. The meeting of Monday was continued by adjournment to Tuesday, the thirtieth, when Mr. Sheriff Greenleaf[90] read a proclamation from the Governour, requiring the people to disperse, at their utmost peril. This produced no other effect than a general hiss. A pledge was exacted from Mr. Rotch, the owner of one or more of the vessels, that the tea should be returned to England in the same bottom in which it came. Mr. Rotch, after protesting against the people's proceedings, yielded to what he considered the necessity of the case, and gave the required promise. After the adjournment of this meeting, nothing of a decisive nature took place, till about the middle of the ensuing month. Mr. Rotch, who had been observed to be dilatory in his preparations for sending back the vessels, was then again summoned before a great assembly at the Old South Church, and enjoined forthwith to demand a clearance from the Collector of the Customs. The result was to be communicated to the people the next day at ten o'clock, till which hour the meeting was adjourned. It was now necessary that prompt measures should be adopted, because, were the duties to remain unpaid beyond

---

[90] Stephen Greenleaf (1704–95), sheriff of Suffolk County before the Revolution, remained a loyalist and protested vigorously against the Whigs.

twenty days from the arrival of the ships, the Collector would be authorized to seize their cargoes.

At the appointed hour, on Thursday, the sixteenth of December, Mr. Rotch made his appearance at the Old South, and declared himself unable to obtain a clearance, until all the merchandise liable to duty should be landed. He was directed to enter a formal protest against the Collector of the Customs, and then to demand a passport from the Governour. To await the success of this latter application, the people adjourned till three o'clock of the same day.

At this crisis of our narrative, we may take a momentary glance at the various parties, whose feelings or interests were affected by the circumstances which we have related. The affair had now arrived at that point, where the whole weight of official responsibility was made to press upon Governour Hutchinson. His situation must have been a most irksome one. He was of course a loyalist, a partisan of the ministry in its most offensive measures, and had already suffered, as well as acted, in its behalf. But he was also a New England man, and possessed the sentiments proper to his birth. The tone of his writings proves him to have been deeply imbued with native patriotism, which, had he come to office in earlier times, when there was yet no conflict between the power of Britain and the rights of the Colonies, would have made him as good and just a ruler as New England ever had. A writer of his country's annals,[91] he must have shrunk from the idea, that future historians would pourtray him as one of those few colonial Britons, who had shown themselves more English than American. It was undoubtedly with inward trouble, that Governour Hutchinson made his choice between the will of his king and the interests of his country, and with painful reluctance, that he hardened his heart to incur the whole odium of ministerial tyranny. His adherents were scarcely more at ease. The favourite Councillors, the officers under the Crown, the Judges, the tory gentlemen; all, in short, who seemed

---

[91] An allusion to Hutchinson's *The History of the Colony of Massachusetts Bay* (see n. 43). In *Grandfather's Chair* (*Writings,* XII, 181–88) Hutchinson's position, his background, and his relations with the colonists are treated in much the same manner as here.

to have the power of the realm on their side, were now cowering beneath the acknowledged supremacy of the people. No advocate of despotism dared speak above his breath; none but the aristocratic dames, who, sipping a decoction of the forbidden herb from diminutive china cups, and snuffing up its exquisite fragrance, declaimed more bitterly against the disloyal mob, with every snuff and every sip.

In estimating the situation of the provincial metropolis, we must not forget the military and naval force, which was as completely at the Governour's command, as if the armed ships had been moored within pistol-shot of Griffin's wharf, and the troops quartered in the churches, or their tents pitched upon the Common. The officers and men, feeling no interest in the country which they were sent to overawe, would smile at the rising tumult of affairs, and nourish, perhaps, an idle hope, that the audacity of the people might not be quelled without the glitter of bayonets in the streets, and at least a volley over their heads. Looking townward from their vessels and the ramparts of Castle William, they ridiculed alike the menaces of the mob, and the imbecility of the Governour for not crushing the sedition with a word and a blow.

We cannot better describe the circumstances of the people, than by resuming our narrative from the point at which we left it. The Freemen of Massachusetts, in public assembly, at the Old South, were awaiting the arrival of Mr. Rotch, with the Governour's ultimate decision on their demands. Would that we might picture them, as if we leaned from the gallery of the sacred edifice, looking down upon a dense mass of visages, old and young, all expressive of the stern determination which made but one heart throughout that great multitude! Perhaps, standing so much nearer to our Puritan forefathers than we do, they had a more imposing mien than their descendants will ever wear. The old original spirit was potent within them. Had it been otherwise, they could not, for a series of years, have braved the threats, and been neither depressed nor maddened by the injustice of Britain, and at length have been forced into an attitude of defiance by the efforts of her strong arm to bend them upon their knees. In that attitude—not upon their knees, but offering a bold front to the oppressor—we find them now.

Mr. Rotch had been directed to re-appear before the assembly, at three o'clock. At that hour, the people had again met, expecting the Governour's reply. If favourable, it would have given a truce to the Colonial troubles. On the other hand, there was probably, a general understanding, that, should their demands be negatived, the Freemen were to enforce their will by some immediate act. Wild spirits were among them, doubtless, whom one inflammatory word of their leaders might have excited to burn the vessels at the wharf. But it was the noble characteristic of all the movements of our fathers, by which they wrought out our freedom, that, possessing the energy of popular action, they yet secured the result of sage and deliberate councils. The will of the wisest among the people was universally diffused, and became the people's will. There was an example of this truth, even on the verge of the meditated act of violence. As the afternoon declined, and the early December evening began to shed its gloom within the meeting-house, there were murmurs at the delay of Mr. Rotch, who had already long exceeded the time allotted for his absence. The leading men restrained the impatience of the people, by representing the propriety of doing all in their power to send back the tea to England, nor proceeding to a more violent measure, till it should be undeniably the sole alternative. Light being brought, an address from Josiah Quincy [92] filled up the interval of a third hour. At last, after a course of patient determination, which, had it been rightly interpreted, might alone have taught the ministry to despair of subduing such a people, there went a whisper that Mr. Rotch was crossing the threshold. It was a moment of breathless interest. Would the Governour yield? Then might the British king have had one other loyal shout from his New England subjects, such as greeted his ancestors of the Hanover line, when it was proclaimed in Boston, that they had elbowed the Stuarts from their throne!

But that huzza was never to be heard again—'Long live King

[92] Josiah Quincy (1744–75), a prominent lawyer and patriot in Boston, went to England late in 1774 to explain the grievances of the colonists. His mission achieved very little, and he died on the return voyage.

George' was a cry of departed years—no echo there would answer it. Mr. Rotch announced, as Governour Hutchinson's ultimate reply, that, for the honour of the king, the vessels would not be permitted to leave the port, without a regular settlement of the custom-house dues.

It was a singular proof of the just estimation in which Mr. Rotch held this assembly, that he dared to appear in the midst of it, with so utter and decisive a negative to its demands. Nothing of injury or insult was offered him. But the dead hush, that pervaded the multitude after hearing the Governour's resolve, was suddenly broken by what seemed an Indian war-cry from the gallery. Thitherward all raised their eyes, and perceived a figure in the garb of the old forest-chiefs, who had not then been so long banished from their ancient haunts, but that a solitary survivor might have found his way into the church. The signal shout was immediately responded by twenty voices in the street. That loud, wild cry of a departed race must have pealed ominously in the ears of the ministerial party, as if the unnatural calmness of the mob were at length flung away, and savage violence were now to rush madly through the town. By the people, such a signal appears to have been expected. No sooner was it given, than they sallied forth, and made their way towards the tea-ships with continually increasing numbers, so that the wharves were blackened with the multitude.

Already, when the crowd reached the spot, a score of Indian figures were at work aboard the vessels, heaving up the tea-chests from the holds, tearing off the lids, and scattering their precious contents on the tide. But it was the people's deed, they had all a part in it; for they kept watch while their champions wrought, and presented an impenetrable bulwark against disturbance on the landward side. Three hours were thus employed, under the batteries of the armed vessels, and within cannon-shot of Castle William, without so much as a finger lifted in opposition. In this passive acquiescence, the government chose the wisest part. Had the troops been landed, the green at Lexington would not have been hallowed with the first blood of the Revolution; and perhaps another royal Governour might have been sent to prison, by the same law of the people's will that imposed such a sentence on Sir Edmund Andros.[93]

Thus were the tea-ships emptied. Their rich cargoes floated to and fro upon the tide, or lay mingled with the sea-weed at the bottom of the harbour. Having done their work, the Indian figures vanished, and the crowd, with a thrill, as if ghosts had walked among them, asked whither they had gone, and who those bold men were. The generations that have followed since this famous deed was done, have still asked who they were, and had no answer. Perhaps it is better that it should be so—that the actors in the scene should sleep without their fame—or glide dimly through a tale of wild, romantic mystery. We will not strive to wipe away the war-paint, nor remove the Indian robe and feathery crest, and show what features of the Renowned were hid beneath—what shapes were in that garb, of men who afterwards rode leaders in the battle-field—or became the people's chosen rulers, when Britain had sullenly left our land to its freedom. But, of those whom the world calls illustrious, there are few whose marble monuments bear such a proud inscription, as would the humblest grave-stone, with only this simple legend under the dead man's name—HE WAS OF THE BOSTON TEA-PARTY!

(April, pp. 317–19)

St. John's Grave

St. Augustin relates,[94] that some Ephesians assured him that St. John, though buried at Ephesus, was not dead, but that, as the bedclothes move up and down by the breathing of a man asleep, so does the earth of the grave where Saint John lies buried. Doubtless, this fable was imagined in honour of the 'beloved apostle'; but we

---

[93] Sir Edmund Andros (1637–1714) was governor of New England from 1686 to 1689; of Virginia from 1692 to 1697. Learning of William's accession to the throne in 1688, the colonists had seized Andros and sent him to England as a prisoner.

[94] An entry in *The American Notebooks* for September, 1835, indicates that Hawthorne was then reading Saint Augustine. The notebook item tells of a dead body's rising and leaving the church while Saint Augustine was holding mass (*Writings*, XVIII, 10).

honour him more by the belief, that he spends no such dreary night in the grave—that he left only his dust in Ephesus, and went straight to Heaven. We do wrong to our departed friends, and clog our own heavenward aspirations, by connecting the idea of the grave with that of death. Our thoughts should follow the celestial soul, and not the earthly corpse. Sepulchral monuments, from the costliest marble of Mount Auburn to the humblest slate in a country graveyard, are but memorials of human infirmity—of affection grovelling among dust and ashes, instead of soaring to the sky.[95]

(*April, p. 319*)

Unrecorded Crimes

In a speech of Lord Morpeth, about a century ago, on the impeachment of the Earl of Macclesfield [96] for illegal practices in his office of Chancellor, we find this striking passage.—'My Lords, there have been crimes so unexampled, and of so horrid a nature, that the male-

[95] This attitude toward graves and tombstones is presented more fully in "Chippings with a Chisel" (1838), where the narrator says to Mr. Wigglesworth, the monument carver (*ibid.*, II, 253–54): " 'I care little or nothing about a stone for my own grave, and am somewhat inclined to scepticism as to the propriety of erecting monuments at all over the dust that once was human. The weight of these heavy marbles, though unfelt by the dead corpse of the enfranchised soul, presses drearily upon the spirit of the survivor, and causes him to connect the idea of death with the dungeon-like imprisonment of the tomb, instead of with the freedom of the skies. Every grave-stone that you ever made is the visible symbol of a mistaken system. Our thoughts should soar upward with the butterfly—not linger with the exuviae that confined him. In truth and reason, neither those whom we call the living, and still less the departed, have anything to do with the grave. . . .

" 'They are not under the sod . . . ; then why should I mark the spot where there is no treasure hidden! Forget them? No! But to remember them aright, I would forget what they have cast off. And to gain the truer conception of DEATH, I would forget the GRAVE!' "

[96] Thomas Parker, first Earl of Macclesfield (*c.* 1666–1732), was impeached in the House of Lords in 1725. Impeachment proceedings were commenced in Commons on February 12, and the trial was held before the Lords from May 6 to 26. Lord Morpeth was one of the principal managers for the Commons at the trial. Hawthorne found a full report of the trial, including the passage he quotes from Morpeth's speech, in Howell, *A Complete Collection of State Trials*, XVI, 1031. See also *A Collection of the Parliamentary Debates in England*, London, 1740, IX, 100–79.

factors have been tried at midnight, and immediately drowned, and the journal-books burnt, in compassion to mankind, that the memory of the proceeding being destroyed, the crime itself might not be propagated.' It would be a blessed thing for the world, if the neces-sity of unvarying laws, and of established precedents, would permit the crimes of each successive age to pass into oblivion, and leave to the next generation the task of contriving its own modes of iniquity. But now, much of the evil of the past remains as an inheritance to the future; [97] there are whole libraries, the volumes of which con-tain nothing but crime. It is not good to read such books; for, to our sinful nature,[98] guilt is contagious, and may be said to com-municate its contagion to the paper on which it is recorded. The ex-tensive circulation of criminal trials is both a sign of something evil in the public mind, and a cause of new evil.

(April, p. 322)

Warriours, Ancient and Modern [99]

We have here a motley troop of warlike figures, whom we pro-pose to display upon the pages of the Magazine, without much re-gard to military order. They will resemble a company, composed of the shattered fragments of several regiments; or a throng of horse and foot, pursuers and pursued, in the confusion of a lost battle; or perhaps they will remind the reader of the scene on a muster-ground, after dismissal, when soldiers in many different uniforms are mingled together. But here, the old iron-clad knight, who fought under the

[97] Cf. the attitude toward the past set forth in *The House of the Seven Gables,* expressed chiefly by Holgrave; also the fear voiced by Hawthorne in the preface to *Peter Parley's Universal History* that children may be influenced by the evil deeds recorded in history.

[98] Cf. the idea of man's predisposition to sin and the universality of sin in such stories as "Young Goodman Brown," "The Procession of Life," and "The Minister's Black Veil."

[99] This discussion of warriors is clearly one of the contributions which Hawthorne wrote most unwillingly (see n. 75). That he wrote reluctantly here may be inferred from the generous repetition of materials from the article entitled "The French Soldiery" (see text, pp. 78–88). The article is embellished with ten woodcuts.

walls of Jerusalem, will be the comrade of the modern hussar; the
man-at-arms of the eleventh century will ride in the same rank with
the carabinier of the nineteenth; and every figure that wears a
sword, will be liable to the conscription in our troop.

Here, in the first place, come a knight and a foot-soldier, both of
whom were Crusaders. It will be observed that the defensive armour
of the knight is greatly superiour to that of the common soldier. He
wears, over all his other garments, a sur-coat, on which are embroidered the arms of his family; beneath this external covering is
his hauberk, or shirt of mail, formed of ringlets of steel linked together; under the hauberk, is a cuirass of forged iron, composed of
breast-plate and back-plate; and under the cuirass is a gambeson,
or quilted coat, stuffed with cotton, to preserve his body from bruises.
He also carries a wooden shield, covered with leather and strength-
ened with iron or brass, which, in time of action, he suspends round
his neck, and passes his left arm through two handles on the inside.
The defensive armour may be seen to better advantage on the next
figure.

This is a man-at-arms, probably a gentleman by birth, but who
has not yet attained the dignity of knighthood. He is clad in complete steel from head to foot, except a portion of his face, which can
also be covered by closing the vizor of his helmet; when his head will
be literally shut up in an iron box. His offensive weapons are a
sword, and a heavy lance of ash-wood, which should be represented
as eighteen or twenty feet in length. The immense weight of their
equipment, and its want of pliability, must have greatly embarrassed
the knights and men-at-arms in battle. Their ordinary and best
mode of fighting was, to seat themselves firm in the saddle, direct
their lances, and then gallop headlong to meet the advancing foe,
who came onward in the same style. Sometimes the lances were
splintered on both sides, without the overthrow of either champion;
but generally, one or other of them was borne off his horse, and
measured his length on the field. Here, unless stunned by the fall,
or suffocated by the closeness of his helmet, the warrior lay pretty
safe. It is related, that, at a certain battle, in Italy, the vanquished
knights could not possibly be slain, but remained stretched on the

field like huge lobsters, till several men were set to work upon each of them with wood-cutter's axes. King James the First, who was a dear lover of peace, remarked, in praise of armour, that it not only protected the wearer, but, by impeding his movements, prevented him from hurting any body else.

The war-horses were almost as heavily armed as their riders; they wore an iron mask over the face, and frequently a breast-plate; their legs were sometimes defended, either by iron or stiff leather. It was likewise the fashion to cover them completely with chain-mail, or with quilted linen. An animal thus accoutred must have been very unwilling to move; nor can we wonder that the knights were compelled to use spurs, the rowels of which were six inches long. Some remnant of the ancient armour may be seen in the next cut, which represents a soldier of Louis the Sixteenth's guard.

Defensive armour was also worn, and probably still continues to be so, by the French carabiniers. The first of the two following figures has a breast-plate under his coat, and his immense boot sufficiently protects the whole leg and thigh. This corps did excellent service in the wars of Louis the Fourteenth.

The breast-plates of the Carabiniers are now of burnished copper, as are likewise their helmets, which are surmounted with a red crest.

The hussars were probably the first mounted troops who entirely laid aside defensive armour. This corps was formed in 1692, of Hungarian refugees in the service of France. Their uniform was a sky-blue vest and pantaloons, and a bonnet, boots, and scarf, all of scarlet. Each hussar had a right to wear as many plumes as he had cut off foemen's heads.

The hussars fought without any sort of order, or system of tactics. They charged their adversaries in a confused throng, surrounded them, and affrighted them with their shouts and gestures. If repulsed, they were promptly rallied, and came again to the charge. They were very adroit in the management of their horses, all of which were small and light. About the year 1750, they wore a species of fur cap, called schakos, and a blue pelisse with red trimmings.

Until the French Revolution, the hussars had many singular customs; one of which was, to pull the ears and tails of their horses, whenever they made a halt—a process which was supposed to remove their weariness. When the corps was subjected to the same discipline as the rest of the army, all these usages were abandoned. Their dress however, had still a wild and singular appearance.

There were, at one period, fourteen regiments of hussars in the French service. At the restoration of the Bourbons, these were reduced to six, which is the number retained under the present government. Their uniform, as will be seen by the cut at the head of the next column, has nothing of the stiffness which is usual in the military garb. In this respect, they form the most perfect contrast that could be imagined, to the knights and men-at-arms whose figures lead the van of this article.

It is a sad thought, that men of the sword, whether as individuals or in armies, should hitherto have filled so large space in the annals of every nation. Will the time never come, when all, that pertains to war, shall be merely a matter of antiquarian curiosity?

(*April, pp. 329–31*)

Ancient Pilgrims

In the year 1407, some heretics having spoken against the popish custom of making pilgrimages to the shrines of Saints, and particularly objecting to the merry music which accompanied the march of the pilgrims, the Archbishop of Canterbury made the following reply. We give it with all its antique diction, and uncouth and disorderly spelling—

'When one of them that goeth barfote striketh his Too upon a stone, and hurteth hym sore, and maketh hym to blede, it is well done that he or his Felow begyn then a songe, or else take out of his Bosome a Bagge-pype, for to drive away with soche Myrthe the hurte of his Felowe. For, whith soche solace, the Travell and Werinesse of Pylgremes is lightely and merily broughte forthe.'

We are inclined to take the side of the jovial Archbishop against the heretics, who, by the way, were soon after burnt for their misbelief in regard to this, and other sacred matters. It would have been almost worth while to live in those old days of papistry, for the sake of riding in the company of Chaucer's pilgrims, beguiling the way with tales mirthful or melancholy; or even to go on foot, dancing along to the sound of the bag-pipe, with the comfortable idea that every step of this merry journey was a step towards heaven. Sometimes, it is true, the pilgrims walked with peas in their shoes, or crept over the stony roads on their bare knees—modes of travelling which the merriest music could hardly render tolerable. But generally, a pilgrimage, though imposed or undertaken as a religious penance, must have been a very pleasant interlude in a man's life. On such occasions, all the daily cares, that harassed him at home, were thrown aside, and it was inevitable that his disburdened mind should grow cheerful and frisky. And except to visit the distant shrine of a saint, it was seldom, in those times, that people strayed a dozen miles from their birthplace; so that these pious journeys afforded them almost their sole opportunities for seeing the world; and when completed, the pilgrim was a travelled man, and had a stock of fireside stories for the remainder of his days. Should the Romish faith, as some forebode, be established in America, there is no part of its rites, ceremonies, and customs that our locomotive countrymen would more readily adopt, than this of pilgrimages. But it would not be the same thing now, as in those good old times. The pilgrim would neither provide himself a staff, nor seek out a good stout horse—he would simply put down his name at the coach office, or get on board a steamboat, with a vallise under his arm—or, perchance, he would do his pilgrimage in a rail-road car. No bag-pipe nor song would enliven his way; he would be graver than the ancient pilgrims, but with earthly cares, not heavenly meditations—and a pilgrimage, thus modernised, would be as dull as a trip to Saratoga Springs.[100]

(April, p. 332)

---

[100] In this connection one recalls Hawthorne's own rambles in the 1830's and the tale of "The Seven Vagabonds." Here is a hint of "The Celestial Railroad." For other examples of the author's fondness for putting persons and actions of the past in a modern environment, see "The New Adam and Eve" and "P.'s Correspondence."

Fidelity

Captain Walcot, at his execution for being concerned in one of the plots, in Charles the Second's time, advised his friends, 'that they would neither hear any man speak, nor speak themselves, that which they would not have repeated; for there is no such thing as faith in man to man, whatever there is in man to God: Either the tears of a wife, or a family of little helpless children, something or other, will attempt or provoke men to betray one another.' These are the bitter words of one about to die for a friend's breach of confidence. We do not concur with Captain Walcot, as to the universal faithlessness of mankind:—there are many single men whom we would trust, even when their truth to us might be ruin to themselves; but, to speak frankly, no husbands, no fathers. Not that a man's love of wife or child is stronger than his self-love—but with the former love, he patches up a much more plausible excuse to his conscience.

(*April, p. 336*)

April Fools [101]

It is a curious fact, that the custom of making April Fools prevails in the most widely separated regions of the globe, and that, everywhere, its origin is hidden in remote antiquity. The Hindoos on the Ganges practise it; in all the European countries it exists, in one shape or another; the French make what they call April Fish; and, in America, it is one of the few mirthful customs which our fathers brought from merry Old England. When once such a fashion was established, we should suppose that human nature might be pretty safely trusted to keep it up. It is desirable to have the privilege of saying, on one day in the year—what we perhaps think, every day—that our acquaintances are fools. But the false refinement of the present age has occasioned the rites of the holyday to fall

[101] Reprinted in [A. H. Japp's] *Memoir of Nathaniel Hawthorne*, London, 1872, pp. 238–42. Accompanying the essay is a quarter-page engraving.

somewhat into desuetude. It is not unreasonable to conjecture, that this child's play, as it has now become, was, when originally instituted, a vehicle of the strongest satire which mankind could wreak upon itself. The people of antiquity, we may imagine, used to watch each other's conduct throughout the year, and assemble on All Fools' Day, to pass judgment on what they had observed. Whoever, in any respect, had gone astray from reason and common sense, the community were licensed to point the finger, and laugh at him for an April Fool. How many, we wonder, whether smooth-chinned or gray-bearded, would be found so wise in great and little matters, as to escape the pointed finger and the laugh.

It is a pity that this excellent old custom has so degenerated. Much good might still result from such a festival of foolery; for though our own individual follies are too intimately blended with our natures to be seen or felt, yet the dullest of us are sufficiently acute in detecting the foolery of our neighbours. Let us, by way of example, point our finger at a few of the sage candidates for the honours of All Fools' Day.

He who has wasted the past year in idleness, neglecting his opportunities of honourable exertion; he who has learnt nothing good, nor weeded his mind of anything evil; he who has been heaping up gold, and thereby gained as many cares and inquietudes as there are coins in his strong-box; he who has reduced himself from affluence to poverty, whether by riotous living or desperate speculations: these four are April Fools. He who has climbed, or suffered himself to be lifted, to a station for which he is unfit, does but stand upon a pedestal, to show the world an April Fool. The gray-haired man, who has sought the joys of wedlock with a girl in her teens, and the young girl who has wedded an old man for his wealth, are a pair of April Fools. The married couple, who have linked themselves for life, on the strength of a week's liking; the ill-matched pair, who turn their roughest sides towards each other, instead of making the best of a bad bargain; the young man who has doomed himself to a life of difficulties by a too early marriage; the middle-aged bachelor who is waiting to be rich; the damsel who has trusted her lover too far; the lover who is downcast for a damsel's fickleness;—all these are

April Fools. The farmer, who has left a good homestead in New England, to migrate to the Mississippi Valley, or any where else, on this side of Heaven; the fresh-cheeked youth who has gone to find his grave at New Orleans; the Yankees who have enlisted for Texas; [102] the merchant who has speculated on a French war; [103] the author who writes for fame—or for bread, if he can do better: the student who has turned aside from the path of his profession, and gone astray in poetry and fancifulness: [104]—what are these, but a motley group of April Fools? And the wiseacre who thinks himself a fool in nothing—Oh, superlative April Fool!

But what a fool are we, to waste our ink and paper in making out a catalogue of April Fools. We will add but one or two more. He who, for any earthly consideration, inflicts a wrong on his own conscience, is a most egregious April Fool. The mortal man, who has neglected to think of Eternity, till he finds himself at the utmost bourn of Time,—Death points at him for an April Fool. And now let the whole world, discerning its own nonsense, and humbug, and charlatanism, and how in all things, or most, it is both a deceiver and deceived—let it point its innumerable fingers, and shout in its own ear—Oh, World, you April Fool! Lastly, if the reader in turning over this page, have not profited by the moral truths which it contains, must we not write him down in our list of April Fools? But if there be no truths, nothing well said, nor worth saying, we shall find it out anon; and whisper to ourself,—'Mr. Editor, you are an April Fool.'

(*April, pp. 339–40*)

---

[102] The reference is to the men who were enlisting in the struggle of Texas for independence from Mexico.

[103] See n. 76.

[104] For others of Hawthorne's comments on the futility of striving for fame, particularly in literary endeavors, see the story "The Ambitious Guest," and also *Writings*, I, 207, 222, 258; II, 102–3, 305–6; III, 171–72; IV, 90, 94, 255, 306–7; V, 64, 110, 192, 250–51; XVII, 256, 286–87.

Martha's Vineyard

It is not generally known, that, in ancient times, the Vineyard, with Nantucket and the neighbouring islets, constituted a separate colony, wholly independent of any other jurisdiction in America. This territory was granted by William, Earl of Stirling,[105] to Thomas Mayhew,[106] formerly a merchant in the province of Massachusetts Bay, but whose fame, rather traditionary than historical, has brought him down to posterity under the title of Governour Mayhew. He appears to have had as real and legal a claim to the gubernatorial dignity, as any of the French, Dutch, Swedish, or English potentates, who then bore sway within what are now the limits of the United States and Canada. Governour Mayhew came into office in 1642; at which time, there were a few English families at one extremity of the island, whom Providence had brought thither, while their vessel was wandering along the coast in search of Virginia. The descendants of the Nortons,[107] who were among these early settlers, are now very numerous in the Vineyard. The rest of Governour Mayhew's territory was inhabited by the red men,[108] whose sachems seem to be independent chiefs, yet owed a species of feudal homage to the great Sachem of the Wampanoags, who ruled on the main

[105] Sir William Alexander, Earl of Stirling (c. 1567–1640), poet and courtier, held large grants of land in America after 1621, including New Brunswick and Nova Scotia until they were ceded to France in 1632.

[106] Thomas Mayhew lived from 1593 to 1682—Hawthorne is incorrect as to both his age and the date of his death. Though avowedly recounting historical facts in this sketch, Hawthorne did not let the facts hinder the full play of his imagination on the "dynasty of the Mayhews." The record is that Mayhew acquired Martha's Vineyard, Nantucket, and the Elizabeth Islands in 1641 and moved to the Vineyard as magistrate in 1646. His only son, Thomas (c. 1621–57), began in 1642 colonization and missionary work among the Indians. He was lost at sea on his way to England in 1657; hence the successor of the elder Mayhew was his grandson, John Mayhew, who died in 1689 and was in turn followed by Matthew Mayhew, another grandson, who lived until 1710.

[107] The Nortons are mentioned along with the Mayhews in "Chippings with a Chisel" (*Writings*, II, 242).

[108] See the reference in "Chippings with a Chisel" to the Indians under the rule of Governor Mayhew (*ibid.*, II, 250).

land. The Governour had been partly induced to emigrate to Martha's Vineyard, by the hope of converting the Indians to Christianity; and contemporary writers give such statements of his success, as we might find it difficult to believe; if the French missionaries had not also proved, at about the same period, that the red man had a soul for the white man's Heaven. Be that as it may, Governour Mayhew undoubtedly gained an influence over the Indians of the isles, which was exerted equally for their good as his own, and that of his countrymen in Plymouth and Massachusetts. During his rule, there were no wars in the Vineyard; by the mild energy of his character, the Indians there were kept quiet, while king Philip [109] was stirring up the savages to their last great struggle with the civilized invader; and when the good old Governour was called away, the martial spirit of the race had long been fled.

We love to dwell upon the history of the little province, and eke out its unwritten portions by the aid of fancy. We wonder whether the inhabitants ever troubled themselves about a constitution, a charter, or a bill of rights? Did they grumble at the sovereignty of Great Britain, and bluster about independence? Did the people send representatives to the General Court of Martha's Vineyard, or was it the custom, as formerly in Massachusetts, for the whole body of the freemen to legislate in person? Or, as appears more probable, was Governour Mayhew's head the legislative, and his hand the executive branch of power? If so, the good old man must be set down in the list of despots, and, but for a kind and upright heart, might have been as black a tyrant as the worst of them. How large a standing army did this potentate maintain, and what portion of the troops kept guard before his palace-gates, or attended him, when he marched through his dominions? Where did the prison stand, and where the scaffold, and how many traitors, or other criminals, were executed under Governour Mayhew's warrant? What rebellions or intestine commotions disturbed the Vineyard, and what hostilities

[109] King Philip (d. 1676), a sachem of the Wampanoag Indians, led the Indians in the hostilities which from June, 1675, to August of the following year reached the proportions of a war. During the hostilities the Indians on Martha's Vineyard remained loyal to Mayhew and the British.

with the rival powers across the Sound? What were the alliances of
this Commonwealth, and what the general system of its foreign policy? For the support of his administration, did the Governour levy
taxes at his own pleasure? And did he, like his brethren of Massachusetts, assume the regal prerogative of coining money? On his
death-bed, did he nominate his successor?—or was it by Divine
Right that Thomas the Second succeeded to his father's chair of
state? For certain it is, that the dynasty of the Mayhews was continued in the person of the first ruler's son, who also, we believe,
combined Church with State, and was himself the whole clergy of
the province. Legislator! Captain-General! Chief-Priest! All that
monarchs aspire to be, such were the Mayhews of Martha's Vineyard.*

The separate sovereignty of this little insular nation was more
than once disputed by the large provinces in its neighbourhood. In
1644, the Commissioners of the United Colonies (on what pretence,
save the right of the strongest, does not appear) annexed Martha's
Vineyard to the jurisdiction of Massachusetts. This was during the
civil war in England, when an appeal to the King must have been
fruitless, and one to the Parliament would have resulted in its sanction of the Puritan usurpation. It is probable, however, as we do not
trace its strong character in the early history of the island, that Massachusetts was satisfied with asserting its title, and made no attempt to

---

* Governour Mayhew died in 1681, at the great age of ninety-
three. Gookin [110] says, that Thomas Mayhew, the eldest son of the
Governour, was lost on his passage to England, before his father's
death. It must therefore have been Matthew,[111] the second son, who
succeeded to the family honours and prerogatives. There are many
of the name of Mayhew still in the Vineyard, and they appear to
feel a proper pride in their origin.

[110] Daniel Gookin (1612–87) included material relating to Martha's Vineyard in
his *Historical Collections of the Indians in New England,* which was ready for the
printer in 1674 but was not published until 1792, in the first volume of the *Collections
of the Massachusetts Historical Society.* Hawthorne drew some volume of the *Collections* from the Salem Athenaeum Library fifteen times or more in the year 1830
(see "Books Read by Nathaniel Hawthorne").

[111] Matthew Mayhew was not a son but a grandson of Governor Mayhew. See n. 106.

deprive the Ma[y]hews of their just authority. Whenever the energetic government of the Bay-province did actually bear sway, its influence was too perceptible to be overlooked, and too peculiar to be mistaken. In after years, the claim was either withdrawn or forgotten, and the Mayhews ruled the Vineyard in peace, till late in the reign of Charles the Second. The island, without regard to the previous title of Governour Mayhew, was then granted to the King's brother James, and annexed to the province of New York, which had recently been taken from the Dutch. But neither in this case, was the external jurisdiction much more than nominal; and Martha's Vineyard still remained a separate dominion, merely paying the Duke of York an annual tribute of two barrels of pickled cod-fish. His Royal Highness being a Catholic, the object of this arrangement was doubtless to obtain a good supply of fish for his table, in Lent and other seasons of abstinence from flesh. A Whale would have been a tax more honourable to the bold hunters of the deep. The cod-fish subsidy was however done away in 1692, by a final union between Martha's Vineyard and Massachusetts, and the effective exercise of the authority of the latter province within the limits of the island. Thus ended the rule of the peaceful Mayhews.*

In time of peace, the jurisdiction of Massachusetts has ever since had the same supremacy in Martha's Vineyard, or Duke's county, as in any of the counties on the main land. But a province, which is indefensible in war, cannot strictly be said to form an integral part of the country with which it is politically connected. It must always be allowed a degree of independence, in holding intercourse with the enemy; it would be its utter ruin, to take an active part in hostilities; and however inoffensive in this respect, it will be likely to suffer more, save in the slaughter of inhabitants, than any other portion of the territory. This has been the case with Martha's Vineyard. We are not informed of the extent to which its prosperity was

---

* The writer in the Massachusetts Historical Collections,[112] from whom we have drawn most of the foregoing statements, speaks of the cod-fish tax, on the authority of tradition.

[112] Daniel Gookin; see n. 110.

affected by the old wars between France and England; but in the Revolutionary contest, it was a severe sufferer, without the satisfaction of taking any revenge on its oppressors, or of helping to establish the liberties of America. The sons of the Vineyard were captured, and confined in the British prison-ships, where many of them died. The whaling business was entirely broken up. The island was continually exposed to the ravages of the enemy's cruisers; and in 1779, the English General Gray robbed it of one hundred and twenty oxen and ten thousand sheep, leaving the grass to grow uncropped on its desolate pastures. Before the close of the war, Martha's Vineyard exercised one of its ancient rights, as a separate colony, by sending an agent or ambassadour to London, to represent the proceedings of this wholesale cattle-stealer, and negociate a settlement of the claims which had thereby accrued. About a third of the value of the sheep and oxen was repaid by the British government. The Vineyard long suffered under the depressing influence of its Revolutionary misfortunes, and perhaps had not entirely recovered from them, when they were in some measure renewed by the war of 1812.

Thus much for the history of the island. In regard to its present condition, a month's residence [113] enables us to give a few hasty sketches, which perhaps may entertain the reader; as Martha's Vineyard lies somewhat out of the beaten track of tourists and description-mongers. The settlement nearest to the main land is that of Holmes's Hole; a name familiar to the wives of New England seamen, when, searching the ship-news, they are gladdened with the intelligence that their husbands have arrived thither, and are only awaiting a fair wind to bring them home. The port is separated from Falmouth, on the main, by the Vineyard sound, which is here about nine miles across. It is a small and rather shabby-looking town, with a few streets, which plough through such a heavy sand that the inhabitants have acquired a peculiar gait, by the constant habit of trudging ankle-deep along the side-walks. The young girls manage to perform

---

[113] This leaves no doubt that Hawthorne visited Martha's Vineyard, possibly in the summer of 1830 or 1831. For a fuller discussion of this matter and of parallels between this sketch and "Chippings with a Chisel," see an article of mine on "Hawthorne at Martha's Vineyard," in *The New England Quarterly*, XI (June, 1938), 394–400.

it very gracefully. Some of the houses are painted yellow; others have a greenish tinge; but generally they present a dark and weather-beaten aspect, betokening that the inhabitants care little for out-ward show. The meeting-house has the same neglected look, and might, whether fairly or not, convey the idea that religion has gone somewhat out of fashion. Altogether, the town offers a strange con-trast to one of our white inland villages, with the architectural pretti-nesses of the dwellings, and the neat church, looking as if it were painted anew every Saturday in readiness for the Sabbath. The sandy lanes of Holmes's Hole will as little bear a comparison with a smooth village street, extending between two broad and verdant margins, and overshadowed by lofty elms, which almost intermingle their heavy boughs across it. In fact, there is a terrible deficiency of green grass and tall trees. Behind the town, the land rises in gentle swells, on the side of one of which may be discerned a small company of slate and marble grave-stones, marking the site of an ancient burial place.

There are several shoe-maker's shops in the town, one or two variety stores, a shop for the sale of ready-made clothing, and a post-office, where every mail-day, the whole correspondence of Holmes's Hole and the vicinity is displayed at a window. There are two school-houses, each looking like a church in miniature, with a little tower and cupola; and a bell which jingles as regularly as that of a college chapel. In school-hours, the voices of the children might be heard a long way off, all reciting their lesson together, in a sort of half-musical chant. Several times in the course of a day, a red flag was displayed at the door of an auction-room, and the auctioneer rang a handbell with such prodigious emphasis, that at least half a dozen maids and matrons waded through the sand to bid upon his goods. Sometimes, an old fashioned chaise drove into town, or else a wagon toiled heavily along, lugged by a yoke of the fine cattle of the Vine-yard. Next, perhaps, the village doctor would be seen on horseback, plodding forth ten miles or more, to spend all the night abroad, for a scanty fee. And now, should there chance to be any passengers to-day—for its arrival depends upon that contingency—now appears the stage-coach from Edgartown,[114] the insular metropolis. Such are the trifles that serve to amuse the stranger, when the sultry sun and the heavy sand compel him to idle away the day at the window of the inn.

There are two wharves at Holmes's Hole; one extending out from the central part of the town, and the other about a mile below, at the entrance of the harbour. It is pleasant, in a Summer morning, to lean against one of the posts at the end of the inner wharf, and watch the boys angling for cunners, eels, scaupog, and other fish with Indian names; or to mark the arrival and departure of the packets, that ply between this port and New Bedford or Nantucket. The masters of these sloops seem to take more pride in them than in their dwelling-houses, if we may judge by the decorations and pretty flourishes of paint about the stern and bows. Before the steam-boat came into competition with them, they had a great run of business, both as to freight and passengers, and still have not much cause to grumble. The flag being set—that is to say, lowered a little from the mast-head, as a signal of sailing orders—down come the passengers, with their trunks and great-coats, and step hastily aboard. But one old gentleman, bethinking himself that he has left a bundle ashore, entreats the skipper for time to run and fetch it. 'Well, well! But bear a hand!' cries the impatient skipper; and off sets the old man at full speed. Meantime, the mainsail is hoisted; a horn is blown repeatedly to hasten the loitering passenger; the boys, playing about the deck, are ordered to bundle ashore; the moorings are on the point of being cast off—one instant more, and the old man will be too late. 'Stop! Stop!' he bellows from afar, and is now seen at the upper end of the wharf, with his baggage and sea-stores, consisting of a pan of gingerbread and the bundle aforesaid. He tumbles aboard, and the sloop, with her broad sail fluttering and shaking, glides slowly from the wharf; when up goes the jib, and she begins to feel the wind.

Then we turn elsewhere for amusement, and perceive an old whaler standing in the shade of one of the warehouses. He has weathered Cape Horn some half a dozen times, but now makes it his business

[114] Edgartown is the setting of "Chippings with a Chisel."

to catch fish along shore, and this morning, off Gay Head, has captured a prize that may be worth looking at. It is a sword-fish, the body already cut up, but the head entire, and with the sword protruding from the snout, five feet in length, flat, two-edged—an awful weapon! Speak to the old man, and he will explain how he harpooned the monster, and tell us, moreover, that, once upon a time, sitting in the stern of his boat, she was staggered with a sudden shock; and up came a sword through the bottom, directly between the astounded fisherman's legs. The sword-fish is very common in these waters; its meat is dry, but not ill-flavoured, and somewhat resembles halibut.

But the greatest incident of the day, is the arrival of the steamboat from New Bedford, bound to Nantucket. A flag at the lower wharf is the signal of a single passenger, and will call her into the entrance of the harbour; another flag at the upper wharf denotes three passengers or more, and will bring her all the way up to town. Both signals are set to-day. And here she comes round the point, already audible by the distant beating of her wheels, and whiz of steam, which rapidly grows more distinct. Up she drives, right against the wind, nears the wharf, runs foul of a sloop's bowsprit, lands a gentleman, a lady, and a horse, takes on board three or four of the Vineyard people—and is off again! But the curses of the packet-masters follow her, as she goes snorting on her way. 'May her boiler burst!' they say in their hearts; and we say, 'Heaven forgive them!' For our own part, however, we prefer a vessel that voyages in the good old way, by the favour of the wind, instead of one that tears her passage through the deep in spite of wind and tide, snorting and groaning, as if tormented by the fire that rages in her entrails.

If a person can muster resolution to wade through the sands of the village and reach the neighbouring pastures, he may then walk pleasantly on a soil thinly bestrewn with grass, and intermingled with moss, which gives an elastic spring beneath the feet. In a ramble, one Sabbath afternoon, we came to a secluded spot, hidden among the surrounding hills, and found three grave-stones, of which the inscriptions were not likely to be often read. Yet one of them was worth reading. It was consecrated to the memory of John and Lydia Claghorne, a young whaler and his wife, the former of whom had perished on the farther side of Cape Horn, about the same time that Lydia had died in childbed. The monumental verse ran thus:—

> John and Lydia, that lovely pair,
> A whale killed him, her body lies here;
> Their souls, we hope, with Christ shall reign—
> So our great loss is their great gain.

John Claghorne has now slept beneath the sea, and Lydia here in her lonesome bed, between sixty and seventy years. One of the rarest things in the world, is an appropriate and characteristic epitaph, marked with the truth and simplicity which a sorrowing heart would pour into the effusion of an unlettered mind; an expression, in unaffected language, of what would be the natural feelings of friends and relatives, were they standing above the grave. It seems to us, that this rude and homely verse may be ranked among the masterpieces of monumental literature.[115]

The general cemetery of Holmes's Hole is at some distance from these three stones, and in open sight of the town, which here looks prettier than elsewhere, especially when brightened by the declining sunshine. On the left appears the sea, the sound, and Falmouth on the main, far enough off to be shrouded with mist; on the right is a salt-water lake, separated from the harbour by an isthmus of sand; and before us, at the foot of the hill, lies the village, its windows kindling cheerfully in the western sun. We stand among the graves, and do not much wonder that the dead people retained their attachment to their native island, through every change of clime, and came back hither to be buried under its sandy sods—all, save those who rest in the caves of ocean. There is here a collection of about fifty grave-stones, and a far greater number of nameless graves, many of which are so old as to be hardly discernible. Some are crossed by an immense foot-path. A few of the monuments were marble, and inscribed with deeply cut letters, which had been painted black, but were now washed nearly white again by the moisture of the climate.

---

[115] See Hawthorne's account of his visit to the graveyard in "Chippings with a Chisel" (*Writings*, II, 239–40). In the story (*ibid.*, II, 248) he reiterates the preference expressed here for the crude and simple verses on the tombstones.

The moss soon gathers on a grave-stone here. Many of the stones were admirable specimens of antique sculpture—the antiquity of a hundred years, or more—and were carved all round with a border of funeral emblems, and a death's head or a cherubim on top. All these had been imported from the main-land, or some, perhaps, from England. But there was one rough gray stone which bore scarcely any marks of having been touched by a human hand, except that the initials S. L. and an ancient date, were rudely inscribed upon it. This humble memorial, wrought painfully by Grief herself, and doubtless bedewed with tears, was more honourable both to the mourner and the dead, than the costliest monument that ever was bought and sold. In a spot where there were several children's graves together, almost obliterated by time, a wild rose, red, fragrant, and very small, had either sprouted from one of the little mounds, or been planted there by the forgotten parents of the forgotten child, and had now spread over the whole group of those small graves. The mother's dust had long ago been mingled with the dust over which she wept—the nameless infant, had it lived would have been hoary and decrepit now—yet, all this while, though marble would have decayed, the rose had been faithful to its trust.—It told of affection still.[116]

(*April, pp. 341–44*)

Wolfe's Monument

Before Lord Aylmer,[117] the late Governour of Canada, left Quebec, he caused a monument to be erected to General Wolfe, on the plains of Abraham. The base is seven feet square and three feet high, and is formed of granite boulders, which inclose the very stone against which Wolfe was leaning, when he breathed his last.[118] These masses

[116] The details of this paragraph are followed very closely in "Chippings with a Chisel" (*ibid.*, II, 239–40); see the article referred to in n. 113.

[117] Mathew Aylmer (1775–1850), the popular governor-general of Canada from 1830 to 1833, was responsible for erecting monuments in Quebec to both James Wolfe (1727–59) and Louis Joseph Montcalm (1712–59).

[118] See the narrative "Wolfe, on the Heights of Abraham" (text, pp. 125–30).

of granite are united with blue-water cement. On the base is placed a large square lime-stone, which forms the plinth of the column; next, there are polished marble rings, from which rises a circular pillar of polished dark blue marble to the height of about seven feet, and with a diameter of two and a half feet. The height of the whole monument is twelve feet. The inscription is in large capitals, and cut deep into the stone—HERE DIED WOLFE VICTORIOUS. The monument stands on the left of the city, and at the distance of about one hundred yards. It has been assigned as a reason for not sooner erecting a memorial to a man, whose life and death conferred so much glory on his country, that such a trophy would continually have reminded the conquered Canadians of their defeat and sub-jection. But now, after a lapse of seventy-seven years, the descendants of the vanquished will not feel sore on the subject. Ought not Mont-calm also to have a monument on the field of his honourable defeat and death?

(April, p. 344)

Note on the Tea Party

In drawing up our sketch of the Boston Tea Party,[119] we have derived great assistance from a manuscript volume of letters and other documents, now in the possession of Mr. Abel Bowen.[120] The collection appears to have been made with a view to publication. It contains letters to the East India Company, relative to the condition and prospects of the Tea-trade in America, and proposing methods of carrying it on:—other letters from American merchants in London, soliciting the agency in the disposal of the tea, for themselves or their friends;—and letters, also, from the agents in Boston and other ports, detailing the people's proceedings and their own. There are also copies of most of the public documents relative to the affair. The whole forms a mass of valuable information, a great part of which

[119] See text, pp. 91–99.

[120] Abel Bowen (1790–1850), printer and wood engraver of Boston, was one of the proprietors of the Boston Bewick Company. He did the engravings for Caleb H. Snow's *History of Boston* and projected various similar volumes.

could not easily be found elsewhere, if at all. The manuscript came into Mr. Bowen's hands from a person who obtained it in Halifax; whither many New England papers, both public and domestic, were conveyed when the British evacuated Boston.

(April, p. 351)

Viscount Exmouth

This was the British admiral who fought the battle of Algiers.[121] His family name was Pellew. From his boyhood, he was remarkable for courage, and early gave proof of the ability which afterwards made him a distinguished ornament of the British navy. When General Burgoyne was ascending the side of the ship which brought him to America, the yards were manned to receive him; and happening to look upward, the General saw a midshipman standing on his head, at the very extremity of the yard-arm. This was one of young Pellew's ordinary feats. After his arrival in America, he served with the army, and by his skill, a bridge was constructed across the Mohawk, over which Burgoyne marched to Saratoga. He was afterwards engaged in the battle of Bemis's Heights, and came near capturing General Arnold, whose stock and buckle remained in Pellew's hands as a trophy of the encounter. Had Arnold then been made prisoner, some of the most striking and melancholy incidents of our Revolutionary war might never have occurred, and that wretched traitor might still have borne the name of patriot.

(May, p. 358)

Coinage

Coins have been made of pewter, brass, copper, silver, gold, and platinum. Money has recently been coined of the latter metal in Russia. Pewter coins were issued by King James II, during his wars

---

[121] Edward Pellew, Viscount Exmouth (1757–1833), admiral in the British navy, was knighted by several European countries for his victory at Algiers (1816), where he led a British squadron, along with Dutch ships, to subdue the Algiers pirates.

in Ireland, after abdicating the English throne. Leathern coins, if such they may be called, have been in use in some countries. The Spartans, we believe, used iron money. The most ancient pieces of coin were impressed by placing the blank metal under the die, and giving it a blow with a hammer. They appear to have been very carelessly manufactured; for the blank piece of metal was often imperfectly rounded, and sometimes was not placed directly underneath the die; so that only a portion of the inscription or device was stamped upon the coin. Occasionally, coins were cast; and ancient moulds have been found with metal remaining in them. The form has generally been circular in all ages; but we have seen specimens of coin from the East Indies in the shape of little copper cubes. The size of pieces of money varies extremely in different ages and countries. Some Russian copper coins are almost big and heavy enough to crush a man, should they fall upon his head. The gold doubloon is a ponderous coin. On the other hand, there used formerly to be a coinage of silver pennies and half-pence, in England, which were so small that it was difficult to find one of them in the pocket. In fact, they could not have been much bigger than silver spangles, and must have looked as if they came from the royal mint of Lilliput. Medals, struck in honour of distinguished personages, or to commemorate remarkable events, are often several inches in diameter—the size of an ordinary saucer.

Gold bullion for the English coinage is imported by the Bank of England, and transmitted to the mint in the shape of ingots. It is there melted in black lead crucibles, each of which will contain about a hundred pounds of metal. When in a state of fusion, the gold is stirred with a stick of black-lead, in order to mingle the pure metal with the alloy, the proportion of which is two carats to twenty-two. It is then poured into moulds, which give it the shape of bars, ten inches long, seven wide, and one thick. Silver bullion is imported in ingots, of from fifty to sixty pounds troy-weight. At the mint, it is melted in very strong cast-iron pots, shaped like the letter U, each containing from four hundred to four hundred and fifty pounds of the metal. After being mixed with alloy, at the rate of eighteen penny weights to every eleven ounces and two penny weights, it is cast into iron ingot moulds. The bars of silver must then be annealed, by heating them red-hot. Gold does not undergo this process.

Having been thus prepared, the bars of silver and gold are passed between rollers, in order to reduce them to sheets of the necessary thickness for coinage. These sheets are cut into slips, each of the bigness of two coins; and pieces of a circular form are struck out, which must be sized, or brought to the standard weight, by filing the heavier ones, and throwing the light ones aside to be re-melted. This process of sizing is rendered much less troublesome than formerly, by the great perfection of the machinery which is now used for flattening the bars, and cutting out the circular pieces. After being sized, the pieces, or blanks, as they are called, are heated red-hot, and are then pickled, by boiling them in sulphuric acid, which renders them clean and brilliant. The next operation, is milling; the use of which is, to preserve the coins from being filed or clipped round the edges. Lastly, they are stamped on both sides at once, by means of a screw-press. Such is the accuracy with which coin is now manufactured in England, that, of 1000 sovereigns, 500 were found to be perfectly correct, 200 varied only half a grain from the standard, 100 varied three-fourths of a grain, and the remaining 100, in the aggregate, one grain. Medals are produced by a succession of operations, similar to the above. When they are very large, and the figures are to be much elevated above the surface, it is sometimes necessary to give them fifteen or twenty strokes of the die. Some have been cast in plaster moulds. They have also been cast in sand, and finished by striking with the die.

In this country, the earliest coinage was that of shillings, in Massachusetts, in 1652. By manufacturing and issuing these coins, the government of the colony infringed a royal prerogative, and made themselves liable, for aught we see, to the pains and penalties of forgery. King Charles the Second took umbrage at the fact, but was pacified by being shown one of the coins, whereon was represented a tree, which his Majesty mistook for the Royal Oak that had concealed him from his enemies;—the truth being, that the New England coiner had done his best to give the image of a pine-tree. There is a well-known story, that the mint-master grew very rich by his contract with [the] government; and at the marriage of his daughter, a stout, plump lass, he put her into one side of a pair of scales, and heaped Massachusetts shillings into the other, till they weighed her down. This was the girl's portion. If young ladies of modern times were to be thus portioned according to their weight in silver, a slender waist would stand but a poor chance in the matrimonial market.[122]

(*May, p. 365*)

Tower of Babel [123]

On the banks of the Euphrates is the site of a ruined city, which is supposed to have been Babylon, that mighty capital of ancient Chaldea. Among the ruins, and about four miles from the river, there is an immense mound, to which the Arabs have given the name of El Mujellibah, or 'The Overthrown.' Scholars, deeply versed in ancient history and geography, are of opinion that this mound was the foundation of the Tower of Babel. In shape, it is a vast oblong square, and is composed of sun-dried and kiln-burnt bricks, which are laid in regular courses, with layers of unbroken reeds between each course. The material of most of the bricks appears to have been mud, which was beaten up with chopped straw, and baked in the burning sun of that Eastern clime. This was the sort of brick which the Israelites were compelled to make without straw—a very difficult task; for the straw was necessary to keep the mud or clay from crumbling to pieces. Instead of mortar, asphaltus or bitumen was used; this is the slime which is referred to in the following passage from Scripture—

---

[122] This story is retold, in more detail, in *Grandfather's Chair* (*Writings*, XII, 38–43); and after it has been concluded by Grandfather, Clara says: "Well, Grandfather, . . . if wedding portions nowadays were paid as Miss Betsey's was, young ladies would not pride themselves upon an airy figure, as many of them do." In composing this essay for the magazine, Hawthorne drew heavily on John W. Draper's "Coins and Medals," *The American Journal of Science and Arts*, XXIX (1836), 157–60.

[123] "Where the devil are my clothes?" Hawthorne wrote to Louisa (n.d.). "I could not go to meeting today because I had but one clean shirt, which I was afraid to expend till tomorrow; and so I staid at home and wrote a dissertation on the Tower of Babel."

'And they had brick for stone, and slime had they for mortar.' [124]
Such of the bricks as remain entire are thirteen inches square and
three inches thick, and are generally marked with ancient characters.

The mound is a solid mass, the sides of which face the four
cardinal points. The northern side is 274 yards in length; the southern 256; the eastern 226; and the western 240. In its most elevated
part, the ruin is 139 feet high. The summit is an uneven surface,
strewn with whole and broken bricks, some of which are vitrified
or petrified, and with pottery, bitumen, shells, and glass. The base
of the mound is greatly injured by time and the elements. Towards
the southeast, it is cloven asunder by a deep furrow, extending from
top to bottom. In the sides of the structure deep cavities are visible,
which have been partly worn by the weather, but chiefly hollowed
out by the Arabs, in search of bricks and other antiquities. Within
these caves, there is an offensive smell, and they are strewn with
the bones of sheep and goats, which have been dragged thither and
devoured by jackals. Numberless bats and owls inhabit their dismal
recesses. Lions have béen said to make their lair among the ruins;
but it is believed that there are no lions in that part of the East. The
natives can hardly be prevailed on to follow strangers into the cavities of the wall, or to remain in the vicinity of the mound after sun-
set, for fear of the demons with whom their superstitious fancies
have peopled this place of mystery and decay. Besides its name of El
Mujellibah, the mound is also called Haroot and Maroot, from a
tradition that two rebel angels, who bore those appellations, are confined thereabouts in a certain invisible well, within which they have
been hanging by their heels for ages, and will continue so to hang till
the day of judgment. It is natural that legends of this character
should be connected with the ruins, and throw a shadowy dread
around them; but the only real danger, incurred by a visit to El
Mujellibah, is that of being stung by the venomous reptiles which
infest the spot. The situation of this, and other parts of the once
magnificent and populous city of Babylon, corresponds well with the
prophecy of Jeremiah.—'And Babylon shall become heaps, a dwelling-
place for dragons, an astonishment and a hissing, without an in-

[124] Genesis 11: 3.

habitant.'[125] The traveller in the East finds, at every step, proofs equally strong of the prophetic truth of the Bible. It is not too much to say, that all the countries, where the old prophets dwelt, are now strewn with accomplished prophecies.

This is not the place for an erudite discussion, whether the ruinous mound of El Mujellibah—The Overthrown—be really the remains of the Tower of Babel, where mankind, till then constituting one race and people, were first divided into nations of various tongues. But there is nothing, either in the structure itself, or its local situa tion, to controvert that opinion; and if any person, by adopting it, will gain a livelier faith in Scripture history, there are fair and reasonable grounds for him to do so.[126]

(May, p. 366)

Wolfe, on the Heights of Abraham [127]

In 1759, the American forests had been for about four years the battle-ground of France and England. The war had lingered, and its events had done little credit to the British generals hitherto employed; less, perhaps, from any remarkable deficiency on their part, than from the great military talents of Montcalm, the French commander. But Sir Jeffrey Amherst had now [128] succeeded General Abercrombie [*sic*] [129] in the chief command, and had formed a plan for the reduction of Canada, by means of three armies, which should enter the province by as many different routes, and simultaneously attack all the strong-holds of the French. Brigadier General Wolfe, a

[125] Jeremiah 51: 37.

[126] Hawthorne included in *Peter Parley's Universal History* (I, 36–38) a note on the present ruins of the Tower of Babel.

[127] The account of the fall of Quebec in *Grandfather's Chair* (*Writings*, XII, 158–60) bears considerable similarity of detail to this narrative, and some identity of expression. The narrative in the magazine is illustrated by an engraving, "The approach of Wolfe to the Heights of Abraham."

[128] This was in 1758. Sir Jeffrey Amherst (1719–97) fought throughout the French and Indian Wars.

[129] General James Abercromby (1706–81), after a successful career in the British army in America, was recalled in the fall of 1758 after his defeat at Ticonderoga.

young but distinguished officer, was placed at the head of the division which was destined to besiege Quebec. It was near midsummer, when he ascended the St. Lawrence, under convoy of Admirals Saunders [130] and Holmes,[131] and disembarked his men on the island of Orleans, a few leagues below the Canadian capital.

Quebec, by its position, is a natural fortress, and much military science had even then been employed in strengthening it. The city occupies a table land, on the tongue of a peninsula, formed by the junction of the river St. Charles with the St. Lawrence. At that period, it contained ten thousand inhabitants, and covered a space about three miles in circumference, two-thirds of which were defended by the height of the precipices and the rapidity of the streams, and the remainder by a fortification across the peninsula. On the summit of Cape Diamond, three hundred and fifty feet above the level of the water, stood a citadel, the cannon of which commanded the whole town. This citadel, as well as the ramparts which it looked down upon, was strongly garrisoned. Armed vessels and floating batteries were moored in the river of St. Charles; and on its eastern shore, and extending to the Montmorenci, lay the French army, under the famous, and hitherto fortunate, Marquis de Montcalm. His troops were composed partly of regulars, and partly of provincials, either of whom had the strongest motives to fight valiantly; the latter for their native city, the former for the capital and key of the French dominion in America. On the whole, the defences of Quebec were proportioned to the importance of the city.

Wolfe saw the difficulties of his undertaking, and that none but the most daring measures offered even a chance of success. He had, in the first place, taken possession of Point Levi, on the opposite shore of the St. Lawrence, and thence battered the city with cannon-shot and bombs, which beat down many of the houses, but produced no impression on the ramparts. His next attempt was made against

[130] Sir Charles Saunders (c. 1713–75) was commander-in-chief of the fleet on the St. Lawrence during the French and Indian Wars and ably supplemented Wolfe's movements.

[131] Charles Holmes (1711–61) was, at the siege of Quebec, third in command of the fleet on the St. Lawrence.

the army of Montcalm in its entrenchments, by landing on the eastern shore of the Montmorenci river, and attempting to storm the lines. Here he was repulsed, with the loss of five hundred slain. It was the policy of Montcalm to avoid a general engagement in the open field, and lengthen out the siege, till the invading army should be routed by the severe and early winter of that region. Autumn had already commenced, and nothing had been effected towards the reduction of the place. Wolfe began to despair of the result, and his anxiety wrought upon his frame, already debilitated by disease, and naturally too weak for the gallant soul that animated it. He was observed to be much depressed, and is said to have resolved not to survive the failure of the expedition. At this juncture, while Wolfe was confined to a sick-bed, his three brigadiers, Moncktor [sic],[132] Townshend,[133] and Murray,[134] conceived a plan for landing the army on the shore of the St. Lawrence, above Quebec, and thence gaining the Heights of Abraham, by means of a narrow passage up the precipice. In that quarter, as the approach of an enemy was deemed next to impossible, the city was less strongly fortified than elsewhere. The project being submitted to the decision of Wolfe, he immediately acceded to it, and deferred the execution only till he should be able to superintend it in person. The time fixed upon was the night preceding the thirteenth of September.*

---

* Wolfe was heard to say, that he should be well contented to give an arm or a leg, to gain possession of Quebec. All things considered, he was probably even better pleased to win the city at the price of his life. Colonel Hamilton, author of Men and Manners in Amer-

---

[132] Robert Monckton (1726–82), a successful commander through a long military career, was in command at the expulsion of the Acadians in 1755 and was second in command at the siege of Quebec. He was later governor of New York, 1761–65.

[133] George Townshend (1724–1807) was an arrogant and boastful brigadier general who, after the death of Wolfe, attempted to appropriate for himself chief credit for the victory at Quebec.

[134] James Murray (c. 1725–94) was singled out by Wolfe for his ability and was assigned the most dangerous tasks during the siege of Quebec. He remained to hold the city during the winter following Wolfe's victory. He was governor of Quebec, 1760–63, and of Canada, 1763–66.

Montcalm had previously been induced, by the motions of the British, to detach fifteen hundred of his men to a distance, under the command of M. de Bougainville.[135] On the appointed night, the fleet moved three leagues up the river, with Wolfe and the troops on board, and made demonstrations of landing detachments at various points. Meantime, the general and his army embarked in boats, and fell down the river with the tide, undiscovered by the French sentinels who were ranged along the shore. Owing to the darkness of the night, a part of the troops were landed somewhat below the point that had been selected. The Scottish Highlanders, however, accustomed to climb among the rugged passes of their native mountains, led the way up the darksome and dangerous path, followed by the remainder of the battalions, as fast as the boats touched the shore. General Wolfe was among the foremost. The ascent was scaled, by catching hold of the projections of the almost perpendicular precipice, clinging to the plants which had rooted themselves into the crevices of the rocks, and swinging from one precarious foothold to another, aided by the branches of the trees. At the summit, there was an entrenched party of the enemy, whom the van of the British put to flight. It appears not improbable, that, had a few resolute men taken their stand at one of the turns of this wild path, with sword and bayonet, they might have defended it against Wolfe's whole army, have thrust the assailants down the cliff, and thus have rescued the province from its fate. But no such gallant stand was made.

ica,[136] has questioned the military abilities of Wolfe. On this point we can pass no opinion; but, so far as we are qualified to judge, Wolfe showed a mixture of enthusiasm and good sense, which composed a very rare and lofty character, and indicated great talent of some kind or other. It was perfectly characteristic of Colonel Hamilton, that he should stand on the Heights of Abraham, and endeavour to depreciate the fame of Wolfe.

[135] Louis Antoine de Bougainville (1729–1811) was an aide-de-camp to Montcalm at Quebec and later an illustrious navigator and explorer in the South Seas.

[136] Thomas Hamilton writes of Wolfe (*Men and Manners in America*, Edinburgh, 1833, II, 354), "Yet there appear no grounds for attributing to him the qualities of a great general. His first attempt was a failure, and the second was successful only from the blunder of his opponent."

The troops reached the verge of the precipice in safety, and with little opposition, and stood, at daybreak, on the Heights of Abraham, within a mile of the hostile city. Between them and the ramparts, the ground rose and fell in abrupt inequalities. So near was this adventurous army to Quebec, that they could hear the bells of the Cathedral pealing the hour. Their commander had led his troops where there was no retreat down the headlong precipice, nor any alternative for himself or them, save victory or utter ruin.*

When tidings came to Montcalm, that Wolfe and the British forces waited to give him battle on the Heights of Abraham, he could not at first believe the tale. It was [as] if an army had flown thither through the air. But, as one messenger after another assured him that the foe was really under the ramparts of Quebec, he resolved that the fate of Canada should now be decided by one great battle. It would still, no doubt, have been the best policy of the gallant Frenchman to avoid a general engagement, and trust the defence of Quebec to its walls and citadel; which latter fortress, at least, was capable of sustaining a regular siege. The enterprise of the British commander, was, in fact, the ultimate resource of a desperate man; without a battle, he was almost certainly lost; but there appears to have been no need that his adversary, whose situation was so different, should play the desperate game which gave Wolfe his only chance. Such, however, were not the reflections of Montcalm. When convinced that the British had actually gained the Height, he lost no time in passing his army across the river St. Charles, which lay between him and the city. Wolfe, aware of the enemy's movements, immediately arranged his order of battle, placing himself on the right of the line. Montcalm, in person, commanded the left wing of the French. Thus, when the two armies met, their generals encountered each other amid the smoke, and dust, and fury of the conflict, where it raged the fiercest.

---

* It is stated that there were thirty boats, and sixteen hundred men; but this number is probably less than the truth. The morning was overcast and showery. The precipitous ascent, by which the army reached the summit of the cliff, is now used as a path down to the timber-rafts, which generally cover the surface of Wolfe's Cove.

We shall describe the battle on the Heights of Abraham, no farther than as it was connected with the fate of Wolfe. Early in the action, a bullet struck his wrist; around which he wrapped his handkerchief, and waved the wounded arm to encourage his men onward. Not long afterwards, he received a second shot, in the groin, but continued to advance, without betraying that he was again wounded. While the fate of the day was still doubtful, a third ball passed through his body, and stretched him on the field. Even then, he would scarcely allow himself to be conveyed to the rear. Reclining against a rock, which, in after times, was venerated as a hero's death-pillow, he had sunk into a stupor, no longer mindful of the din of arms. But a shout came pealing across the battle-field—'They fly! They fly!'—and starting as from sleep, Wolfe looked earnestly round on his kneeling attendants. 'Who fly?' he inquired. 'The French!' replied the lieutenant who supported him. The martial enthusiasm of Wolfe gleamed forth upon his countenance, like the effulgence of the sun, and changed his expiring agony to transport. 'Then I die happy!' he exclaimed; and there lay his corpse upon the victorious field, while his spirit was borne away upon the very shout that announced his triumph.

Never—never—was there a death more glorious! If a man's heart do not throb higher at the tale, he has not the heart of a man within his breast. Rank and honours, all that his King could give, awaited Wolfe in England; but no such glorious moment could have come to him again; and it was better for him then and there to die, leaning against his stony pillow, listening to the peal of his own triumph— and consecrating, with his life-blood, the soil which he had added to the dominion of Britain.*

(May, pp. 381–83)

---

*Wolfe died at the age of thirty-three. It was said, that, at the period of his victory and death, he was suffering under a mortal disease, and could have survived but a few months. A monument (as we have stated elsewhere in this Magazine) has recently been erected to his memory by Lord Aylmer, the late Governour-General of Canada.[137]

[137] See text, pp. 118–19; also n. 117.

The Martyr's Path

It is recorded, as an old superstition, that the grass along the way, by which a Martyr had gone to execution, always afterwards remained paler than other grass; and it was the same with whatever tree or shrub chanced to grow there—the foliage would never wear a gladsome green. Were there any truth in this, there is more than one foot track in New England, where the grass ought to look pale, in spite of the rain and dew of ages. Boston, if grass grew in its streets, would show such a pathway, leading from the ancient prison place to the gibbet of the Quakers—a pale wavy line would be drawn across some of the green fields of Connecticut—and for Salem, there would be a blighted track, up Gallows Hill, as broad as the highway.[138] But there are many, whose whole walk through life is a path of martyrdom; who are the martyrs of uncharitableness, which does not indeed kill the body, but grieves the heart; and yet the grass is none the paler, where their feet have been.

(*May, p. 394*)

The Duston Family [139]

Goodman Duston and his wife, somewhat less than a century and a half ago, dwelt in Haverhill, at that time a small frontier settlement in the province of Massachusetts Bay. They had already added seven children to the King's liege subjects in America; and Mrs. Duston about a week before the period of our narrative, had blessed her husband with an eighth. One day in March, 1698, when Mr. Dus-

---

[138] See Hawthorne's treatment of the Quaker persecutions at Boston and of the Salem witch persecutions in "Main Street" (*Writings*, III, 92–94, 99–105); also the idea of the Bloody Footstep used in *Doctor Grimshawe's Secret* and *The Ancestral Footstep*.

[139] Reprinted in *Writings*, XVII, 229–38. In this sketch Hawthorne leaned heavily on the account in Cotton Mather's *Magnalia Christi Americana* (see an article of mine on "Hawthorne's Literary Borrowings," *PMLA*, LI [June, 1936], 547). The account is preceded in the magazine by a half-page woodcut.

ton had gone forth about his ordinary business, there fell out an event, which had nearly left him a childless man, and a widower besides. An Indian war party, after traversing the trackless forest all the way from Canada, broke in upon their remote and defenceless town. Goodman Duston heard the war whoop and alarm, and, being on horseback, immediately set off full speed to look after the safety of his family. As he dashed along, he beheld dark wreaths of smoke eddying from the roofs of several dwellings near the road side; while the groans of dying men,—the shrieks of affrighted women, and the screams of children, pierced his ear, all mingled with the horrid yell of the raging savages. The poor man trembled yet spurred on so much the faster, dreading that he should find his own cottage in a blaze, his wife murdered in her bed, and his little ones tossed into the flames. But, drawing near the door, he saw his seven elder children, of all ages between two years and seventeen, issuing out together, and running down the road to meet him. The father only bade them make the best of their way to the nearest garrison, and, without a moment's pause, flung himself from his horse, and rushed into Mrs. Duston's bedchamber.

The good woman, as we have before hinted, had lately added an eighth to the seven former proofs of her conjugal affection; and she now lay with the infant in her arms, and her nurse, the widow Mary Neff, watching by her bedside. Such was Mrs. Duston's helpless state, when her pale and breathless husband burst into the chamber, bidding her instantly to rise and flee for her life. Scarcely were the words out of his mouth, when the Indian yell was heard: and staring wildly out of the window, Goodman Duston saw that the blood-thirsty foe was close at hand. At this terrible instant, it appears that the thought of his children's danger rushed so powerfully upon his heart, that he quite forgot the still more perilous situation of his wife; or, as is not improbable, he had such knowledge of the good lady's character, as afforded him a comfortable hope that she would hold her own, even in a contest with a whole tribe of Indians. However that might be, he seized his gun and rushed out of doors again, meaning to gallop after his seven children, and snatch up one of them in his flight, lest his whole race and generation should be blotted from the earth, in that fatal hour. With this idea, he rode up behind them, swift as the wind. They had, by this time, got about forty rods from the house, all pressing forward in a group; and though the younger children tripped and stumbled, yet the elder ones were not prevailed upon, by the fear of death, to take to their heels and leave these poor little souls to perish. Hearing the tramp of hoofs in their rear, they looked round, and espying Goodman Duston, all suddenly stopped. The little ones stretched out their arms; while the elder boys and girls, as it were, resigned their charge into his hands; and all the seven children seemed to say.—'Here is our father! Now we are safe!'

But if ever a poor mortal was in trouble, and perplexity, and anguish of spirit, that man was Mr. Duston! He felt his heart yearn towards these seven poor helpless children, as if each were singly possessed of his whole affections; for not one among them all, but had some peculiar claim to their dear father's love. There was his first-born; there, too, the little one who, till within a week past, had been the baby; there was a girl with her mother's features, and a boy, the picture of himself, and another in whom the looks of both parents were mingled; there was one child, whom he loved for his mild, quiet, and holy disposition, and destined him to be a minister; and another, whom he loved not less for his rough and fearless spirit, and who, could he live to be a man, would do a man's part against these bloody Indians. Goodman Duston looked at the poor things, one by one; and with yearning fondness, he looked at them all, together; then he gazed up to Heaven for a moment, and finally waved his hand to his seven beloved ones. 'Go on, my children,' said he, calmly. 'We will live or die together!'

He reined in his horse, and caused him to walk behind the children, who, hand in hand, went onward, hushing their sobs and wailings, lest these sounds should bring the savages upon them. Nor was it long, before the fugitives had proof that the red devils had found their track. There was a curl of smoke from behind the huge trunk of a tree—a sudden and sharp report echoed through the woods— and a bullet hissed over Goodman Duston's shoulder, and passed above the children's heads. The father, turning half round on his horse, took aim and fired at the skulking foe, with such effect as to cause a momentary delay of the pursuit. Another shot—and another —whistled from the covert of the forest; but still the little band pressed on, unharmed; and the stealthy nature of the Indians forbade them to rush boldly forward, in the face of so firm an enemy as Goodman Duston. Thus he and his seven children continued their retreat, creeping along, as Cotton Mather observes, 'at the pace of a child of five years old,' till the stockades of a little frontier fortress appeared in view, and the savages gave up the chase.

We must not forget Mrs. Duston, in her distress. Scarcely had her husband fled from the house, ere the chamber was thronged with the horrible visages of the wild Indians, bedaubed with paint and besmeared with blood, brandishing their tomahawks in her face, and threatening to add her scalp to those that were already hanging at their girdles. It was, however, their interest to save her alive, if the thing might be, in order to exact a ransom. Our great-great-grand-mothers, when taken captive in the old times of Indian warfare, appear, in nine cases out of ten, to have been in pretty much such a delicate situation as Mrs. Duston; notwithstanding which, they were wonderfully sustained through long, rough, and hurried marches, amid toil, weariness, and starvation, such as the Indians themselves could hardly endure. Seeing that there was no help for it, Mrs. Duston rose, and she and the widow Neff, with the infant in her arms, followed their captors out of doors. As they crossed the threshold, the poor babe set up a feeble wail; it was its death cry. In an instant, an Indian seized it by the heels, swung it in the air, dashed out its brains against the trunk of the nearest tree, and threw the little corpse at the mother's feet. Perhaps it was the remembrance of that moment, that hardened Hannah Duston's heart, when her time of vengeance came. But now, nothing could be done, but to stifle her grief and rage within her bosom, and follow the Indians into the dark gloom of the forest, hardly venturing to throw a parting glance at the blazing cottage, where she had dwelt happily with her husband, and had borne him eight children—the seven, of whose fate she knew nothing, and the infant, whom she had just seen murdered.

The first day's march was fifteen miles; and during that, and many succeeding days, Mrs. Duston kept pace with her captors; for, had she lagged behind, a tomahawk would at once have been sunk into her brains. More than one terrible warning was given her; more than one of her fellow captives,—of whom there were many,—after tottering feebly, at length sank upon the ground; the next moment, the death groan was breathed, and the scalp was reeking at an Indian's girdle. The unburied corpse was left in the forest, till the rites of sepulture should be performed by the autumnal gales, strewing the withered leaves upon the whitened bones. When out of danger of immediate pursuit, the prisoners, according to Indian custom, were divided among different parties of the savages, each of whom were to shift for themselves. Mrs. Duston, the widow Neff, and an English lad, fell to the lot of a family, consisting of two stout warriours, three squaws, and seven children. These Indians, like most with whom the French had held intercourse, were Catholics; and Cotton Mather affirms, on Mrs. Duston's authority, that they prayed at morning, noon, and night, nor ever partook of food without a prayer; nor suffered their children to sleep, till they had prayed to the christian's God. Mather, like an old hard-hearted, pedantic bigot, as he was, seems trebly to exult in the destruction of these poor wretches, on account of their Popish superstitions. Yet what can be more touching than to think of these wild Indians, in their loneliness and their wanderings, wherever they went among the dark, mysterious woods, still keeping up domestic worship, with all the regularity of a household at its peaceful fireside.

They were travelling to a rendezvous of the savages, somewhere in the northeast. One night, being now above a hundred miles from Haverhill, the red men and women, and the little red children, and the three pale faces, Mrs. Duston, the widow Neff, and the English lad, made their encampment, and kindled a fire beneath the gloomy old trees, on a small island in Contocook river. The barbarians sat down to what scanty food Providence had sent them, and shared it with their prisoners, as if they had all been the children of one wigwam, and had grown up together on the margin of the same river within the shadow of the forest. Then the Indians said their prayers— the prayers that the Romish priests had taught them—and made the sign of the cross upon their dusky breasts, and composed themselves to rest. But the three prisoners prayed apart; and when their petitions were ended, they likewise lay down, with their feet to the fire. The night wore on; and the light and cautious slumbers of the red men were often broken, by the rush and ripple of the stream, or the groaning and moaning of the forest, as if nature were wailing over her wild children; and sometimes, too, the little red skins cried in sleep, and the Indian mothers awoke to hush them. But, a little before break of day, a deep, dead slumber fell upon the Indians. 'See,' cries Cotton Mather, triumphantly, 'if it prove not so!'

Uprose Mrs. Duston, holding her own breath, to listen to the long, deep breathing of her captors. Then she stirred the widow Neff, whose place was by her own, and likewise the English lad; and all three stood up, with the doubtful gleam of the decaying fire hovering upon their ghastly visages, as they stared round at the fated slumberers. The next instant, each of the three captives held a tomahawk. Hark! that low moan, as of one in a troubled dream—it told a warrior's death pang! Another!—Another!—and the third half-uttered groan was from a woman's lips. But, Oh, the children! Their skins are red; yet spare them, Hannah Duston, spare those seven little ones, for the sake of the seven that have fed at your own breast. 'Seven,' quoth Mrs. Duston to herself. 'Eight children have I borne—and where are the seven, and where is the eighth!' The thought nerved her arm; and the copper coloured babes slept the same dead sleep with their Indian mothers. Of all that family, only one woman escaped, dreadfully wounded, and fled shrieking into the wilderness! and a boy, whom, it is said, Mrs. Duston had meant to save alive. But he did well to flee from the raging tigress! There was little safety for a red skin, when Hannah Duston's blood was up.

The work being finished, Mrs. Duston laid hold of the long black hair of the warriors, and the women, and the children, and took all their ten scalps, and left the island, which bears her name to this very day. According to our notion, it should be held accursed, for her sake. Would that the bloody old hag had been drowned in crossing Contocook river, or that she had sunk over head and ears in a swamp, and been there buried, till summoned forth to confront her victims at the Day of Judgment; or that she had gone astray and been starved to death in the forest, and nothing ever seen of her again, save her skeleton, with the ten scalps twisted round it for a girdle! But, on the contrary, she and her companions came safe home, and received the bounty on the dead Indians, besides liberal presents from private gentlemen, and fifty pounds from the Governour of Maryland. In her old age, being sunk into decayed circumstances, she claimed, and, we believe, received a pension, as a further price of blood.

This awful woman, and that tender hearted, yet valiant man, her husband, will be remembered as long as the deeds of old times are told round a New England fireside. But how different is her renown from his!

(*May, pp. 395-97*)

Chantrey's Washington [140]

The statue of Washington (of which the preceding sketch will give the reader an accurate, though necessarily imperfect idea) was placed in its present situation [141] in the latter part of October, 1827. It is constructed of white Italian marble, from the quarries of Carrara, and was completed at an expense of about fifteen thousand dollars. Chantrey,[142] the most eminent of British sculptors, had been long employed upon this noble specimen of art, which, by the opinion of competent judges, is ranked among the best productions of his chisel. The edifice in which it stands, was built expressly for the reception of the statue, and is attached to the rear of the State-House, ascending as high as the second story of that structure. The interiour is an oblong square, thirty feet long by thirteen broad, with a dome at the top, throwing its light into the vaulted recess, ten feet by thirteen, where the statue is placed. The whole edifice appears like a recess in

---

[140] The preceding page is devoted to an engraving of Chantrey's statue.
[141] In the vestibule of the State House at Boston.
[142] Sir Francis Legatt Chantrey (1781–1842) was an English painter and sculptor, noted especially for his attainment of characteristic expressions in his portrait busts.

the large and lofty hall of the State-House, with which it communicates by means of three arched entrances.

As we ascend the successive flights of steps, which give access from Beacon Street to the portal of the State-House, we perceive the figure of Washington, in the long vista between the pillars of the hall. Even at that distance, its aspect of calm and thoughtful dignity impresses the beholder, and causes him to advance with some faint semblance of the feeling, with which he would have approached the presence of the illustrious original. The statue, which is seven feet in height, stands on a pedestal, with the left foot somewhat advanced, and the weight of the body resting chiefly on the right. The head is slightly turned towards the left. The right hand grasps a roll of manuscript, and the left supports the heavy folds of the ample cloak, which forms the drapery of the statue. The arrangement of this cloak was a most fortunate conception, on the part of the sculptor. Had he arrayed the modern Hero and Statesman in the garb of ancient Greece or Rome, or had he given him the stiff military coat, the flapped waistcoat, and small clothes, of a Revolutionary general, the effect would, in either case, have been almost equally objectionable. Canova's statue,[143] which was recently destroyed by fire, at Raleigh, in North Carolina, represented Washington in the Roman military dress, with short curled hair, a garment shaped somewhat like a shirt, naked legs, and sandals on his feet. The garb of an Indian Chief would have been quite as graceful, and more appropriate to the American warriour. But Chantrey, while clothing the statue in the Revolutionary uniform, has taken advantage of the voluminous folds of the cloak, to give the figure of Washington a classic grace and dignity, and to hide all those details which, as belonging to a fashion so recently passed away, might excite ludicrous emotions in the spectator.[144]

This statue is one of the chief objects of interest in the city of Boston; and there are few hours of the day, in which some admiring group may not be seen near its pedestal.

(*June, p. 402*)

---

[143] Antonio Canova (1757–1822) was an Italian sculptor of the neoclassical school.
[144] Hawthorne again expressed his preference for modern raiment for statues in *The Italian Notebooks* (*Writings*, XXI, 367–68; XXII, 44). See n. 1.

The Royal Household Book

Thirty or forty years ago, the society of Antiquaries in London published a volume,[145] containing the regulations and ordinances for the government of the royal household, during the reigns of several English sovereigns. We derive from it the most minute and curious details concerning the domestic affairs of the Court; and (though such knowledge can hardly be deemed useful, in our democratic age, and republican country) we should feel qualified to act either as groom of the bed-chamber to Henry the Seventh, or as Maid of Honour to his Queen. We could likewise superintend the preparations for a royal feast, both on fish-days, and flesh-days, and enumerate the ingredients of every dish that was set before the King. The following list of eatables would answer for an ordinary occasion.[146] Pottage, a chine of beef, venison, cooked in various ways, mutton, young veal, goose or stork, capons of grease and conies of grease, together with baked carp, as the first course; and for the second, jellies, wild-fowl, tarts, pastry, and fruit. On Fridays and Saturdays, nothing but fish was to be served, and, among other varieties, congar-eels, porpoises, and seals.[147] Captain Basil Hall [148] mentions having eaten part of a porpoise, and that it resembled very coarse beef; but we are not aware that the flesh of seals is reckoned among modern articles of food. Nothing is more remarkable, in the domestic economy of the middle ages, than the absence of tea and coffee, and the consumption

[145] *A Collection of Ordinances and Regulations for the Government of the Royal Household, Made in Divers Reigns from King Edward III to King William and Queen Mary. Also Receipts in Ancient Cookery*, London, 1790. This volume is listed in the *Catalogue of the Library of the Boston Athenaeum, 1807–71*. Hawthorne found most of the information for this sketch in a section of the *Collection of Ordinances* entitled "Articles Ordained by King Henry VII for the Regulation of His Household" and in a similar section on the regulations of Henry VIII.

[146] For these remarks on foods Hawthorne was indebted to a chapter on "Ancient Cookery" (*ibid.*, pp. 423–73), which preserves the early fifteenth century orthography, and "A List of the Dishes of the Ancient Cookery" (*ibid.*, pp. 474–76).

[147] See *ibid.*, pp. 449–50.

[148] Captain Basil Hall (1788–1844), of the British navy, traveled in China and the Americas and published several accounts of his travels.

of ale and wine, in large quantities, by the Queen and all the court ladies. The maids of honour, were allowed one gallon of ale in the morning, another gallon in the afternoon, and two gallons of ale and a pitcher of wine in the evening; and all this appears to be over and above what they drank at their regular meals.

Other entries enable us to form an estimate of the style in which great personages appeared at court. Dukes and Archbishops were allowed stabling and 'herbage' for twenty-four horses, and nine beds for their servants, who probably were accustomed to sleep double or treble. A Dutchess, if a widow, was allowed twenty horses and seven beds. The Queen's maids of honour, among them all, had six horses and three beds. The whole number of the King's horses (this was in the reign of Henry the Eighth) was one hundred and nine.

Among the ordinances of Henry the Seventh, are particular directions for making the king's bed,[149] prescribing the exact manner in which the feather-bed was to be beat up, the placing of the bolster and pillows, and the spreading of the sheets and other bed-clothes; and when this important affair was happily accomplished, 'then shall the Usher draw together the bed-curtains, and an Esquire for the body shall cast holy water on the bed; then shall the Esquires and Ushers, and all other that were at the making of the bed, goe without the chamber; and there to meet them bread, ale, and wine; and soe to drink together.' Henry the Seventh appears to have set more weight upon such ceremonious trifles, than any monarch before or since his time. He ordains the method that was to be observed at the coronation of the King, the reception and coronation of the Queen, her delivery in child-bed, the marriage of a princess, and every other event that could befall the royal family. Nor does he neglect to prescribe the method of conducting the king's obsequies; but, as if to conceal from the vulgar crowd, that a monarch must finally humble himself to undergo the same fate with the meanest of them, the directions on this subject are given in Latin.[150] It was not fit that ordinary men should know, that perfumes and spices were

---

[149] See the *Collection of Ordinances,* pp. 121–22.

[150] See *ibid.,* pp. 129–30. These directions have the title "De Apparatu Principis Quam Migraverit ex Hoc Seculo."

requisite to stifle the smell of mortality, in a royal corpse. We, however, shall be irreverent enough to translate the passage.

When an anointed king shall pass from this temporal to the eternal state, first of all, in his bed-chamber, shall his body be washed with warm water. Then shall it be anointed all over with balsam and aromatics, and, afterwards, enveloped in a waxed linen-cloth, so that only the face and beard shall remain uncovered. Waxed linen shall likewise be wound about his hands and fingers, in such manner that each finger and thumb shall be separately covered, and the hands, covered with the waxed cloth, shall remain open. But the groom of the bed-chamber must take care of the king's brains and bowels. Moreover, the corpse must be clothed in a garment extending from head to foot, above which must be spread a regal pall. The beard must be carefully combed over the breast, and then a royal crown or diadem shall be placed on the dead monarch's head. Afterwards, a ring of gold is to be put upon the middle finger of his right hand; and the same hand shall hold a golden ball, in which shall be fixed a gilded rod, having the sign of the holy cross at the top, which must rest upon the bosom of the corpse. In the left hand shall be a gilded sceptre, extending from the hand to the left ear. And lastly, the legs and feet must be clothed in stockings and shoes. The king being adorned after this fashion, and honourably attended by the prelates and nobles of his realm, shall be borne to the place appointed for his sepulture.

(June, pp. 405–6)

Kissing a Queen

Pepys, in his diary,[151] states that, in 1668, he went to Westminster Abbey, where by particular favour, he was permitted to see the body of Catherine of Valois, the Queen of Henry the Fifth. The upper part of her body was put into his hands; 'and,' says Pepys, 'I did kiss her mouth, reflecting upon it that I did kiss a queen; and that

[151] See Richard, Lord Braybrooke's edition of Pepys's *Diary*, London, 1858, IV, 107–8.

this was my birth-day, thirty-six years old, and that I did kiss a Queen!' Did her Majesty's half-decayed corpse we wonder, smell differently from meaner clay?

(*June, p. 426*)

Village of Economy [152]

The village of Economy is situated on the Ohio, eighteen miles below Pittsburgh, on a bluff, elevated about fifty feet above the low-water mark of the river. A colony of German emigrants originally settled in this vicinity, but afterwards removed further west; whence, however, they returned, about twelve years since, and laid the foundation of Economy. Factories of various kinds, with steam machinery, were established; the land was brought under high cultivation; and the inhabitants paid considerable attention to the culture of the vine, and produced very tolerable imitations of their native German wines. They called themselves Harmonists,[153] and were subject to the patriarchal authority of Rapp, an aged German, of somewhat visionary notions in politics and religion. The leading characteristics of the sect, or colony, were a community of goods, and the prohibition, or discouragement, of marriage. We do not understand that, as among the Shakers, the latter regulation was based on religious tenets. It had been adopted by Rapp as a means of preventing the too rapid increase of his colony; and all the members were to live together as brethren and sisters, denying themselves a nearer and dearer intimacy, merely from motives of expediency. The ordinance of celibacy was not, however, so strictly observed, but that marriages did sometimes occur; and, even in cases where the ceremony had been

---

[152] With this article appears a small woodcut, "View of the Village of Economy, Penn."

[153] George Rapp (1757–1847) organized the communistic religious body known as Harmonists at Württemberg and in 1803 led his followers to America. The society founded Harmony, Pennsylvania (1805), New Harmony, Indiana (1815), and Economy, Pennsylvania (1825). See in this connection Hawthorne's similar discussion of the Shakers in "The Canterbury Pilgrims," "The Shaker Bridal," and various letters (Julian Hawthorne, *Nathaniel Hawthorne and His Wife*, I, 127, 419–21; George Parsons Lathrop, *A Study of Hawthorne*, pp. 144–45).

omitted, the fruits of connubial intercourse would occasionally make their appearance. Although these infant proselytes to his sect might not be very welcome, Rapp received them graciously, and established a school for their education. We are not aware that any account of the condition of the settlement has recently been given to the public.

(June, p. 430)

Habitations of Man [154]

A description of all the methods by which people have sheltered themselves from the elements, illustrated with engravings of every kind of domestic edifice, would form a curious and interesting work. In some states of society, man has burrowed beneath the earth; in regions where all the year is Summer, he rears a bower of branches; within the Arctic circle, the Esquimaux use the eternal snows as a quarry, whence they hew the building-materials of their huts; in the southern islands, the houses are a kind of basket-work; in parts of India, they are a light fabric of bamboo; and, in more than one country, mud cottages may be seen, at no great distance from marble palaces.

The first habitations of the hardy settlers of our country were constructed of the ruins of the forest, which had fallen beneath their axes. The log-house was a rude, but comfortable dwelling, homely and substantial, like the characters of those who built it. In our memory, there is a vivid picture of such an edifice, which we used to visit in our boyhood, while running wild on the borders of a forest-lake.[155] It had a little square window, the size of four panes of glass; the chimney was built of sticks and clay, like a swallow's

---

[154] This note is illustrated by two small engravings.

[155] An allusion to Hawthorne's wanderings around Lake Sebago during the time he spent with his mother and sisters at Raymond, Maine; see Woodberry, pp. 7–9. In an autobiographical sketch written in 1853 Hawthorne has this to say about his skating excursions on the lake: "When I found myself far away from home, and weary with the exhaustion of skating, I would sometimes take refuge in a log cabin, where half a tree would be burning on the broad hearth. I would sit in the ample chimney, and look at the stars through the great aperture through which the flames went roaring up" (Samuel T. Pickard, *Hawthorne's First Diary,* London, 1897, p. 5).

nest; the hearth was a huge, flat, unhewn stone; and the fire place, where sat an old Revolutionary pensioner and his dame, occupied nearly the whole breadth of the house. Similar dwellings still exist in the remoter parts of New-England; a few of them are scattered along the road that leads through the heart of the White mountains.[156]

The Laplanders build even ruder structures than these. Their wretched hovels, composed of sods, loose stones, turf, and bushes, have a fire-place in the centre, the acrid smoke from which continually circulates through the habitation, and is the only means of stifling its filthy smells. It is a characteristic distinction between these people and the American backwoodsmen, that the former spend their lives in the miserable huts which they inherited from their fathers, and bequeath them to their children; while the latter is almost certain to erect a smart frame-house, if not an edifice of brick or stone, on the site of his log-cottage.

The Kaskaias, who roam through the Far West, have houses of buffalo-skins, which are taken down at every migration in their wandering life, and may be erected again, within a few moments after their evening-halt. There are six or eight poles, twenty or thirty feet in length, to every lodge. Four of these are tied together at the smaller extremities, and are covered with skins, while the but-ends rest upon the ground, and form the main support of the structure, which the remainder of the poles are employed in strengthening. Thus, in a very brief interval, the green space on the banks of a stream is covered with a little village of tall, conical-shaped lodges, the whole labour of constructing which is performed by the squaws. As short a time suffices for their removal; the skins are packed on the horses, belonging to the family; and men, squaws, and children mount, and take a new ramble through the wilderness, dragging their tent-poles at the horses' heels. By the broad traces which they leave behind, a domestic party, carrying their lodges along with them, may always be distinguished from a band of warriors, who leave only the track of their footsteps.

The dwellings constructed by the Beaver are superiour to many

<hr>

156 Hawthorne, in all probability, traveled through the White Mountains in the summers of 1830 and 1831; see Woodberry, pp. 40–41.

which shelter the heads of human beings. But, blessed be God, whether our habitation be a cave, a hut, a lodge of skins, or a marble palace, the name of home has a hallowing influence, which renders it the only spot on earth where true comfort may be found.

(June, p. 431)

Wild Horsemen [157]

Philosophers have always been puzzled to contrive such a definition of man, as should completely distinguish him from every other animal. We are not aware that, among the many attempts of this sort, he has ever been described as an animal that gets on horseback. Yet this is one of the most peculiar characteristics of the human race; for no animal, except man, systematically imposes on another the burden of his conveyance from place to place. This is a natural instinct of mankind; and in whatever country men and horses exist together, the four legs of the latter are compelled to perform the business of the biped's single pair.

Among the most famous horsemen in the world are the Mamelukes. These bold riders are of Turkish or Circassian origin, and at an early age, are imported into Egypt as slaves. They are there instructed in the art of horsemanship, and the practice of arms, and become the only troops of the nation, which is therefore, in a great measure, under their sway. Their whole life being spent in the saddle, they acquire an incredible dexterity in the management of their horses, and, individually, are terrific antagonists in battle. They have no acquaintance, however, with scientific warfare, and may be defeated by a greatly inferiour body of regular cavalry.

The Sioux, otherwise called the Dacotahs, are an Indian people in the region of the Mississippi and Missouri, entirely distinct from any other nation of the red-men. In 1824, their numbers were estimated at twenty-five thousand, of whom six thousand were warriours. They have not, like many Indian tribes, any tradition of having emigrated from another country, but believe that the Great

[157] Two small woodcuts accompany this sketch.

Spirit created their fathers, among the same prairies where they themselves are now riding their wild horses.

To the Sioux the art of horsemanship must have been an acquisition of modern date; for the herds of wild horses, which now trample the vast prairies of the West, are of European origin, and descended from sires, who had immemorially been subjugated to the service of man. Washington Irving, in his Tour on the Prairies,[158] describes the taming of a young horse; a task so easily accomplished, that the steeds of the desert would appear never to have relapsed entirely into the wild state, but still to retain an hereditary fitness for the saddle.

(June, p. 432)

Historical Anecdote

At the commencement of the Revolution, the British officers had a small theatre in Boston. One night, when the performance was a farce called the 'Blockade of Boston,' [159] an orderly sergeant rushed upon the stage, and called out, 'The Yankees are attacking our works on Bunker's Hill!' The audience mistook him for a personage of the farce; but General Howe [160] saw that the man's trepidation was not feigned, and immediately ordered the officers to their alarmposts.

(July, p. 446)

Cincinnati [161]

The city of Cincinnati stands on the north bank of the Ohio, at a spot where the hills, on either side of the river, retire from the shores, leaving an intermediate space of about twelve miles in circumfer-

---

[158] Chapter XX of *A Tour on the Prairies*, 1835.

[159] *The Blockade of Boston* was written by General John Burgoyne and was acted by officers of the British army.

[160] General William Howe (1729–1814) of the British army in America.

[161] This article is illustrated by a half-page "View of Cincinnati, Ohio."

ence. The river flows through the valley which is thus ιormed, di-
viding it into two unequal portions, the larger of which, compre-
hending two thirds of the whole area, and containing about four
square miles, lies on the Ohio shore. The site of Cincinnati is on two
parallel plains, usually termed the Hill and the Bottom, the former
of which is elevated fifty or sixty feet above the latter. The extent
of the valley, from Deer-creek on the east to Mill-creek on the west,
is nearly three miles. Until the year 1788, the Indian or the hunter,
standing on the circular line of hills, above the valley, of which we
have described the outline, would have seen only the gigantic trees,
and the river sundering the primeval forest with its tranquil breadth.
Nearly twenty years later, from the same position, nothing was visible, save a rough backwoods settlement of five hundred people. But
soon a marvellous change was to take place; in 1820, the once solitary
vale had become populous with nearly ten thousand souls; and now,
if the traveller take a view of Cincinnati from its wall of hills, he will
behold busy streets, compact and massive edifices, the spires of
churches, the smoke of manufactories, and all other characteristics
of a city, containing thirty-five thousand inhabitants.

Seven of the streets of Cincinnati are sixty-six feet wide, and
separated from each other by spaces of three hundred and ninety-six
feet, and are intersected, at right angles, by streets of the same
width, and at equal intervals. Among other public buildings are a
Court House, a Jail, four Market Houses, a Bazaar, two Theatres, a
Medical College, a Hospital and Lunatic Asylum, and between
twenty and thirty Churches. A large amount of capital is employed
in manufactures, with steam-machinery; and there is a dense population in the vicinity of the buildings for this purpose. An obscure
portion of the city, Mrs. Trollope [162] informs us, is inhabited by free
negroes, and thence derives the local designation of Little Africa.
The market of Cincinnati, according to the same lady, (whose favourable judgments, at least, are entitled to implicit confidence,) is
hardly surpassed, for its excellence, cheapness, and abundance, by
any in the world. She likewise speaks with admiration of the noble

[162] Frances Trollope, *Domestic Manners of the Americans,* London, 1832. Hawthorne's allusions are to pp. 49–60.

landing-place, more than a quarter of a mile in extent along the river, well-paved, and surrounded with neat buildings. Fifteen steamboats, she observes, have been counted here at once; and there was yet space for fifteen more to be ranged in the same line. The years that have elapsed since Mrs. Trollope resided there, are no small period in the history of so recent a city as Cincinnati, and have doubtless prodigiously improved it.

It is the great trade which is carried on with the East, the West, and the South, and even with foreign countries, in addition to its own internal industry, that has made Cincinnati the largest and wealthiest city, except New Orleans, in the Valley of the Mississippi. Its rapid, yet healthful growth has rendered it famous throughout the world. It is one of those wonders, the result of favourable situation and energetic enterprise, to which the American so proudly points, as peculiar to his own land, when the European boasts the ruined magnificence of other times.

(July, pp. 449–50)

The Devil's Hill

In Don Juan [*sic*] de Ulloa's Travels in South America,[163] (an excellent old book,) a legend is related of a poor man in Spain, who was about to commit suicide, when a courteous stranger accosted him, and inquired the cause of his trouble. Being informed that it proceeded from poverty, he offered to carry him to a country where he should have whatever quantity of gold he pleased. An hour was accordingly appointed for their departure. Meantime the Spaniard, thinking that he must make provision for a considerable journey, bought some loaves of bread, hot from the oven, with the baker's name and residence stamped upon them; he then lay down to sleep,

[163] Don Antonio de Ulloa (1716–95) and Don George Juan (1712–1774) published *A Voyage to South America* at Madrid in 1748. A French version was published at Amsterdam in 1752, and the work was printed several times in an English translation by John Adams of Waltham Abbey (fourth ed., 1806), and was included among Pinkerton's *Voyages* (London, 1813, XIV). The story which Hawthorne retells here occurs in I, 320–22, of the 1806 edition.

in the open air, at the spot assigned for his meeting with the stranger. His nap began in the province of Estramadura, in Old Spain; but when he unclosed his eyes, he found himself on the summit of a hill in South America, with the plain of Chisquipata stretched at his feet. Descending the hill, he was invited to breakfast with an inhabitant of the country, and, at table, produced his loaves of bread, which had not wholly lost the warmth of the Spanish oven. His host, as it happened, had emigrated from Estramadura, and recognised the baker's stamp, and knew that these warm loaves could have been baked nowhere but in Spain. Of course, he looked with no little wonderment at his guest; nor was the latter less perplexed, on discovering that he had journeyed from one side of the globe to the other, while asleep, and without so much as dreaming of it. They could explain the mystery no otherwise, than as a trick of Satan, in the person of the courteous stranger; and the people of Quito have ever since called the height, where the Spaniard started from his sleep, the Devil's Hill. But considering that the poor man was relieved from hopeless poverty, and rescued from suicide, and conveyed, without the peril and wearisomeness of a sea-voyage, to a land where there was gold in every hill, it would rather appear to have been the deed of his patron-saint. Certainly, it has not come within our experience, that the Devil ever did so good-natured a thing.

(*July, p. 458*)

Fashions of Hats [164]

The *Magasin Universel* (A French Penny Magazine, to which we have been indebted for much useful and entertaining matter) observes, in regard to the subject of this article:—

'In few things is fashion so variable as in hats. Whole volumes might be occupied with the history of the innumerable changes, which this one article of the toilet has undergone. These changes must have cost so much the greater efforts of invention, because a hat is a very simple thing in itself, and susceptible of only a limited

---

[164] This essay is illustrated by fifteen small woodcuts.

variety of combinations. Sometimes the crown of the hat has been lowered, and almost flattened; sometimes it has been elevated into a point, like the cap of a magician. By turns the rim has been widened or narrowed, turned up, or slouched down, and always without reference to the season of the year, which ought to be the chief consideration in fixing the shapes of hats. It has often happened that, in the Summer months, the face is exposed to the scorching rays of the sun, by a hat almost without a rim; while in Winter, when not a particle of sunshine can be spared, an immense breadth of brim throws a circular shadow round the wearer. Fashion is not seldom the reverse of comfort; and it is singular that the majority of people should agree in sacrificing the latter to the former.'

We confess that, in examining the following series of cuts, we have been struck rather by the similarity than the diversity of hats, in different ages. In every specimen we observe a round crown and a brim; and it appears to us that all the variations, which the hat has assumed in the course of many centuries, might have been contrived by an active fancy, in one or two hours. In dress, as in everything else, an absolutely new idea is as rare as the discovery of a new planet.

The hat itself, however, or any other separate covering for the head, except for the purpose of defence in battle, appears to have been unknown among the ancients. As a protection against rain or cold, when the hair was insufficient, they probably drew their mantles over their heads. We are indebted for the invention of the hat to the Saxons, who inhabited a country where the great changes of temperature rendered a garment for the head as desirable as for the rest of the body. The first hats mentioned in history were made of wool or felt. The poet Chaucer, at a later period, represents a merchant as wearing a Flemish beaver.[165] Froissart, in his Chronicles, makes frequent mention of hats, although, according to some chronological tables, they were not invented till 1404, many years after the historian flourished, and were first made in London in 1510. Some of the early fashions may be seen in the two following figures.

At a very early period, white hats were worn by the fashionables

[165] The Prologue to *The Canterbury Tales*, l. 272.

of the city of Ghent, in Flanders, and it has been conjectured that the shape and colour of the hat were regulated by the politics of the wearer, and made known the party to which he belonged. Mrs. Trollope, in her recent work,[166] informs us that the same kind of political emblem is now in use at Paris. In an inventory of the personal effects of an English knight, in the year 1459, one entry is of a beaver hat, lined with flowered damask, besides two straw hats. In 1517, hats of enormous size came into fashion, and were worn entirely on one side of the head. Henry VIII, king of England, bought a hat and plume for fifteen shillings, or between three and four dollars—which, considering the relative value of money at that period, was a price that could be afforded only by monarchs and nobles. The hats, in the next cut, are said to be copied from a picture, painted in the year 1544. One of them is of so familiar a shape, that we should not ourself be ashamed to wear it this very day, on the sunny side of Washington Street.

It now became the fashion to line hats with velvet, and to manufacture them with high crowns, and occasionally with very broad brims. Specimens of these may be seen in the following cut, the first figure of which is taken from a portrait of the Earl of Morton,[167] a Scotchman, and the second from that of Sir Philip Sidney, who was the most accomplished gentleman of his age. His hat is one of the oddest in the series.

The wearing of hats appears to have been long a privilege, enjoyed only by lords, knights, and gentlemen. In the reign of Elizabeth, it was enacted that every person, above seven years old, unless of knightly rank, or possessed of a certain property in land, should wear a woollen cap, or pay a fine of three farthings. At this period, the privileged ranks were very extravagant in their hats. Some were made of silk, some of velvet, some of taffeta, some of wool, some of a fine species of fur, which was imported from distant regions. They were adorned with black, white, brown, red, green, or yellow

---

[166] Frances Trollope, *Paris and the Parisians in 1835*, New York, 1835.
[167] Possibly James Douglas, fourth Earl of Morton. He was regent of Scotland, 1572–78, and died in 1581.

ribbons. In course of time, hats became so common as to lose their sacred character, and to be worn not only by knights and nobles, but by their meanest domestics.

In the reign of Charles the First, and until the accession of the Prince of Orange, broad brims were in fashion. The Puritans were distinguished from the Cavaliers by their steeple-crowned hats. Some of the modes which prevailed, during this interval, are represented in the four following figures.

But these broad brims being found troublesome, the inconvenience was remedied, not by cutting them off, but by turning them up against the side of the hat. First one segment of the brim was elevated; then, two.

About the commencement of the last century, or somewhat sooner, the third segment of the brim was raised, and the result was a three-cornered cocked hat.

During the fifty or sixty years that ensued, the three-cornered hat, with unimportant variations of shape, was universally worn by men of all ranks and ages. Children, likewise, were adorned with a pair of breeches at one extremity of their persons, and a triangular hat at the other. Round hats first began to be worn by the common people in 1750, or thereabouts, but were not adopted by the higher classes till nearly thirty years later. In times not long gone by, we used occasionally to be greeted by an apparition of

> 'The old three-cornered hat,
> And the breeches—and all that,' [168]

but now, we are inclined to doubt whether the last of the three-cornered hats be not hung upon a peg.

On reviewing our series of cuts, we do not perceive that a single one of these successive fashions was calculated to add grace to the wearer's aspect, nor very well adapted to the more important purposes of a garment for the head. Nor can the more modern variations be considered as improvements, in either respect. Would it be beneath the dignity of men of science, taste and genius, to turn their attention to this, and other matters of dress? By bringing philosophical principles

[168] Oliver Wendell Holmes, "The Last Leaf," ll. 40–41.

to bear upon the subject, with regard to elegance and utility, they might possibly present the world with fashions, which should be as universal as the difference of climate would permit, and immutable in the countries where they should be once established. We have not much faith, however, in any projects which seek to contravene the maxim, that the 'fashion of this world passeth away.' [169]

(August, pp. 493–94)

Revolutionary Sentiments

There is a good deal of rough energy, and yet a classical turn, in the following passage, which we extract from old Timothy Pickering's 'Easy Plan of Discipline for a Militia,' [170] published in 1775. The introductory remarks, prefixed to the treatise, are well worth reading, because so thoroughly characteristic of the writer and of the times. They give us a perfect idea of the thoughts and feelings of a plain, strong-minded, upright citizen, conscientiously compelled to become a soldier, yet carrying a quaker-like simplicity into the ranks of war.

'Why throw away our money,' cries the Revolutionary colonel, 'for a fool's baubles?—Will a long tail and powdered hair obstruct the passage of the keen-edged sword? Or a rich garment prevent the entrance of the pointed steel?—If an enemy be pierced through the heart with the ball or bayonet of a rough, plain-dressed warriour, would he be more effectually pierced, though the ball or bayonet were sent by the arm of a tinselled beau? Away then with the trappings (as well as tricks) of the parade. Americans need them not, their eyes are not to be dazzled, nor their hearts awed into servility, by the splendour of equipage and dress; their minds are too much enlightened to be duped by a glittering outside.'

[169] I Corinthians 7: 31.
[170] Published at Salem. Pickering (1745–1829) served as lieutenant, colonel, and adjutant general in the Revolutionary War, and was afterward postmaster general, secretary of war, and secretary of state. His *Easy Plan of Discipline* was adopted by the Provincial Congress of Massachusetts in November, 1774 (see Alden Bradford, *History of Massachusetts,* Boston, 1822, p. 361), and was for a time in general use in the Continental army.

The colonel complains of the enormous waste of silk in the manufacture of standards:—

'Two-thirds of the silk imported from Great Britain,' he remarks, 'which is made into colours, would amount to a considerable sum; (for every company has its colour;) and so much, at least, we might save in future, if colours be reduced to a reasonable, and useful size. Three or four square yards of silk are taken to make one. This obliges the Ensigns, whenever they are in the ranks, or the wind blows, to gather up the colours in their hands, till by several folds and doublings, they are reduced to a quarter of their size when fully displayed, and thereby the distinguishing marks, by which the men might find their own regiments or companies, are liable to be wholly or in part concealed. At any rate, all that is thus doubled up is absolutely useless.'

There is something of the old Puritan spirit in the following remarks on military music; they remind us of the Cameronean leader, who ordered his drummer to beat the hundred and nineteenth psalm. As a battle-tune, the author would evidently have preferred Old Hundred [171] to Yankee Doodle.[172]

'Whenever the battalion marches, in order to perform the firings, advancing and retreating, the fifes are to play some tune to regulate the step. And tunes, which have some grandeur and solemnity in them, are undoubtedly to be preferred. The light airs, frequently played for a march, would appear to me as unnatural and improper to be used when a battalion is advancing toward an enemy, as the church music, censured by the poet, is unfit and indecent on those occasions when it is commonly used,—

> 'Light quirks of music, broken and uneven,
> Make the soul dance upon a jig to Heaven.' [173]

[171] The first version of the tune "Old Hundred" appeared as the melody to Psalm CXXXIV in the 1551 edition of the Geneva Psalter. The early New Englanders used the metrical version of the hundredth Psalm by William Kethe, which begins, "All people that on earth do dwell."

[172] "Yankee Doodle" appears to have been sung first by the British soldiers in derision of the Colonial troops, but it was soon adopted by the Revolutionary soldiers as a marching song.

[173] Alexander Pope's *Moral Essays*, Epistle IV, ll. 143–44.

If Colonel Pickering, after spending a few years in the service, had re-written this pamphlet, he would probably have made great alterations, and thereby have destroyed its peculiar and characteristic value. Any practised soldier might form a better system of Military Discipline; but here we see the New England militia-man, putting himself on his defence against the drilled warriours of Britain.

(August, p. 496)

Feminine Characteristics

Bishop Aylmer,[174] preaching a sermon before Queen Elizabeth, spoke in very uncourtly terms of the great body of the female sex. It will not be unfair, perhaps, to consider the first clause of the following passage as merely complimentary to his royal auditress, and to set down the remainder as the Bishop's *bona fide* opinion. 'Women,' observes he, 'are of two sorts:—Some of them are wiser, better learned, discreeter, and more constant than a number of men; but another and a worse sort of them, and the MOST PART, are fond, foolish, wanton flibbergibs, tattlers, triflers, wavering, witless, without counsel, feeble, careless, rash, proud, dainty, nice, tale-bearers, eaves-droppers, rumour-raisers, evil-tongued, worse-minded, and in everywise doltified with the dregs of the Devil's Dunghill!' It would be a bold man, in our day, who should stand up in a pulpit and repeat these words. At the time when they were uttered, and long afterwards, there was a species of cant in vogue, which aspersed the daughters of Eve with all their mother's frailties, and denied their claim to any of her heaven-born virtues. Modern cant (if we may venture to think it such) would produce a very curious counterpart to the above passage from Bishop Aylmer.

(August, p. 500)

[174] Bishop John Aylmer (1521–94) was Bishop of London during Elizabeth's reign. His arrogance and intolerance won for him the hearty disapproval of the puritan elements of his time.

St. Clair's Conqueror

The following description is given of the personal appearance of the Indian Chief, by whom General St. Clair was so disastrously defeated, in 1791:—[175]

'The Messesago Chief is a person six feet high, about forty-five years of age, of a very sour and morose countenance, and apparently very crafty and subtle. His dress was Indian hose and mocassins, a blue petticoat that came half way down his thighs, an European waist-coat, and surtout; his head was bound with an Indian cap, hanging half down his back, and almost entirely filled with plain silver broaches, to the number of more than two hundred. He had two earrings to each ear; the upper part of each was formed of three silver medals, about the size of a dollar; the lower part was formed of quarters of dollars and fell more than twelve inches from his ear; one from each ear over his breast, and the other over his back. He had three very large nose jewels of silver, that were curiously painted. The account he gave of the action was, that they had killed fourteen hundred of the whites, with the loss of only nine of their own party, one of whom had killed himself by accident.'

The leader who gained so complete a triumph as this, over a general trained to war from his youth upward, should hold an honourable place in the list of military men. Had such a victory been achieved by one civilized army over another, the conquerer would have slept beneath a marble column; but none can tell under what tree this warlike savage is taking his final rest. Military glory is so connected with ideas of silken banners, swords, drums, epaulettes, and marshalled lines, that these appear to make up the sum and substance of it, and the grim war-painted Indian is denied a place among the gorgeous heroes who shine in history.

(*August, p. 506*)

[175] General Arthur St. Clair (1736–1818) had an honorable career in the British army during the colonial wars. He later settled in Pennsylvania and served in Washington's army. After the Revolution he was governor of the Northwest Territory. In 1791 he was overwhelmingly defeated by an army of Indians, inferior in numbers, led by Little Turtle (*c.* 1752–1812), a Miami chieftain.

Caverns [176]

Tennessee, Kentucky, and the western parts of Virginia, abound with caves, which, both for their extent and the fantastic magnificence of their sparry petrifactions, may be ranked among the wonders of the world. Weyer's Cave, in Virginia, contains a great number of halls, passages, and galleries, most of which are adorned with concretions of splendid and variously colored spar, formed by the gradual deposit of earthy matter from the water that moistens the roof and walls. Many of these concretions have assumed the shape of fluted columns, pyramids, thrones, and colossal statues, ranged in long colonnades, and, by the dim light of the torches, perfectly resembling the handiwork of mortal sculptors. It might be imagined that some great potentate had here built for himself a deep and secret palace, or perhaps a tomb, and enriched it with all the treasures of art, which he deemed too precious for mankind even to look upon. But, on a nearer view, it is found that these objects have been wrought by no earthly hand: and the whole scene, with all its indescribable splendour, affects the mind like the illusions of a dream. The largest and loftiest hall in the cave has been dedicated to the memory of Washington, and contains, among other gigantic figures, one which bears the name of Washington's Statue.

In Tennessee, caverns are so numerous, and frequently of such vast size, that they are considered hardly worth mentioning to the curious traveller, unless it be possible to wander for miles within their mysterious recesses. At the summit of a lofty peak of the Cumberland Mountains, there is a hollow descending perpendicularly to a depth which has never been sounded; so that here, we might almost believe is the mouth of the Bottomless Pit, or at least a passage-way to the central cavity of the globe.

The Mammoth Cave, in Kentucky, has been explored to the distance of sixteen miles—the longest journey that ever was performed within the bowels of the earth. Through the mouth of the cave there

[176] Three small engravings accompany this sketch.

is a continual current of air, which for six months of the year, is drawn inward, and during the other six, rushes outward with force enough to extinguish a torch. It is one of the breathing-places of our mother Earth, where she performs her long respirations, and heaves her mighty, yet unavailing sighs, for the sin and sorrow of her children. Within the cavern, the spectator beholds hills, plains, and valleys, high precipices, and awful chasms, and deep rivers, broken with waterfalls—the whole presenting a picture of what the external world would be, were the sun extinguished, and only a few torches glimmering amid the darkness of Eternity. In the spacious gloom of this cave, the innumerable wretches who are weary of the light of day, might build a City of Despair; or, should a pestilence depopulate the land, the dead might here find a sepulchre. Should the former of these two projects be adopted, the inhabitants of the subterranean city might hold communication with the outer world by means of a stage-coach, which, it is stated, might be enabled, by a trifling expenditure, to run fifteen miles within the cavern.

The most celebrated cavern of the old world, is the Grotto of Antiparos, in Greece. As regards extent, it cannot compare with the vast caverns of America; although it appears to equal them in the fantastic combinations of its stalactites, and its imitations of natural and artificial objects; and perhaps to excel them in the beauty of its many-coloured spar, and the indescribable brilliancy of its crystals. The roof and walls are festooned and decorated with what seems the richest ornamental sculpture, and the floor is absolutely paved with substances that glow and sparkle like the diamond.

Until the seventeenth century, this resplendent cave remained hidden from the world. To the adventurer whose torch first gleamed upon those glittering walls, the spot must have seemed the treasury of Nature, where she had hoarded up her brightest and choicest jewels, lest man should snatch them from her grasp.

(*August, pp.* 507–8)

Edward Drinker

This person was born in 1680, on the spot where Philadelphia now stands: and died in 1782. Few men have seen greater changes in their travels far and wide, than Edward Drinker, during the century which he spent on his native soil. 'He saw the same spot of earth,' observes one who knew him, 'covered with woods and bushes, the haunt of wild beasts and birds of prey, afterwards become the seat of a great city, not only the first in wealth and arts in America, but equalled by few in Europe. He saw great and regular streets, where he had often pursued hares and wild rabbits. He saw fine churches rise upon morasses, where he used to hear nothing but the croaking of frogs; great wharves and ware-houses, where he had so often seen the Indian savages draw fish from the river; and that river afterwards full of great ships from all parts of the world, which, in his youth, had nothing bigger than an Indian canoe. And on the spot where he had gathered berries, he saw the City Hall erected, and that hall filled with legislators, astonishing the world with their wisdom and virtue!' When the hoary patriarch had seen all this, he must have felt as if he had more than one century on his shoulders; or perhaps these changes appeared dreamy and unsubstantial, like the scenery of a theatre, which shifts many times in an hour or two.[177]

(August, p. 508)

[177] Here seems to be a source and a forestudy for the idea underlying the sketch "Main Street" (1849).

Edward Drinker (1680–1782) went from Philadelphia, his birthplace, to Boston to live at the age of twelve and in 1745 returned to Philadelphia to remain the rest of his life. "He was four times married, and had 18 children, all by his first wife, and before his death he had a grandchild born to one of his grandchildren, being the fifth in succession from himself. He retained all his faculties to the last. . . . His memory continued so perfect that he could relate the minutest events in his youth, and never repeated them twice to the same company. He had the unusual happiness of seeing a place of desolation, the lurking spot of wild beasts and birds of prey, converted to a handsome, populous, and flourishing city, and after living under seven sovereigns, and beholding the great Penn establish his treaty with the Indians, and the congress sign their alliance with France, he hailed the day which made America a free independent republic" (J. L. Blake, *A General Biographical Dictionary*, New York, 1839, second ed., p. 290).

Laplandish Customs [178]

A Lapland Winter begins, at the latest, in November, and seldom closes much before June. During a considerable part of this long interval, the sun continues below the horizon, merely approaching so near its edge as to throw a feeble glimpse of twilight over the snowy desolation. But the absence of the solar rays are [*sic*] in some degree compensated by those mysterious phenomena, the Northern Lights, which dart from the horizon to the zenith, in fantastic and ever-changing shapes, the celestial brilliancy and beauty of which are inconceivable by the inhabitants of other climes. By the light of this etherial illumination, the Laplander makes long journeys across the ice and snow, drawn by a reindeer, which whirls the boat-like sledge along, at the rate of nineteen miles an hour. It is affirmed that a messenger once travelled, with a single reindeer, (which was not changed during the journey,) from the frontiers of Norway to Stockholm, a distance of eight hundred miles, in forty-eight hours. The sledges are so constructed, that an overturn is apt to take place many times in the course of a day's journey; but as the riders are securely fastened in, they manage to right themselves without stopping the reindeer, and seldom incur material damage.

In the month of June, the Laplanders make an annual migration from the mountainous interiour of the country to the seacoast. As the snow has now vanished, they leave their sledges behind, but take with them their entire herds of deer, which are laden with the skins and furs that constitute almost their only articles of traffic. These annual journeys are not, however, undertaken so much for the purposes of trade, as from a tender regard for the health of the rein-deer, which cannot be preserved except by the beneficial influence of the sea-breezes, in Summer. After a few months spent in fishing for cod, coal-fish, huge plaice, and halibut, the emigrants return to their native mountains, still accompanied by their herds, which now carry burdens of meal, cloth, manufactured articles, and spirituous liquors.

---

[178] Three woodcuts embellish this note.

The Laplanders are a dwarfish people, averaging little more than five feet in height. Their life is one of great endurance and hardship, which, however, instead of breaking down their constitutions renders them healthy and active. They are meagre and bony, yet, like most of the northern races, are capable of devouring, at a single meal, such immense quantities of food as might afford them a comfortable subsistence for many days.

The appearance of the two sexes, in their ordinary costumes, may be seen in the preceding cut. Their garments are chiefly composed of the fur of reindeer. They have no shirts nor stockings, the place of the latter being in some measure supplied, by thrusting dried grass into their shoes. It is averred by travellers, that the Lapland ladies are accustomed to wear a certain article of dress, which men in other countries are most anxious to keep to themselves.

(*August, pp. 513–14*)

NATURE, SCIENCE, INDUSTRY
AND ARCHITECTURE

The Science of Noses

Turning over an old book, the other day, we lighted upon a set of rules for discovering people's characters, by the length and formation of their noses. This ancient and forgotten science appears to us, far preferable to the phrenological inventions of later times.[179] It is simple in its application, and comprehensible to the meanest understanding. Its chief advantage[,] however, is, that—whereas the bumps on a man's head are hidden beneath his hair or a wig, and the worse qualities they indicate, the less will he permit them to be examined—here, on the contrary, the index of his character is precisely the most prominent feature of his face. It would seem as if Nature had taken this precaution, in order to render hypocrisy unavailable. A person might endeavour, no doubt, to keep the world in the dark by merely putting his handkerchief to his nose, like a chicken that thrusts its head into a corner and fancies itself invisible. But in a case of this studied concealment, it would not be uncharitable to conclude, that he was characterized by such an atrocious nose, as it would affright mankind to look upon. Without further preface, we shall favour our readers with the elements of the science, beseeching them not only to study their neighbours' noses, but to glance in the looking glass at their own. . . .

(*March, p. 268*)

Comparative Longevity

In the French *Revue Encyclopedique,* we find some interesting statements on longevity and the proportion of deaths to the popula-

---

[179] For another allusion of Hawthorne's to phrenology see *Fanshawe* (*Writings,* XVI, 89). Numerous lectures on phrenology were delivered in Boston during the 1830's (see Joseph B. Felt's *Annals of Salem,* Salem, 1845–49, II, 39).

tion, in the different countries of Europe. It thence appears that the duration and value of human life varies as much between one European nation and another, as it does between people of different races, and inhabiting different quarters of the globe. The number of deaths varies more than the number of births; in respect to the latter, there is never a difference of more than one half between any two countries; while the mortality of one is sometimes nearly triple that of another.

If we were asked what land, of all others on the face of the globe, we should fix upon as the most favourable to human life, our thoughts would probably turn to the sunny clime of Italy, whither consumptive patients go from all parts of the world, to inhale the balm of its atmosphere as their only chance of prolonged existence. Yet this would be a vast mistake; the air may be beneficial as a medicine; but it is apparently too delicious and exhilarating for constant use. It is not in the bleak and almost arctic region of Norway, nor in dreary Iceland, which is literally a land of ice, that human life has its briefest span—but in sunny Italy itself. Perhaps there is a feverish excitement in the blood, which causes the frame to wear out quickly in a southern clime; while, in colder countries, it is preserved from decay by its torpidity. The British islands, and especially Scotland, are very favourable to the life of man; in a million of inhabitants, the annual deaths are somewhat more than eighteen thousand. Sweden and Norway are also salubrious climates; there are only two deaths in that part of Europe for three in the southern countries. In Denmark and the greater part of Germany, the proportion is about the same. Russia and Poland, where the mass of the inhabitants have scarcely the necessaries of life, and can barely claim the rank of civilized people, are astonishingly favourable to the continuation of existence. The population, consisting of sixty-six millions[,] lives, on an average, half as long again as the Italians, and exactly twice as long as the inhabitants of Vienna, the capital city of Austria. The mean rate of mortality is in Switzerland, in the provinces of the Austrian empire, and in Spain, in which countries the annual deaths are about one in every forty. France, Holland, Belgium and Prussia, do not vary much from the same proportion. In other parts of Europe, the deaths are one in thirty, and often more, in the countries that border on the Mediterranean sea.

In all Europe, which contains two hundred and ten millions of inhabitants, about five millions and a half die annually, being one fortieth part of the whole; but these deaths are distributed very unequally between the northern and southern countries. In the former, death takes but one man in every forty-four; in the latter, he lays claim to one in thirty-six. In the north of France there are 22,700 deaths a year, and in the south 27,800 for each million of inhabitants; this is a striking difference, within the limits of one country.

Two great causes are assigned, which influence the duration of life and the number of deaths; these are CLIMATE AND CIVILISATION. A cold and rigorous climate is eminently favourable to existence; and likewise a low or moderate temperature, in the neighbourhood of the sea. In Russia, it is the climate alone that prolongs life, without any aid from civilisation; but, in more temperate regions, civilized habits, are absolutely necessary to produce a similar good effect. Between the tropics, the duration of life varies according to the different breeds of men. Thus in Batavia, the annual amount of deaths, taking all the inhabitants together, is one in twenty-six; but of this amount, the Europeans lose one in eleven, the slaves one in thirteen, the Chinese one in twenty-nine; and the Javanese, who are the natural inhabitants of the country, lose only one in forty-six. In the West Indies, the whites lose one third more, according to their numbers, than the blacks.

The effects of civilisation may be perceived, by contrasting the diminished mortality of the present day with that of former times. In Sweden, it has lessened one third in sixty-one years; in Switzerland one third in sixty-four; in the Pope's dominions, one third in sixty-two; in Prussia, one third in one hundred and six; and in Austria, one third in the short space of seven years. This latter fact, if it be correctly stated, is marvellous, and must have some extraordinary cause. In France, the mortality has diminished one half in the course of a century and a half. In Russia and Norway, during the last thirty years, it has remained at a stand; and in Naples it has increased. In the manufacturing city of Manchester, in England, it has diminished more than one half in sixty-four years, and in Birmingham, nearly one half in ten years. Taking the whole of Europe together, it is supposed that the mortality is less by one third than it formerly was.

The principal causes of a heavy average of deaths may be enumerated as follows;—the dampness of marshy tracts, especially in warm countries;—the want of sufficient food among the lower classes, and of comfortable clothing;—pestilential diseases;—great and sudden changes of the weather;—the insalubrity of private dwellings, prisons, and hospitals, owing to a too confined space, and neglect of cleanliness;—drunkenness, or the habitual use of alcohol;—unhealthy occupations, or too constant labour, especially in the case of children and youth;—war, not merely as producing death in battle, but by fatigue, forced marches, exposure, and an unhealthy mode of life in camp and field. On the other hand, the causes of a diminution of mortality are the drying up of marshes, and the embankment of rivers and streams;—the increased facilities of earning a livelihood; the greater abundance and better quality of food; attention to the wants and comforts of children; vaccination, which has almost eradicated one of the most fearful diseases of past times;—health-regulations at sea-ports, and the general enforcement of cleanliness;—the decreased prices of merchandise and manufactures, which place within the reach of every class those conveniences of life which were formerly confined to the wealthy;—the useful inventions, which have created new comforts. Thus we see that the life of man is not only embellished, but prolonged by civilisation; nor can it be doubted that the process will go on, and that our posterity will live longer, and with less torment of disease, and in a world of greater physical enjoyment, than ourselves. It is not, we hope, irreverent to say, that the Creator gave us our world, in a certain sense, unfinished, and left it to the ingenuity of man to bring it to the highest perfection of which final and physical things are susceptible.

We have not at hand any statements similar to the above, in regard to our own country. It is reasonable to suppose, however, that, within the vast limits of the United States, there is as great a difference in the length of life and number of deaths, as among the nations of Europe. The average of mortality in our cities has generally been stated at one in forty, which is the same as in Europe at large; and as the number of deaths is always greater in cities than elsewhere, this would indicate that the new world is more favourable to human life than the old. The situation of America, in a transition-state from a wild land to a cultivated one, affords opportunity for the solution of many problems, as to the causes which effect the health and longevity of man. It is desirable to know—and we should be glad to state it in this Magazine—what are the different averages of existence, when spent in a clearing of the primeval forest, in a long cultivated part of the country, and in a crowded city;—whether the felling of the western woods and the miraculous growth of towns, operates for good or evil on the old settlers;—what has been the influence, in this respect, of canals, and especially of the Erie Canal, in the long tract through which it drags its torpid current;—what is the effect of the increasing use of coal instead of wood, as fuel. Many other questions might be proposed; but the answers, we fear, would scarcely come to hand while we sit in the chair editorial; since, to be accurate, they must be formed by the comparison of distant communities, and of the present generation with its ancestors and posterity. And whatever may be the duration of this earthly existence, let it ever be in our minds, that another comes hastening on—which is eternal.

(*March, pp. 299–300*)

Snakes

It has been supposed that all snakes produce their young by means of eggs; but a correspondent of the American Journal of Science [180] gives evidence to the contrary. In a water-snake, he found about a hundred young ones of various lengths, and the thickness of a knitting-needle. The same writer observes that the smaller species of snakes cast their skins in the latter part of May or beginning of June;

[180] Judge Samuel Woodruff, "Notices in Natural History," *The American Journal of Science and Arts*, XXIX (1836), 304–6.

the larger species retain their old garments somewhat longer; but all have got rid of them by the end of September. A rattle-snake, in confinement, was observed to rub his head against the wires of his cage, and thrust it between them, as if endeavouring to escape. By this process, the skin on the back of his head began to cleave away and turn downward on his neck. He then knotted himself into several convolutions, the last of which pressed forcibly on the separated portion of the skin; and shooting his head briskly forward, released another length of his body. In this manner, he gradually crept out of his skin, which was left wrong-side outward. The whole race of snakes are turncoats. The reason of this provision of nature is, that a snake's skin is a sort of armour to protect his grovelling body from injury in its continual contact with the earth—and this skin is of a texture which cannot accommodate itself to the increased size of the snake. If he were not thus enabled to creep out of it, he must either burst it asunder, or be confined in an intolerably tight waistcoat.

(April, p. 332)

Coffee House Slip [181]

The engraving represents one of the haunts of business, in the commercial capital of America. Coffee House Slip, so named from its vicinity to the Tontine Coffee House, is situated at the foot of Wall Street. Since the sketch was taken, the Great Fire [182] has swept across this portion of New York, and left smoking ruins in its track, instead of the closely wedged edifices of the day before. It is a singular truth, that the mere shadowy image of a building, on the frail material of paper, which might be annihilated in an instant, is likely to have a longer term of existence than the piled brick and mortar of the building. Take a print like this at the head of our article, and an edifice like the large one on the right hand corner, and the chances are, that, a century hence, the print will be as good as ever; while the edifice, though it may not have crumbled beneath the weight of

---

[181] An engraving of half a page introduces this sketch.
[182] In December, 1835. For another mention of the fire see text, p. 37.

years, will probably have been torn down to make room for modern improvements, or utterly destroyed by fire. Should posterity know where the proud structure stood, it will be indebted for its knowledge to the wood-cut.

To a person of quiet and secluded habits, whether he live in the country or in a retired street of the metropolis, there can be no pleasanter ramble than to the vicinity of one of the principal wharves. He finds himself, as it were, in a different world, and takes note of every thing around him, with the minuteness of a traveller to far distant lands. The great ships, that have come speeding night and day from the uttermost parts of the earth, and are now moored in the dock, their enormous hulls rusty and sea-stained, and their rigging torn by the gales;—other vessels displaying their snowy canvass and proudly marching from the strand, to visit ports that are half the world's width asunder, or perchance to go down into the ocean-depths:—the packets, with their places of destination announced in huge letters on their shrouds, some landing their freight, some stowing it away in their capacious holds, some mustering their passengers for departure;—the bales and bags of precious merchandise, and puncheons and casks of choice liquors, and barrels of flour stamped with different brands, which lie scattered along the wharf, as if any poor devil might have them for the picking up;—the mounted iron cannon, presenting its gaping mouth at the stranger, as if to utter tales of pirates in the West Indies or of Malays in the East;—the other cannon, which has long ago sent forth its last peal of thunder, and now, with its muzzle in the earth and its breech in the air, is converted into a post;—the rumbling of heavily-laden wagons, the clash and clang of bars of Swedish iron, dragged on trucks over the pavement, the quick rattle of gigs, and the slow rattle of handcarts;—all these particulars, and many more, attract the observer's notice, and enter into his recollection of the scene. He snuffs up the scent of tar, to which his nostrils are less accustomed than are those of a sailor to the perfume of the Spice islands.

He observes also the living features of the scene, as well as its inanimate objects. There is the merchant, with his thoughtful brow and anxious eye, musing on the wealth that he has trusted to the uncertain main—doubtful, perhaps, whether, in three months hence, he will be a man of half a million, or a bankrupt;—there are the slender clerks, comparing a ship's cargo with the invoice;—there the sea-captain, with the flush of the salt-breeze still glowing on his cheek:—there the bronzed sailors, in bluejackets and duck trousers, rolling along like ships over uneven billows, and talking hoarsely, as if with speaking-trumpets;—there the truckmen, in frocks no longer white;—there the day-labourers, with their Irish look and accent;—and if any female be brought into the sketch, she must be Irish too, with a rough red cheek and unabashed stare, such as befits the mistress of a sailor's boarding-house. The jabber of foreign tongues is heard around, and the stranger almost doubts whether his short walk have not transported him to Lisbon or Madrid, or some port along the shores of the Mediterranean. And now he hears, issuing from the bowels of the earth, a mingled uproar of laughter and oaths, and tuneless singing, and perhaps the squeak of a fiddle, which, with the fumes of tobacco-smoke and strong liquors, are sure tokens of a victualling cellar and grog-shop.

(April, pp. 345–46)

Shot Tower [183]

This edifice was erected, some years ago, by Mr. George Youle, and is situated on Manhattan island, a few miles from the city of New York. It rises to the height of one hundred and fifty feet, and forms one of the most striking objects amid the picturesque and beautiful scenery with which it is surrounded. The East River, thronged with steam-boats and other vessels, flows at its base. The tower needs nothing but antiquity, and a mantle of clinging ivy, and above all, the charm of legend and tradition, in order to afford as good a subject for the pen of the poet or novelist, as it already does for the pencil of the artist.[184] Or if it were (as might well beseem its stately height)

---

[183] With this article appears an engraving of half a page.

[184] See Hawthorne's assertions elsewhere that a dim past and ivy-covered ruins are essential for literary productions (*Writings,* VII, xxi–xxii; VIII, xxix–xxxi).

the monument of a hero, or even a light-house, to guide benighted mariners to their haven, nothing would be easier than to surround it with romantic associations. But it is almost impossible to connect the sentiment of romance with a Shot Tower.

When we consider the small size of the article, to the manufacture of which this lofty structure is devoted, the means appear greatly out of proportion with the result. Formerly, in casting shot, the apparatus was merely a plate of copper, in the bottom of which were punched a number of small holes. This was placed a few feet above a kettle of water, into which the melted lead descended, after passing through the holes in the plate. But in falling so short a distance, and being so suddenly cooled and hardened, the shot did not acquire a perfectly globular form,—a desideratum which is now attained by means of Shot Towers. In that of Mr. Youle, the largest size of shot falls from the summit of the edifice to the bottom of a well, twenty-five feet below the surface of the earth, making the whole descent about one hundred and seventy-five feet. The size of the shot is determined by the size of the holes through which it passes. The furnaces, for melting the lead, are situated near the summit of the tower. Three tons of shot is the quantity usually manufactured per day.

This method of casting shot was invented by Mr. Watt,[185] the celebrated engineer, in consequence, it is said, of a dream. He tried the experiment from the tower of the church of St. Mary Redcliffe,[186] and, finding it successful, obtained a patent, which he afterwards sold for ten thousand pounds. There are now several shot-towers in the vicinity of London. The loftiest of these is one hundred and fifty feet high, and gives a fall of one hundred and thirty feet to the melted lead. An iron staircase ascends from the base to the summit of the tower: Arsenic is mingled with the molten lead, in the proportion of forty pounds to one ton. In casting, the metal is not poured through a tube, but descends through the open space of the tower, in a continual stream of silvery drops. As the weight of the lead prevents it from scattering, or being blown about like water-drops,

---

[185] James Watt (1736–1819), Scotch engineer and inventor.
[186] Redcliffe, it will be noted, is the name Hawthorne gave to one of the chief characters in *Doctor Grimshawe's Secret.*

the workmen pass to and fro, without danger, close beside this fiery cascade. The shot is of different sizes, from No. 1, or Swan Shot, to No. 12, which is called Dust Shot. When first manufactured, they are of a dull white colour, without lustre, and are polished by being shaken together in an iron barrel which is made to revolve by machinery. This process gives them their black lustre, and they are then ready for sale.

(*April, p. 349*)

Pennsylvania Hospital [187]

This Institution had its origin in the charity of private individuals, and was the first of the kind in the Anglo-American dominions; although, at an earlier date, there were probably hospitals under the direction of the Catholic priesthood, in the French colonies. The corner-stone of the eastern wing was laid in the year 1755. As since enlarged and completed, it consists of a central part and of two wings, which are united to the main structure by two buildings, each eighty-one feet in length. The central part is sixty-three feet long, and sixty-one in depth; the wings extend each about thirty feet in front, by one hundred and eleven feet deep; and the length of the whole edifice is two hundred and eighty-five feet, fronting southward, on Pine street. There are other buildings belonging to the Hospital; and the space of ground, covered by its edifices, its groves, and gardens, is nearly fifteen acres, and occupies the entire square between Spruce and Pine, and Eighth and Ninth streets. Venerable trees throw their shadow round about the structure, and a statue of the illustrious Quaker, William Penn, presented by his grandson, stands on a pedestal in front. In all respects, the exteriour of the Hospital is on a scale of magnificence and beauty, that fills the beholder's mind with the pleasantest impressions, in spite of the associations of human misery, connected with a remembrance of the objects to which this stately structure is devoted.

The internal arrangements are equally admirable. The central

---

[187] Opposite this essay is a full page woodcut of the hospital.

edifice contains a library of six thousand volumes; an apothecary's establishment; an amphitheatre for surgical operations and lectures; a lying-in ward; a female sick ward; chambers for the resident physicians; and apartments for the steward's family. The western part of the Hospital is occupied exclusively by insane patients, one hundred of whom can there be accommodated. On the east of the central edifice are the medical and surgical wards, calculated for the reception of one hundred and sixty patients. From the foundation of the Hospital, down to the year 1828, the number of individuals, admitted within its walls, had been hardly less than twenty-five thousand.

The foundation of Hospitals was an early result of Christianity, until the appearance of which, there was no such thing as systematic benevolence on earth. In the first years of the Church, the bishops provided for the poor, both in health and when diseased; and after the priesthood had acquired a stated revenue, one fourth of the whole was appropriated for similar purposes. The Catholic religious institutions, although greatly perverted from the pristine purity of their origin, accomplished a vast deal of good, during the dark and bloody centuries in which they flourished. The only friends of the sick and miserable were then to be sought under the hood of the monk and the veil of the nun. In course of time, many persons, when conscious of the approach of death, devoted their wealth to the foundation of Hospitals, thus hoping to perpetuate their names and memory, which would otherwise have been lost for want of children —or perhaps to make amends for an evil life, by applying to this sacred purpose their unjust gains, which they could no longer hoard in their coffers, nor spend upon themselves. Other Hospitals were endowed by governments; others, as in the present instance, by the contribution of charitable individuals. At the present day, there are few or no civilized countries, where the homeless sick may not find the shelter of a roof, the skill of a physician, the care of a nurse, and a pallet to stretch their wasted forms upon;—every thing, in short, save the sedulous affection which, at a sick bed, is worth them all.

The most powerful description of a Hospital that ever was, or can be given, is contained in Milton's Paradise Lost. The Archangel Michael leads Adam, after his fall, to the summit of a high hill, and

brings before him a series of pictures, portraying the future destinies
of the world;—and among the rest, the following,—the dark and fearful painting of which is worthy of the pencil that had successfully
depicted the torments of the fallen angels:—

'Immediately a place
Before his eyes appeared, sad, noisome, dark,
A Lazar-House it seemed, wherein were laid
Numbers of all diseased, all maladies
Of ghastly spasms, or racking torture, qualms
Of heart-sick agony, all feverous kinds,
Convulsions, epilepsies, fierce catarrhs,
Intestine stone and ulcer, colic pangs,
Demoniac frenzy, moping melancholy,
And moon-struck madness, pining atrophy,
Marasmus, and wide-wasting pestilence,
Dropsies, and asthmas, and joint-racking rheums.
Dire was the tossing, deep the groans; Despair
Tended the sick, busied from couch to couch;
And over them triumphant Death his dart
Shook, but delayed to strike, though oft invoked
With vows, as their chief good, and final hope.
Sight so deform what heart of rock could long
Dry-eyed behold? Adam could not, but wept,
Though not of woman born; compassion quelled
His best of man, and gave him up to tears.[188]

No marvel that Adam wept!—no marvel, if he failed to discern,
in this dreadful misery of his descendants, the hand of a beneficent
Creator! But Michael tells him, in substance, that these many varieties
of loathsome sickness were the punishment of intemperance and un-
governed appetite. Adam inquires, if there be no easier mode of
death than those which he beholds in the Lazar-House; and receives
the following answer.—

'There is, said Michael, if thou well observe
The rule of not too much, by temperance taught,

[188] *Paradise Lost,* XI, ll. 477-97.

In what thou eat'st and drink'st, seeking from thence
Due nourishment, not gluttonous delight,
Till many years over thy head return:
So may'st thou live, till like ripe fruit thou drop
Into thy mother's lap, or be with ease
Gathered, not harshly plucked, for death mature.' [189]

The above lines contain the whole doctrine of Temperance, and are worthy of the Archangel's lips. And were mankind wise enough to seek, in their food and drink, 'due nourishment, not gluttonous delight,' there would be many a vacant bed in the wards of the Pennsylvania Hospital.

(*May, p. 371*)

Nature of Sleep [190]

Scientific men have been infinitely puzzled to explain the phenomena of sleep; the reason being, perhaps, that they cannot examine into its nature, at the same time that they are undergoing its influence. If a person, while asleep, were capable of noticing and recording his own sensations, a correct theory of the matter would probably soon be attained. Most of the present theories are dreams, it is true; but they have the great disadvantage of being merely the dreams of waking men.

Dr. Philip,[191] an English physician, has paid much attention to the subject, and appears to have thrown considerable light upon it. His observations on the nature of sleep are so connected with his

---

[189] *Ibid.*, ll. 530–37.   [190] Reprinted in *Writings*, XVII, 219–23.

[191] Dr. Alexander P. W. Philip (*c.* 1770–*c.* 1851) was an assiduous investigator in physiology and pathology. He was one of the first to use the microscope in the study of inflammation. The work by Philip to which Hawthorne alludes here is a paper "On the Nature of Sleep" contributed to the *Transactions of the Royal Philosophical Society of London*, 1833, pp. 73–87. Philip read the paper before the Society on March 7, 1833. He also published at London in 1834 a book entitled *Inquiry into the Nature of Sleep and Death*. Philip's other researches alluded to by Hawthorne were on the circulation of the blood and the relations between the nervous and the muscular systems; see the *Transactions*, 1833, pp. 55–72.

researches on other points of animal physiology, that the former can-not be fully understood without an acquaintance with the latter. An abstract, however, may be attempted, and perhaps be made sufficiently intelligible to interest the reader.

He observes, that, in the more perfect animals, there are two systems, in a great degree distinct from each other; one is the sensi-tive system, by means of which we perceive, and act, and hold inter-course with the external world; the other is the vital system, by which existence is maintained. The sensitive system, alone, is subject to sleep. When the reasoning powers are fatigued by attention, the feel-ings by the indulgence of passion, the eye by objects of sight, the ear by sounds, and the muscles of voluntary motion by powerful and re-peated exercise, they cease to be excited by ordinary stimulants; and, unless stronger stimulants are applied, they fall into a state of rest. This is sleep; and during its continuance, the excitability, which had previously been exhausted, is restored, and the nerves can be again acted upon by the usual stimulants. It is a law of the sensitive system, that it is subject to be thus alternately excited and exhausted; and unless the exhaustion is excessive, it does not interfere with health, but is entirely in the natural course of things. But that sleep alone is healthy, which is easily broken. If from fatigue, or any other cause, it be unusually profound, such sleep partakes of disease; because then the vital system, though it does not sleep, is affected by the tor-por of the sensitive system. Thus, in very profound sleep, the move-ments of the respiratory organs are sluggish, and the blood, in con-sequence, is less frequently renovated at the lungs, and therefore acts with diminished power in keeping up the motion of the heart.

As we have stated, it is the nature of the sensitive system to be alternately excited and exhausted. Now, there is this great differ-ence between it and the vital system, that the latter is continually excited, but never, in its natural and healthy state, undergoes ex-haustion, or needs repose in order to fit it for the performance of its duties. It is continually at work, from the first moment of our lives till the last, and is never tired; or if it be so, its weariness is the symp-tom of disease; it does not resemble the healthy exhaustion of the sensitive system, but manifests itself in debility, whence the sufferer very slowly recovers, if at all. The heart belongs to the vital system; it is continually in a state of excitement and action, and is never weary of throbbing; it works for a whole lifetime together, and never sleeps till it has done its task. Its sleep—the sleep of the vital system —is death; for when it has once fairly sunk under exhaustion, there is no possibility of arousing it. The sensitive system, on the contrary, is aroused from its sleep by means of the vital system; from which, during its repose, it has been collecting and accumulating fresh excitability, to supply the place of what was wasted in the hours of wakefulness. The vital powers reinvigorate the exhausted sensitive powers; and therefore the latter may safely fall asleep; but Nature has provided no method of reinvigorating the exhausted vital powers, because she did not contemplate that they should ever need repose. Had we been created without this faculty of continual wakefulness, in our hearts and the rest of our vital systems—had these organs been liable to fall asleep, like the sensitive ones—the first nap, which we might happen to take, would last till the day of Judgment —for the simple reason, that there would be no possibility of awaking us. Hence we may infer, that no living creature has ever been more than half asleep, and that only the dead sleep sound; their bodies, we mean; for their spirits are then more wide-awake than ever.

How strange and mysterious is our love of sleep! Fond as we are of life, we are yet content to spend a third of its little space in what, so far as relates to our own consciousness, is a daily, or nightly, annihilation. We congratulate ourselves when we have slept soundly; as if it were a matter of rejoicing that thus much of time has been snatched from the sum total of our existence—that we are several steps nearer to our graves, without perceiving how we arrived thither, or gaining either knowledge or enjoyment on the way. Well!—Eternity will make up the loss; on no other consideration can a wise man reconcile himself to the necessity of sleep.

(*May, p. 385*)

Effect of Colour on Heat

Many of our readers will recollect Dr. Franklin's experiment,[192] by placing pieces of cloth, of different colours, on the snow, in order to test which of them would absorb the greatest quantity of heat from the sun. It was found, after some hours' exposure, that the black cloth had sunk deepest in the snow, and that the other pieces had sunk to depths which corresponded to the darkness of their colours; while the snow beneath the white cloth had not been melted at all. From this result, Dr. Franklin drew the inference that dark-coloured garments were unfit to be worn in hot countries; and that the dress of the inhabitants, and of sailors, and the uniform of soldiers, between the tropics, should be of some light hue. Their hats, especially, in his opinion, should be white, that the intense heat of the sun might not be absorbed through a dark surface into their brains.

Nevertheless, the observations of other distinguished philosophers led them to a very different conclusion. Among these were Count Rumford [193] and Sir Everard Home.[194] The Count affirmed, that, if he were to become a resident in the torrid zone, he would either blacken his skin, or wear a black shirt. Sir Everard, by actual experiments on his own person and that of a negro, discovered that the black skin was far less affected by the sun's rays than the white; although the absorption of heat by the black was very considerably greater. In other words, the negro's skin remained cooler, while yet it undeniably imbibed the largest quantity of heat. No satisfactory

---

[192] This experiment of Franklin's and his conclusions were recorded in his letter to Miss Mary Stevenson, Sept. 20, 1761 (see *The Writings of Benjamin Franklin*, ed. Albert Henry Smyth, New York, 1907, IV, 111–16).

[193] Sir Benjamin Thompson, Count Rumford (1753–1814), was the instigator of numerous reforms in public service and social economy while in the service of the Elector of Bavaria. He published several essays on the subject of light, and is credited with originating the theory of heat as a mode of action.

[194] Sir Everard Home (1756–1832) made valuable contributions to the study of comparative anatomy and wrote several books on medicine. In his work he used the papers of John Hunter and later burned them to conceal the evidence of his dependence on them.

explanation of this phenomenon was offered; and even Sir Humphrey Davy,[195] though the fact was undisputed, failed to assign a reasonable cause. In a recent volume of the London Philosophical Transactions,[196] there is an able and interesting paper, which brings forward what appears to be a correct solution of the mystery. The author states, that, although a greater quantity of heat is absorbed by dark-coloured surfaces than by light ones, yet a proportionably greater quantity is given out. Thus, in the case of the negro, there is a brisk circulation of heat, which, passing into and out of the skin, promotes insensible perspiration, and keeps the body cool. Hence, too, the peculiar odour of the coloured race; it being disengaged from their persons together with the heat which is given out.

We may readily conclude, that Nature would not have given the African his sable skin, unless it had been his best protection against the burning clime of his nativity. The ingenious writer, whose essay forms the basis of this article, supposes that the shades of colour in the human race correspond to the differences of climate; and that thus the mean temperature of the body is kept about the same in Greenland, for instance, as in Calcutta. On this theory, however, he would find it difficult to account for the unvarying hue of our Indians; whose skins, we believe, are of as deep a copper colour at the sources of the Mississippi as in Florida. Setting aside the red men, we should suppose that, with all other varieties of mankind, his system might hold good. In regard to the lower orders of animal life, there are even stronger evidences, that their colour is regulated by the degree of heat or cold which they are to endure. Many of the quadrupeds of northern climates change their Summer garments, of various hues, to a Winter dress of white; in the arctic regions, there are white foxes, white hares, and white ermine. In England, similar changes

[195] Sir Humphrey Davy (1778–1829), the noted chemist.

[196] James Stark, "On the Influence of Colour on Heat and Odours," *Transactions of the Royal Philosophical Society of London*, 1833, pp. 285–312. This article, which is divided into two parts, the first treating the effect on heat and the second the effect on odors, also supplied the information for Hawthorne's essay on the "Effect of Colour on Odours"; see text, pp. 201–3. Hawthorne's allusions to Rumford, Home, and Davy are based on Stark's discussion of their observations (*ibid.*, p. 296).

occasionally take place; and in our own country, the rabbit, at least, turns white in Winter. The feathered tribes, in climates where there is a great difference of temperature between Winter and Summer, undergo still more striking variations of hue. Their Winter dress is so unlike that which they assume in Summer, and both, in some cases, are so little similar to what they wear in Spring or Autumn, that Ornithologists, describing the same birds at different seasons, have supposed them to belong to various species. The ptarmigan may be taken as an instance; the dark richness of its Summer plumage gradually gives place to a grayish white, in Autumn; its black spots are changed to zig-zag lines and specks; and it continues to fade, till, in the depth of Winter, it is seen of a pure immaculate white. There is a vast difference of hue between tropical birds and those of an arctic climate; it would exhaust the richest colours of a painter's palette to depict the former; while black and white would suffice for the Summer and Winter dresses of the latter. Humming birds, by the metallic reflection and polished surfaces of their plumage, are admirably fitted to flit through the Summer sunshine. Insects, whose existence begins and ends with Summer, are painted with a gorgeous depth of hue. In like manner, it is supposed that the temperature of flowers is regulated by the colours of their petals; so that there is an important use, in what we have been accustomed to consider merely ornamental. The flowers of mid-summer glow deeply bright; those of the early Spring are pale.

Had black been the colour best fitted to retain heat, there is no doubt, strange as the idea may seem, that the earth would have been defended against the inclemency of Winter by a garment of black snow. But, in the present constitution of things, the soil, and the roots of the herbage and plants, are protected by precisely the proper covering; which, though its spotless whiteness absorbs little or no heat from the sun, gives off as little from the earth. Would it not be wise, then, if we were to reverse the rules that have hitherto guided us, and follow Nature in her fashions—putting on garments white as her snow, for Winter-wear, and decking ourselves, in Summer, with the deepest hues of her verdure and her flowers?

(*May, p. 386*)

Bells [197]

Cowper, in the person of Alexander Selkirk, finds no stronger mode of expressing the dreary desolation of the island of Juan Fernandez, than the following:—

> 'The sound of the church-going bell
> These valleys and rocks never heard,
> Never sighed at the sound of a knell,
> Nor smiled when the Sabbath appeared.' [198]

The idea, contained in these lines, is true and powerful; we immediately feel all the loneliness of the desert isle, 'far mid the melancholy main,' [199] where man dwells not now, nor ever did dwell, nor has hallowed the hills and groves by his earthly sorrows, nor his hopes of immortality. All ears delight in the music of a bell. Milton, for instance, numbers it among his pensive pleasures:—

> 'Oft on a plat of rising ground,
> I hear the far-off Curfew sound,
> Over some wide-watered shore,
> Swinging slow with sullen roar.' [200]

The accents of its iron tongue have a strange influence over human sympathies; or rather, they chime in with every tone of sentiment, and make religion more venerable, grief more tender, and joy more gladsome. Such an effect has been recognised from the earliest times. The Egyptians ushered in the festal days of their deities by the ringing of bells; and bells were rung, too, in some of the religious solemnities of the ancient Greeks.

It is supposed that bells were first introduced into Christian churches about the year 400; although they were not brought into general use, till three or four centuries afterwards. They were given

[197] Reprinted in *Writings*, XVII, 224–28.
[198] William Cowper's "Lines Supposed to Be Written by Alexander Selkirk during His Solitary Abode on the Island of Juan Fernandez," ll. 29–32.
[199] James Thomson, *The Castle of Indolence*, Canto I, stanza 30.
[200] "Il Penseroso," ll. 73–76.

by princes and great men to religious communities; and, in the early ages of the Catholic faith, it was usual to baptize the bells, with great ceremony; the crossing, benediction, and other rites, being performed by a bishop. Many marvellous virtues were attributed to them; and among the rest, that of dispelling thunder storms, in order to effect which, they were generally rung amid the roar of the tempest. The church bells were also sounded, at the moment when the soul of a dying person was passing from his body; a custom for which there were two reasons—one, that all Christians might be reminded to pray for their departing brother; and the other, because the knell was believed to chase away the evil spirits, who watched around the sinner's death-bed.

Bells have the same general shape in all countries; and it is conjectured that their form was imitated from that of a pot or kettle. They have recently been made without any curvature of the sides, but straight up and down, like a tub. The largest bells in the world, are in Nankin, and in Moscow. In the former city, there were four bells, of such size, that, though they were never swung in the belfry, but merely struck with a wooden mallet, they caused the tower to fall, and are said to be still lying amid the ruins. In Moscow, there is a bell which was presented to the cathedral of that city by the Empress Anne, the height of which is twenty-one feet, its circumference near the bottom more than sixty-seven, and its weight at least four hundred and thirty-two thousand pounds. It remains in a deep pit, where it was cast, and has a fissure in its side through which two persons may pass abreast, without stooping. This enormous bell is worth above three hundred thousand dollars, considering it merely as a mass of old bell-metal, and without reckoning the gold and silver, a large amount of which is supposed to be mingled . with its materials; for tradition affirms that, while the metal was in a state of fusion, many of the Russian nobility and people threw in their plate and coin. The tone of a bell is thought to be greatly improved by a mixture of silver.[201] Bell-metal is composed of copper and tin, generally in the proportion of twenty-three pounds of the latter to one hundred of the former; and it is a singular fact, that not only

---

[201] For an account of another bell of Moscow see text, p. 229.

is the compound more sonorous than either of the metals separately, but is also heavier than their aggregate weight.

Bells of moderate size are moulded in the manner of large pots. In the manufacture of larger ones, pits are dug in the earth, and they are cast in a sort of plaster moulds. A cracked bell is generally considered as irremediably ruined; but attempts have recently been made, and sometimes with success, to restore the proper tone by cutting out the fractured part. While the Great Tom of Lincoln was undergoing this operation, a piece was broken off the rim, eight feet in length, and weighing six hundred pounds.

It would have been by no means wonderful, if our pious ancestors, when they emigrated to New England, had rejected the use of bells, and refused to be thus summoned to public worship, because the same mode was practised in the churches and high cathedrals of the ancient faith. They do, in fact, in some of the country towns, and probably in Boston, during the first years of its settlement, appear to have substituted the beat of a drum, instead of the ringing of a bell, on Sabbaths and Lecture-days. This, however, was attributable to the necessity of the case; and bells were imported from England, almost as soon as the pilgrims had exchanged the canopy of forest-boughs for a temple built with hands. The earliest use of bells, in North America, was probably in the French and Catholic city of Quebec. Every little chapel in the wilderness, where the French Jesuits preached to the red-men, had its bell. We recollect to have seen, in the museum of Bowdoin College, one, which we believe, had belonged to the chapel of the martyred Father Ralle. After the priest was slain, and his altar desecrated, by the bloody hands of the New England rangers, this bell, if we mistake not, lay hidden many years beneath the forest-leaves; until being accidentally brought to light, it was suspended in the belfry of the College-chapel. The adventures of this bell would form a pretty and fanciful story, which we should be glad to write, if it were in our nature to be guilty of such nonsensical scribblings.[202]

(May, p. 387)

---

[202] Hawthorne later elaborated "the adventures of this bell" into the "pretty and fanciful story" which he suggests here—"A Bell's Biography" (1837), which follows closely the outline set down in this sketch.

The Precious Metals, as Applied to Articles of Use and Ornament

The consumption of the precious metals, in other modes than by converting them into coin, has greatly increased in recent times. Some articles of plate, such as silver tea-urns and tureens, have been introduced in modern days. Silver table-forks, also, were unknown, even among the higher classes, until the commencement of the reign of George the Third; although, at present, one half the silver used in England, is consumed in the manufacture of forks and spoons. It probably is not two centuries, since table spoons of silver were substituted for pewter, as the latter material had formerly been for horn or wood. Tea-spoons were of course introduced subsequently to the use of tea; the date of which was in Queen Anne's reign. They are now manufactured by millions. Silver plates, dishes, and vessels, the use of which was formerly confined to people of rank, are now common throughout a much wider class. Watches, which are worn by almost every body above the lowest rank, employ a vast amount of gold and silver, far the greater part of which has been applied to this use within half a century. Only a small quantity of the precious metals is now used in lace and embroidery, which were formerly worn in great profusion on the garments of the nobility and gentry; but what is saved, in this respect, is expended, and a great deal besides, in the number and variety of gold ornaments that are now fashionable. For instance, there are gold chains and seals, broaches, breast-pins, and waist-coat buttons; large golden combs, and other ornaments for the head; ear-rings and necklaces; eye-glasses set in gold, and spectacles with gold bows; buttons, clasps, and hooks and eyes of gold, for ladies' gowns. No small portion of gold goes to the manufacture of finger-rings; of which, we presume, almost every man, not absolutely in a state of poverty, has occasion to present at least one to some object of his tender regards, and probably to receive one in exchange.

Much gold is consumed in the various branches of gilding. In

London alone, there are eighty gold-beaters, some of whom use up no less than twenty ounces per week; the average quantity, among the whole trade, is about three ounces. The gold-leaf, after being beaten out to the requisite thinness, is placed between the leaves of books, each of which is three and three-eighths of an inch square, and contains twenty-five leaves. These books are sold by the thousand, at different prices, according to the thickness of the leaves. Only eight penny-worths of gold is used in manufacturing a thousand of the cheapest kind. Silver leaf is sometimes made in the same manner; but the thinnest is at least two and a half times as thick as the thinnest gold; and a thousand books cannot be made with less than an ounce of silver. In what is called water-gilding, gold dust is mingled with quicksilver, and applied like paste to the buttons or toys, which are to be gilded. An enormous quantity of these articles are scattered from the workshops of England over all the markets in the world. A great deal of gold is also used in the porcelain potteries, for gilding tea-sets, table-services, and ornamental china. Plating with gold is performed by applying a thin plate of gold to a thicker one of inferiour metal; the two metals are made to adhere, by means of a strong pressure; and seals and other articles are manufactured in this way, at a comparatively trifling expense. For ten or twelve years, or more, they look as well as solid gold. Silver is likewise rolled in contact with other metals; and ornaments for coaches and coach-harnesses are thus manufactured.

The frames of pictures and looking-glasses require still further portions of gold; and much, also, is expended on the epaulettes and lace of uniforms. A mighty mass of silver is manufactured into thimbles, which are turned out by the bushel and cart-load. Then there are silver pencil-cases, and a host of gew-gaws and knick-knacks, too numerous to mention.

The value of the silver, drawn from all sources, since the discovery of America, has been three times that of the gold; but the loss by wear, on gold, is only a fourth part what it is on silver. An ounce of gold is now worth about fifteen ounces of silver; but, in the days of ancient Rome, it was worth only from nine to eleven ounces. By far the larger part of the immense amount of the precious metals, consumed in the above manufactures, comes fresh from the mines, or is obtained by melting down light guineas, or doubloons, Portugal-pieces, and other foreign coin. About one-fortieth part of the whole is supplied by burning old gold and silver lace, and picture frames, melting unfashionable plate, and from the sweepings of goldsmith's shops, and all such sources. Vast as is the expenditure of the precious metals, they might, however, in case of urgent necessity, be, in a great measure, dispensed with; for the artists of Birmingham are so skilful in the manufacture of alloyed gold, that ornaments of this material may be afforded at from one half to one quarter the standard cost; yet look altogether as well, to an ordinary observer, as the pure metal. Jeweller's gold is not looked upon as the pure gold of Ophir, in any part of the world; and, for aught we know, Birmingham might meet its match on this side of the Atlantic. We recollect a story of an old and wealthy goldsmith, who, being asked by one of his younger brethren how he had managed to grow so rich by his handicraft, made the following oracular response:—'When I set up in business, my young friend, my stock of the precious metals consisted of a gold doubloon and old brass-kettle;—and the doubloon lasted longer than the brass-kettle!'

(*May, pp. 387–88*)

Rainbows

It has been observed by the ancients, that where a rainbow seems to hang over, or to touch, a sweet smell may be perceived.[203] It will be found a somewhat difficult matter to reach the spot which a rainbow touches, in order to test this experiment. Like all other bright things, the gorgeous pageant will remove as we advance, and at last fade into the sky—where, if we follow it thither, we shall doubtless find it.[204]

(*May, p. 389*)

[203] The source of this is Bacon's *Sylva Sylvarum* (*The Works of Francis Bacon*, Boston, 1857, V, 74): "It hath been observed by the ancients, that where a rainbow seemeth to hang over or to touch, there breatheth forth a sweet smell."

[204] An approximation of the idea that Hawthorne was to put into "The Great Carbuncle" the following year.

Salt; Its Origin and Manufacture

Salt is obtained from various sources; as from sea water, from lakes and springs, and from solid masses of the substance, either above or beneath the surface of the earth. It is estimated that the thirtieth part of the water of the ocean consists of salt; but the proportion is largest at the equator, and decreases towards the poles. In hot countries, where the earth is dry and sandy, the surface of large tracts is frequently covered with a layer of salt. In Persia, there are very extensive plains, strewn with salt in flakes; it is often met with in the deserts of Arabia; and in Abyssinia, the traveller journeys four days over a plain of salt. The appearance, probably, is somewhat like that of our fields in winter, beneath their shroud of snow. In the south of Africa, there are abundance of salt lakes, where the salt crystallizes in masses as hard and solid as rock. In Spain, there is a mountain, between four and five hundred feet high, and nearly three miles in circumference, which is one enormous lump of solid salt; as it is transparent, extremely hard, and not easily soluble in water, the people apply it to the manufacture of various kinds of ornaments and utensils, such as vases, urns, and candlesticks. In some parts of Turkey, salt is said to be used, like blocks of granite, to build houses with. There are also mines of salt, among which that of Weliska, in Poland, is the most extensive, and affords the most fruitful supply. This mine is, in fact, a subterranean city, containing chapels and palaces, and colonnades which, by the blaze of torches, gleam with all the colours of the rainbow.

Salt springs are found in Switzerland, France, England, and America. The whole of the valley of the Ohio, from its head waters to Shawnee town in Illinois, according to a writer in the American Journal of Science,[205] is based on a saliferous rock, which lies at the depth of from five to twelve hundred feet beneath the surface, and

[205] "The Salt Mountains of Ischil; in a Letter from an Officer in the American Navy," *The American Journal of Science and Arts,* XXIX (1836), 225–29. Hawthorne also drew from S. P. Hildreth's "Observations on the Bituminous Coal Deposits of the Valley of the Ohio, and the Accompanying Rock Strata," *ibid.,* XXIX, 1–148.

when perforated, yields water of extreme saltness. There are tokens
of its existence along the course of the Alleghanies, over a tract one
hundred miles wide, and several hundred miles in length. It is supposed that the ancient inhabitants of the West were acquainted with
the use and manufacture of salt; for, in digging wells at the Scioto
salines and elsewhere, the remains of furnaces, and fragments of
earthen vessels, have been found at considerable depths. The tusks
and grinders of the Elephant and Mastodon have likewise been met
with in similar situations, whither they had doubtless resorted to
eat salt.

The American writer, to whom we have just alluded, has given a
copious and interesting account of the salt manufacture in the valley
of the Ohio. For many years after the settlement of that region, all
the salt was obtained from the Atlantic states, and was transported
across the mountains on horse-back. The price was then so high,
that salt was almost considered a luxury, rather than an article of
common and necessary use. Its manufacture was first attempted in
1798, at the Old Scioto salt works, where wells were dug to the depth
of twenty or thirty feet, into which the water oozed, through fissures
in the saliferous rock, or bed of salt. The water was but weakly im-
pregnated with the saline substance; and from six to eight hundred
gallons were required, to make one bushel of salt weighing fifty
pounds. This salt, though very dark coloured and impure, sold at
the rate of three or four dollars per bushel. In 1808, the present
method of obtaining the saline fluid, by boring or drilling, was first
put in practice, on the Great Kenawha. The lowest depth, to which
the auger was then driven, was seventy or eighty feet; but as it was
found that, at greater depths, the water increased in strength, the
bores were gradually deepened to three hundred and fifty feet. The
water became so powerfully saline, that seventy-five gallons would
now produce a bushel, or fifty pounds weight, of salt. In 1817, salt
was first manufactured on the Muskingum; and two years afterwards, Mr. Fairlamb contrived a method of boring for it by machinery, connected with a water mill. On some parts of this river,
below Zanesville, the salt rock lay eight hundred and fifty feet
beneath the surface of the earth, and the water was so intensely

strong, that fifty gallons yielded fifty pounds of salt. It was sometimes necessary to bore through a bed of flint, from nine to twelve feet deep, before reaching the salt rock. This flint is so hard and sharp grained, that it wears out the steel of the auger, nearly as fast as it is cut by it; and three weeks of constant labour, by day and night, are required to perforate a thickness of ten feet. Except through those beds of flint the boring is not difficult. The auger is pointed with the best cast steel, from twelve to fourteen inches in length, and three or four inches wide; its progress downward through the various strata is from one inch to six feet per day, proceeding more slowly as the depth increases.

The water is drawn from the wells by pumps, and is evaporated in large iron kettles, by means of furnaces. From five to six cords of wood per day will suffice for a furnace of thirty or forty kettles, producing weekly three hundred bushels of salt, which is sold at twenty five cents per bushel. There is no perceptible difference in the quantity of salt obtained from the water, whether a well have lain idle a few weeks, or be worked continually; nor, in the time that has elapsed since salt was first manufactured in the West, is there the slightest diminution of the supply; although, for several years past, upwards of a million of bushels have been annually produced. Undoubtedly, a sufficient quantity of salt is laid beneath the valley of the Ohio, to last till the inhabitants shall cease to need it—till the earth's means of supplying sustenance to her children shall be entirely exhausted; when, being destitute of food, they may dispense with salt.

On Cape Cod, and in Martha's Vineyard, and perhaps elsewhere on the seacoast of New England, salt is made from the ocean water, by exposure to the sun in ranges of broad and shallow wooden troughs, which may be covered in rainy weather. The pumps, connected with these salt works, are set in motion by sails, like those of wind mills; which, as they briskly revolve, contribute much to enliven the scenery of the barren shores. Salt making in this part of the country, is rather a tedious process.

From the bountiful scale on which Nature has distributed salt throughout the earth, both on its surface and beneath it, and in the ocean that surrounds it, we might at once conclude, that it is almost as necessary to our existence as vital air. It is applied to many uses in the arts; among others, to the manufacture of glass, to bleaching, the glazing of earthenware, assaying metals, casehardening steel, and rendering iron malleable. Salt is indispensable to the health, and indeed to the life of man; it is probable that saline particles, from various sources, are diffused through the air, even at a distance from the sea, and being inhaled with the breath, preserve the blood from corruption. Without this seasoning, no sort of prepared food would be either palatable or wholesome. 'With every bushel of flour,' says the English Penny Magazine,[206] 'about one pound of salt is used in making bread; thus it may be presumed that, in bread alone, every adult consumes about two ounces weekly.' There is an old saying, in derision of an idle and good-for-nothing person,—'He cannot earn his salt;'—and considering what a heap of salt a man devours, during his lifetime, it certainly requires some industry to earn it. Homer and Plato have termed salt DIVINE. Our Saviour, in his Sermon on the Mount, to express to his disciples the relation which they bore towards the mass of mankind, as counteracting its tendency to corruption, told them,—'Ye are the SALT of the earth.'

(*May, pp. 393–94*)

The Dog

Buffon says of the Dog:—'Without enjoying, like man, the light of intellect, the Dog has all the warmth of sentiment; he possesses, in a higher degree than man, fidelity and constancy in his affections; he is all zeal, all ardour, and all obedience. He is more mindful of benefits than of injuries; he is not repelled by bad treatment. If a wrong be offered him, he bears it patiently, and forgets it; or only remembers it as a motive to stronger attachment.' [207] Can this beau-

---

[206] "Common Salt," *The Penny Magazine of the Society for the Diffusion of Useful Knowledge,* IV (Feb. 21, 1835), 66–67.

[207] Buffon, *Histoire Naturelle,* Paris, 1801–08, XXIII, 165–66.

tiful character belong to a creature without a soul?—to one of the brutes that perish, and whose virtues perish with them? How high, then, should be the excellence of beings endowed with immortal souls, and whose virtues might also be immortal!

(*May, p. 397*)

Chinese Pyramid [208]

The cut represents a Chinese feat of strength and dexterity, superiour to any thing that may be witnessed among our amusements of the Circus; although many of these are astonishing specimens of the extent to which the physical powers of man may be improved. The spectacle, here exhibited, is called the Pyramid, and is constructed in the following number. Four men, of great strength, place themselves side by side, sufficiently close together to form a solid base for the structure, which is to be reared upon them. Two others, mounting on their four shoulders, compose the second story of the edifice, and, in their turn, support a third person, who likewise sustains a fourth. The latter reaches this elevation by means of a double ladder. Standing at the summit of this human pyramid, he causes another man (who is probably the slenderest and lightest of the party) to be hoisted up, and seizing the poor fellow with his right hand, elevates him above his head. After holding him, a considerable time, in this position, and balancing him in the air, while he balances himself on his right foot, he suddenly tosses him upward, leaving him to find his way to the earth as he best can. Down he comes, head foremost, into the midst of the spectators, who spread out their arms to receive him, amid the loud acclamations of the multitude. Whether he invariably reaches the ground with whole bones, we cannot say; but his position, like that of all men who are elevated above the heads of the multitude, and sustained on the shoulders of their fellow-beings, can be considered neither safe nor agreeable.

(*June, p. 405*)

[208] This note was written to accompany an unusually crude woodcut.

New York University

This University is an institution of recent date.[209] The building, of which we give a sketch, has a front of one hundred and eighty feet, by one hundred feet wide, and is situated on Washington Square, in the city of New York. It is constructed of marble from the quarries at Sing Sing. The central edifice is fifty-five feet broad and eighty-five deep, and is loftier than the adjacent wings; it contains the chapel, which is lighted principally by one spacious and noble window, twenty-four feet wide, and fifty feet high. The wings of the structure, on each side of the chapel, are of four stories, and are flanked by towers which ascend one story higher, and are embattled at the top. The wings and central building have likewise an embattled parapet. In the interiour, arrangements have been made, on the most extensive scale, for the accommodation of professors, and of classes in the different branches of science, as well as for libraries, and museums of natural history, the fine arts, and antiquities. The style of architecture is similar to that of the collegiate edifices, in the venerable Universities of Oxford and Cambridge.

The officers of government and instruction, in the New York University, form a numerous list, comprising not a few names of eminent men. A greater amount of preparatory learning, than has heretofore been usual in American colleges, is required of those students who intend to pursue the whole academical course, and to become candidates for a degree. The system of instruction is such, that a young man, to whom it may not be necessary or expedient to learn all that is taught in the University, may apply himself exclusively to any of the various branches. This arrangement is in accordance with the spirit of the age, and is likely to extend the usefulness of the institution, by relieving practical knowledge from the incumbrance of dead literature.

Uneducated persons are apt to form very exaggerated ideas of the advantages of what is termed a liberal education. They consider it

[209] New York University was founded in 1831. An engraving of the University building precedes this sketch.

impossible that young men should not be deeply learned, after spending years within the walls of a University, in constant intercourse
with the best qualified instructors, and with every facility for the
acquisition of knowledge. In all these matters, however, there is more
show than substance. Without personal experience and observation,
it is difficult to realise how empty a head may be covered by an academical cap, and how gross a degree of ignorance may be rewarded
with a Latin diploma.[210] The advantages of a University are absolutely nothing, unless the student go thither with an earnest wish,
and steadfast resolution, to profit by them to the utmost. Now such
a wish and resolution will enable any young man, in whatever situation of life, to bring his mind to a degree of improvement, which
may be even the greater for the difficulties that seemed to impede it.
Tutors and professors are comparatively unimportant accessories,
in the business of education. All really educated men, whether they
have studied in the halls of a University, or in a cottage or a work-
shop, are essentially self-educated. Whatever knowledge they have
acquired, it must all have been gained by the vigorous toil of their
own intellects; and such toil never fails of its reward, in the increase
of mental aliment, and of the mind's capacity to digest it. Let no
youth, therefore, be turned back from the field of science, by the idea
that the only path thither leads through the portal of a collegiate
edifice, and that his guide must wear a professor's gown. Such a guide
may indeed be desirable; but where none such is at hand, let the
student go boldly and firmly onward, and he will seldom go astray.

(June, p. 409)

Uses of Dead Animals

In a number of Silliman's Journal of Science, we find an article,[211]
translated from the French, which treats of the various uses that may

[210] It may not be going too far to see in this plea for practical education and contact with the actualities of life a reflection of Hawthorne's realization and his regret
that his training had failed to give him a place in the world of reality. For another
note of Hawthorne's on education see text, p. 38.

[211] M. Payen, "Notice of the Most Simple Means of Employing Dead Animals" (tr.
from the French), *The American Journal of Science and Arts*, XXIV (1833), 326–41.

be made of dead animals. Some of the details, we confess, are calculated to produce an unpleasant effect on delicate stomachs; but they include a great deal of curious information, which we shall endeavour to abstract for the benefit of our readers.

The writer states that there is only one disease among animals, of a nature that renders them absolutely unfit for food. This is called the Carbuncle, deriving its name from the tumours that take place on the diseased animal, and which, when accompanied with sores, are generally covered with a black crust. The body of a creature, that has died of carbuncle, should be buried without handling it, or permitting the blood to drop upon the soil; but grain may be sown over the grave, where it will thrive luxuriantly; and after two years, the bones should be dug up, and applied to several valuable purposes. But it has been proved in various ways, and especially by the provisioning of armies, that no ill-effect results from eating cattle that have died of any other disease, even though it be contagious. Animals, the carcasses of which have communicated mortal sickness to the persons who cut them up, may be eaten without danger. In general, no harm is to be apprehended, either from handling the dead bodies, or using them as food. The workmen in cat-gut manufactories, and in glue-maker's shops, where animal matter, often diseased and putrescent, is boiled down, experience no deleterious effects. Sheep affected with the rot (a kind of small pox) have no unwholesome qualities.

The skin of a dead animal, if damaged so as to be unfit for the tanner, should be cut into small pieces, and boiled in six times the quantity of water, over a small fire, for seven or eight hours. With salt and seasoning, it makes an agreeable and nutritious jelly. The bristles, hair, wool, or feathers, should be dried in an oven, after the bread is taken out. Horse-hair may be used without any preparation of this sort; the longest hairs make excellent clothes' lines, which are very durable, and do not spot the clothes that are hung upon them, and the short hair is fit for stuffing saddles, sofas, and mattresses. Or, together with fur, it forms an admirable manure, which operates mildly, and for a great length of time. Feathers, mixed with

moist earth, answer the same purpose; and a profit may thus be
derived from such feathers as are fit for nothing else. The shoes of
oxen, horses, asses, and mules, are taken off and preserved. The
spurs of fowls, and the horns and hoofs of animals, if sufficiently
large, and free from defect, and of a light colour, are sold to toy-
men; or, if unfit for their purposes, they find a market among the
manufacturers of Prussian blue. They may also be rasped very fine
and converted into manure, which is so powerful, that the four hoofs
of a horse are considered equal to a small load of dung. The bones
are sold to factories of ivory-black, or of toys, if there be any such
establishments within a convenient distance; if otherwise, they are
reduced to small pieces and thrown upon the land, where their
beneficial effect is experienced for five or six years afterwards. If the
soil be very poor and dry, this species of manure does not begin to
operate in less time than fifteen or twenty years. Another kind of
animal manure is made by heating the blood in a large kettle, and
stirring it constantly with an iron rod, until reduced to a moist
powder, in which state it is to be mixed with dry mould, and spread
upon the soil. Raw blood may be used in a similar manner. The
putrid flesh of animals may be torn from the bones, with long-
handled instruments, and strewn over the land, as manure; it should
be slightly covered with earth.

The fat is to be cut into small pieces, melted, and set aside for
greasing axle-trees, harnesses, and shoe-leather. But the most singular
purpose, in our opinion, to which dead animals are applied in France,
is yet to be mentioned. The flesh, blood, and bowels, are kept pur-
posely for the sake of producing maggots, which are sold in Paris
at the rate of about a dollar a bushel, and are used as food for
pheasants, and also for fattening fish in ponds.

Even the smallest animals may afford some profit. The skins of
rats sell at seventy-five cents per hundred, and those of moles at
more than double that price. The entire carcass of a horse is worth
above ten dollars in the country, and a still higher sum at Paris. Cats
and dogs, also, are valuable articles, not only on account of their
skins, but of their fat. The flesh of horses, cats, and dogs, when of a

fine red colour, and sullied by no brown or livid spots, is secretly made use of as food for man—probably by keepers of eating-houses at Paris. But the French writer appears to see no harm in all this. He states, apparently from his personal knowledge, that rats and pole-cats are good and wholesome eating; although they require (espe-cially the polecats) an unusual quantity of pepper and spice to counteract their very peculiar taste and odour. Beseeching Heaven to defend our readers and ourself from the heathenish devices of French cooks, we shall here drop the subject.

(June, p. 410)

Lightning Rods

In Belgium and the Netherlands, buildings are defended by light-ning-rods of a peculiar construction, which, instead of relieving a thunder-cloud of its electricity, drive it into a distant region of the air. It would appear, however, that the effect is not invariably benefi-cial. From a manuscript letter of Professor Van Mons,[212] the dis-tinguished horticulturalist of 'Antwerp, we translate the following passage:—'We have had two Winters successively without frost, and two Summers without rain. In the course of each Summer, thirty storms have threatened to burst upon us, but have invariably been prevented from exploding by the lightning-rods. Finally, the clouds have gathered in regions so high, as to be beyond the controul of the rods, and have there burst forth, sending their moisture to the earth in the shape of huge hail-stones. Before the introduction of lightning-rods, we had, at every change of the moon, in Summer, a storm in the lower regions of the air, accompanied with an abundance of warm rain. These rains are now no longer known.'— This, truly, is a most remarkable instance of a change of climate effected by human agency. A modification of the temperature of the air, so as to render the seasons colder or warmer, would have been hardly more wonderful. Yet we derive the same moral from the re-

---

[212] Jean Baptiste van Mons (1765–1842), Belgian chemist, was the author of various books on chemistry. At Brussels he published in 1803 *Principes d'Electricité ou confirmation de la théorie électrique de Franklin.*

sult, as from the tale of the astronomer, in Rasselas,[213]—that the administration of the Elemental Kingdom would only be changed for the worse, by the interference of man.

(*July, p. 442*)

Influence of Music on Animals

Dogs, says a French writer, are affected in a very lively manner by music; but it is difficult to determine the nature of the impressions which they receive from it. Many naturalists believe that its effect is disagreeable; an opinion which is strongly supported by the fact, that dogs, if left at liberty, take to flight, with howls, as soon as the music reaches their ears. It has even been noticed, that those dogs who are insensible to ordinary noises, and whom the explosion of a cannon would not startle, will nevertheless shudder, and give utterance to involuntary groans, on hearing an instrument of music. Doctor Mead [214] affirms that a dog died of the painful sensations excited by music, which he had been compelled to hear for a considerable time, and which caused him to utter piercing cries. Examples are given of many other animals, and likewise of owls, killed in a similar manner. Cats, also, mew loudly on hearing the sound of musical instruments; but they appear to be more seldom and less painfully affected than dogs.

It is well known, on the other hand, that birds, and especially the canary-bird, testify the liveliest pleasure when airs are played to them. They sometimes approach the instrument, and remain immovable so long as the sounds continue, and then clap their wings, as we should our hands, in testimony of their approbation of the performance.

The horse, also, is extremely sensible to music. The trumpet, and all kinds of copper or brazen instruments, appear most to his liking.

---

[213] The astronomer in *Rasselas* possessed the power for "the regulation of the weather, and the distribution of the seasons." But he remarked, "I have found it impossible to make a disposition by which the world may be advantaged; what one region gains, another loses" (chaps. XLI and XLIII).

[214] Dr. Richard Mead (1673–1754), an English physician, published several books on medicine.

Martial airs animate and excite his ardour; his mane bristles; his eyes sparkle; he snuffs and snorts with his nostrils, pricks up his ears, and beats time, as it were, with his feet. In equestrian performances, horses dance, with perfect accuracy, in cadence to the sound of instruments. Some wild animals are likewise susceptible to the influence of musical tones. The hunters in the Tyrol, and in certain parts of Germany, affirm that they are acquainted with a method of enticing stags by singing, and female deer by playing on the flute. Beavers and rats are also said to possess a musical taste; and eight of the latter animals have been seen to dance the rope, at a fair in France.

Neither are reptiles, nor insects, destitute of a musical ear. The lizard displays tokens of being singularly fond of harmony. The instant that he hears vocal or instrumental music, his movements betray the most agreeable emotions. He turns over, lying now on his back, now on his belly, now on his side, as if to expose all parts of his body to the action of the sonorous fluid, which he finds so delightful. He does not, however, bestow his approbation on all sorts of music, but is very refined in his taste. Soft voices, and tender and plaintive airs, are his favourites; but hoarse singing and noisy instruments disgust him.

An account is given, in a book of travels, of the taming of rattlesnakes in Guiana, by playing tunes on a flageolet, or whistling so as to resemble that instrument. M. dé [*sic*] Chateaubriand, in his travels in Upper Canada, positively affirms, that he saw a furious rattle-snake, which had penetrated into his encampment, lay aside his rage on hearing the music of a flute, and that the serpent followed the musician to a considerable distance.

Among insects, the spider shows the greatest sensibility to music. Immediately on hearing the sound of instruments, she descends rapidly along her thread, and approaches the quarter whence it proceeds; there she remains immovable for whole hours, if the music continue so long. Prisoners, during long confinements, have tamed spiders in this manner, and converted them into companions.[215]

One of the most remarkable instances of the effect of music on animals occurred at the Royal Menagerie in Paris, where a concert

[215] Cf. the use made of spiders in *Doctor Grimshawe's Secret*.

was given, about thirty years ago, and two elephants were among the number of the auditors. The orchestra being placed out of their sight, they could not discover the source of the harmony. The first sensation was surprise; at one moment they gazed earnestly at the spectators; the next, they ran to caress their keeper, and appeared to inquire of him what these strange noises meant. But perceiving that nothing was amiss, they finally gave themselves up to the lively impressions which the music communicated. Each new tune seemed to produce a change of feeling, and caused their gestures and their cries to assume an expression in accordance with it. But it was still more remarkable, that when a piece of music, the correct performance of which had vividly excited their emotions, was incorrectly played, they remained cold and unmoved. They must necessarily have possessed, therefore, if not a discernment, at least a perception of combined sounds, and a distinct sensation resulting from them.

(*July, p. 463*)

Effect of Colour on Odours

In the May number of the American Magazine,[216] we gave an account of the experiments of Dr. Stark,[217] an English physician, in regard to the effect of colour on heat. The same gentleman has instituted a series of experiments, the result of which proves, that varieties of colour greatly modify the capability of substances for imbibing and giving out odours. Dr. Stark's attention was drawn to this subject, by observing that a black dress, which he happened to wear while performing dissections at the anatomical rooms, contracted a most intolerable smell from the dead bodies; whereas, the light olive coloured garments, which he had usually worn, were almost entirely free from the like inconvenience. His first experiment was made by inclosing equal quantities of black and white wool, with a small piece of camphor; the black wool was found to have become much the most odorous of the two. The result was the same, when wool of each colour was shut up in a drawer with assafoetida. He

[216] See text, pp. 180–82.   [217] See n. 196.

afterwards inclosed black, blue, red, green, yellow, and white wool, with assafoetida, and with camphor; the black imbibed the strongest odour; then the blue, then the red, and next the green; the yellow wool was but very faintly scented, and the white scarcely at all. The wool of sheep attracted a stronger odour than cotton-wool; and all animal substances become scented in a greater degree than those of a vegetable nature, and appear to have a particular attraction for fetid odours.

These facts suggest many important hints, as to the regulations which it may be proper to adopt, in cases of contagious disease, and during the prevalence of epidemics. It is usual to purify infected places by raising a high temperature within them, and by the use of chlorine, fumigation with sulphur, washing with quick-lime, and freely ventilating them. Dr. Stark is of opinion, that, in many cases, mere white-washing may be more efficacious than these, or any other measures. When the cholera visited Scotland, most of the narrow lanes, alleys, and staircases of Edinburgh were white-washed; and to this is attributed the mildness of the disease, in that metropolis. The deleterious emanations, meeting with no dark surfaces to absorb them, were swept away by the currents of air. The walls of hospitals, prisons, and of all apartments where a number of occupants are congregated together, should be white-washed; the bedsteads, chairs, tables, and other furniture, should be white, and likewise the garments of the attendants. The black suits, almost invariably worn by physicians, unquestionably render them more liable to communicate disease, in going their daily rounds among the sick and well. Instead of black broadcloth, (which, besides its colour, attracts bad smells the more powerfully, as being an animal substance,) the dress of the medical profession ought to be white cotton—a garb little suited, it must be owned, to the gravity of an M. D.

Most persons have heard of the Black Assize, as it was called, where the Judges, while holding at a court of Oxford, together with a great number of people, were suddenly taken sick and died. This occurred in July, 1577; and Lord Bacon observes,[218] that similar instances of

---

[218] *Sylva Sylvarum* (*The Works of Francis Bacon*, V, 125–26); see nn. 251, 262, and 263.

sickness and mortality happened two or three times, within his memory. There was another instance in 1750, at the Old Bailey in London, where four Judges, several Counsellors, an under Sheriff, with Jurymen and others, to the number of above forty, lost their lives by a sudden attack of some mysterious disorder. In all these cases, the mortality was attributed to a putrid effluvium, which either came from the neighbouring gaol, or was exhaled from the persons of the prisoners, when brought into court. This doubtless was its true origin; and Dr. Stark conceives that the infectious odour was attracted to the judges, counsellors, sheriffs, and other official persons, by the black garments which they wore in the discharge of their duties.

It seems not to have occurred to Dr. Stark to make inquiries as to the respective degrees, in which the black and white varieties of the human race are liable to contagion. It appears, we think, a necessary consequence of his theory, that negroes should suffer more, in proportion to their numbers, than whites, by all sorts of pestilence, and unwholesome smells. Whether such be the fact, we have no means of ascertaining.

(July, pp. 467–68)

Churches and Cathedrals [219]

There is one department of architecture—that of edifices for public worship—in which it does not appear probable that our own country will ever produce such magnificent specimens, as may be seen in many parts of Europe. Those grand and noble structures are the symbols of an established national religion, and could never have had existence, unless a portion of the public wealth, drawn from the people by other than voluntary taxes, had been devoted to the purpose. They may as justly be numbered among edifices of state, as the royal palaces, the fortresses, and the national prisons. They do not form a fair expression of the degree of religious zeal, which influences those who assemble beneath their stupendous domes. In the

[219] Six woodcuts illustrate this article.

United States, on the contrary, every church is a type of the united zeal of private individuals; the building is as much the work of the congregation which worships there, as if each member had laid one of the stones that compose the walls. Thus, our temples, instead of the pride and splendour which state policy imparts to those of other countries, generally possess a neatness and elegance, more analogous to the decorations of private dwellings. Another reason for a simpler style of architecture in our churches, may be found in the simplicity of our faith, divested as it is of those elaborate inventions, which being of earthly origin, require an earthly grandeur in every thing connected with them.

We should be glad to give an engraving of one of the primitive meeting-houses of New England, such as the Puritans first reared, when they ceased to worship beneath the open sky, or the canopy of forest boughs. None such being at hand, we present, instead of the barn-like edifice and humble spire, a view of Trinity Church, in Summer street, Boston. This is a massive structure of rough gray stone, with a square and lofty tower, the whole forming as good a specimen of architecture, in the Gothic style, as may generally be found on this side of the Atlantic. Yet it is chiefly serviceable for our present purpose, as a contrast to those wondrous edifices which have been consecrated to religion in other parts of the world.

In Europe, there are cathedrals of so vast a size that this church might be contained entire within the walls, yet scarcely appear to occupy more room than some of the noble monuments which have been erected there. Five hundred workmen were employed during thirty-five years, in the construction of St. Paul's, in London. Other cathedrals are of unknown antiquity; but, from their immense extent, must have demanded the labour of whole generations of men, and have become venerable with age even before they were completed.

The cathedral of Milan, in Italy, is thought to excel all others in grandeur and magnificence, except St. Peter's, at Rome. It is composed entirely of white marble, and decorated with an innumerable multitude of beautiful ornaments, and according to some authorities, with no less than four thousand five hundred statues. The edifice is surmounted by one hundred and thirty-five spires, each of which sustains twenty-seven statues. At the summit of the principal steeple stands a colossal statue of the Virgin, richly gilt; and from the floor of the cathedral to the top of this statue, the whole height is nearly four hundred feet. The interior of the edifice corresponds with its external magnificence. The vaulted roof is sustained by fifty-two gothic pillars, of prodigious height and circumference, all of which are ornamented with capitals of different designs. The sides of the principal entrance are composed of two columns of granite, each of which was hewn from a single block; and they are supposed to be the loftiest that ever were employed in architecture. This cathedral, though commenced in the middle ages, is still far from being completed. The late Emperor of Austria devoted an annual sum of about one hundred thousand dollars to the progress of the work.

The church of Saint Peter, at Rome,[220] is the wonder of the world, and undoubtedly the most sublime monument that mankind ever consecrated to the Deity, since the creation; nor is it probable that future ages will produce any thing similar to its vast magnificence. This edifice has so often been described, that we will refer our readers to the works of every traveller who has visited Italy, and content ourself with a diminutive representation of its external form, as given in the cut. More than a century was occupied in completing it, at an expense equal to one hundred and sixty millions of dollars. It is said, however, that the structure is now greatly out of repair—that there are many cracks in the cupola, which has been surrounded by an iron hoop of seven millions of pounds in order to prevent it from breaking down—and that large and increasing sums are annually required, to make good the dilapidations of each successive year. Spain formerly paid about four hundred thousand dollars per annum, for this purpose.

The religious edifices of France are less grand than those of Italy, or than the monuments of the Catholic faith in England.

The Church of Notre Dame, however, is a noble structure, nearly

[220] See Hawthorne's remarks on Saint Peter's set down in his notebooks when he visited Rome in 1857 (*Writings*, XXI, 192–93, 216–20; XXII, 309); also the impressions of Saint Peter's recorded in *The Marble Faun* (*ibid.*, X, 201–13).

four hundred feet in length, with two towers, each two hundred and four feet high. It was completed more than six centuries ago, after two hundred years had been spent in building it. The great length of time, that was often consumed in rearing these ancient structures, must be imputed partly to the disadvantages under which the work-men laboured, from the want of proper tools and machinery. It is likewise probable that such works were often interrupted by the public events of the period.

There is one species of religious edifice which should not be for-gotten, in glancing at the various temples of the Christian faith; although the specimens that remain are now consecrated to Pagan-ism. We allude to the ancient Greek churches, in Constantinople and its vicinity, which have only been preserved from destruction by being converted into mosques. Travellers remark that the cross, and other symbols of Christianity, are still visible upon their desecrated walls. The most celebrated of these buildings is the Mosque of St. Sophia, which is two hundred and seventy feet in length, and two hundred and forty in breadth. Its architecture is peculiar, and some-what of an Oriental cast, and is probably less calculated to impress the spectator with devotional awe, than is the sombre sublimity of the churches in western Europe. This mosque, although many cen-turies old, is still in good repair, and may stand till the true faith be again preached beneath its splendid dome.

In conclusion, let us bless God that the narrowest closet may be a temple consecrated to His worship, and that a devout heart may find Him there, as well as in the loftiest cathedral on earth.

(*August, pp. 497–98*)

Coal [221]

. . . Coal, for the purposes of fuel, is fast taking the place of wood. In a few years, its comparative cheapness will have become so decided, that almost all the good old-fashioned fire-places will

[221] A cut of "A Coal Railway" accompanies this note.

probably be succeeded by diminutive grates, filled with red hot lumps of anthracite, diffusing an intense heat, but never gladdening the room with a cheerful blaze.[222] The furnaces of the American steamboats will likewise be replenished with coal, as is already the case with those [of] Europe. Yet even when this change shall have been completed, the only difference will be, that, instead of cutting down the trees which are now flourishing, we shall build our fires with the carbonized forests of past and forgotten ages. . . .

(*August, pp. 498–99*)

[*Suffolk Bank*]

All who have visited State street, within the last year or more, must have noticed the elegant front of the Suffolk Bank,[223] with its range of granite pillars, forming perhaps the most splendid object in that beautiful portion of our city. The edifice occupies, we believe, the site of the ancient Custom House, and looks down upon the spot where the first American blood was shed by the hands of the British soldiery. It may therefore be said to throw its shadow across the very tract of ground, where the Revolution—the progress and consequences of which were to shake the world—began its career of violence. No succession of events, no brilliant nor mournful vicissitudes of our history, can obliterate the remembrance of what once occurred there, nor prevent this spot from being famous, so long as posterity shall feel an interest in the deeds and sufferings of their fathers. The Massacre, if not of primary importance in itself, became so by the use which was made of its anniversary, for many years afterwards, in kindling up the spirit of the people, and renewing as it were, the traces of their kindred blood upon the stones of King street. The event itself was little more than a Riot; but it gave a mighty impulse to a Revolution. When the former building was taken down, there-

[222] For a fuller statement of Hawthorne's preference for the fireplace see his sketch "Fire Worship."

[223] See *Grandfather's Chair* (*Writings,* XII, 198). A view of the bank building precedes this sketch.

fore, it might not have been undesirable to appropriate a part of its site to an historic monument, or to have connected such a design with the modern edifice, so that no stranger, nor school-boy should pass through the street, without being aware that his feet were treading now where the blood-tracks once had been. It would have been in consonance, we think, with the character of New England, to associate a memorial of this nature with the daily business of the people, and to consecrate even the Exchange by some architectural or sculptural device, which should point to the Past, as surely as the clock on the Old State-House points to the noontide hour.

But we have gone somewhat astray from the proper subject of our article. The Suffolk Bank was erected in the course of the year 1834. The cost of the carpenter's work, as we learn from a copy of the survey-bill, was more than eight thousand dollars, and the net cost of the granite, furnished by the Railway Company, was ten thousand, five hundred dollars. The entire cost of the edifice, in its finished state, is estimated at about forty thousand dollars. The architect was Isaiah Rogers,[224] Esq. to' whom the country is indebted for the designs of several of its most admired structures.

(*August, p. 501*)

Longevity of Animals

The average life of a Bull has been estimated at fifteen years; that of an Ox, twenty; of an Ass, thirty; a Horse, from twenty to thirty; a Dog, from fourteen to twenty, or more; a Sheep, a Cat, and a Hare, ten; a Goat, eight; and a Hog, twenty-five. The feathered tribe are generally longer lived. Peacocks, turtle-doves, and partridges, have each a span of twenty-five years. Ravens and Eagles are birds of a whole century. A Goose has been kept in a family from time immemorial; nothing could be said of its age, except that it had been paddling in the same pond, when the great grandsires were infants.

---

[224] Isaiah Rogers (1800–69) was an architect in Boston from 1822 until 1834, when he removed to New York. Among the buildings he designed were the Tremont Hotel in Boston, the Astor House and the Merchant's Exchange in New York, and the second St. Charles Hotel in New Orleans.

Such antediluvian geese, we suspect, are sometimes seen in the market.[225]

(August, p. 506)

Species of Men

Linnaeus,[226] in his classification of the natural world, divided the genus Homo, or Man, into two species. The first was the *Homo Sapiens,* or Man endowed with intellect; this species comprehended all the descendants of Adam. The second species was the *Homo Troglodytes,*—or Orang Outang! The pride of the *Homo Sapiens* certainly revolts at the idea of being placed so nearly on a level with these great monkies; but when the claims of the latter are fairly considered, we might almost allow them to be our cousins, though we deny them the name of brethren. Persons, who are acquainted with the nature and habits of the Orang Outang, entertain no doubt, that their communities are governed by fixed laws, and that punishments are inflicted upon transgressors. Their government and social condition considerably resemble those of an army; and severe penalties are incurred by those who infringe the rules of military discipline. Mr. Holman,[227] the blind traveller, describes the punishment of a baboon for neglecting his duty as a sentinel on guard. It is another remarkable fact, which assimilates this monkey-tribe to the human race, that the female baboons are fond of little children, and delight in giving them food; although, as their dexterity is not equal to their good intentions, they do not make very eligible nurses.

But, however close upon our heels the inferiour tribes of creation may seem to tread, there is one great and invariable mark of distinc-

[225] The author drew the information for this article largely from William Smellie's *The Philosophy of Natural History,* Dublin, 1790 (see the fifth ed., Boston, 1835, pp. 300–2), in which he found even the note about the aged goose.

[226] Carl Linnaeus (1707–78), the noted Swedish naturalist. Hawthorne borrowed a book by Linnaeus, possibly *The Elements of Botany,* from the Salem Athenaeum Library on May 6, 1830 ("Books Read by Nathaniel Hawthorne").

[227] James Holman (1786–1857) became blind at the age of twenty-five, after a short career in the British navy. He spent the remainder of his life in study and travel and published full accounts of his travels (1825 and 1834–35).

tion between the Man with a soul, and the Animal without one. The
latter cannot communicate his intelligence to succeeding generations,
nor accumulate it from age to age; there is no progressive developement of the intellect of the race. It is otherwise with Man; and as he
is capable of adding wisdom to wisdom, throughout Eternity, we
may full surely trust, that an Eternity will be allotted for the infinite
expansion of his capacities.

(August, p. 515)

Church of Saint Sophia

This edifice, of which we have given an engraving in another part
of our Magazine,[228] was built by the Emperor Theodosius. He su-
perintended the work in person, and encouraged the artificers by
gracious words, and promises of recompense. When it was completed, the Emperor was so struck with the grandeur and beauty of
the church, that he named it Saint Sophia, or Holy Wisdom; and
exclaimed,—'Glory to God, who has judged me worthy to achieve this
magnificent work! Oh, Solomon, your temple was nothing to it!'

(August, p. 516)

Weight and Substance of the Globe

There has been much dispute among Philosophers, as to the materials of which the inside of our globe is composed. The composition of its external crust or shell, is known from actual observation;
but no excavations have ever reached the kernel. Some suppose that
the globe is filled with water, whence originate the fountains which
gush so abundantly over its surface. Others believe it to contain nothing more solid than gas, like an inflated balloon. According to the
hypothesis of other theorists, the inside of the world is stuffed with
loadstone, or with solid or molten metal. Our countryman, Captain

228 In connection with the essay on "Churches and Cathedrals"; see text, p. 206.

Symmes,[229] lived and died in the belief, that the globe is hollow, and contains inhabitants; and, in recompense of a life of disappointment, we heartily wish that the poor Captain may now have gone to that inner region, and have found it a better and brighter world than the exterior. But all the above theories, and especially the Symmzonian, are thought to be irreconcileable with the known weight of the globe, which is capable of being accurately ascertained, by means either of natural philosophy or astronomy. We are not, indeed, prepared to say precisely how many pounds the earth does weigh; but its ponderosity is computed to be three or four times as great, as if it were entirely composed of the heaviest stones with which we are acquainted. It therefore follows, that the interior substance of the globe must be extremely dense and heavy.

(*August, p. 518*)

Incurable Disease

Sir Edward Coke [230] being oppressed with infirmities, a friend sent him several physicians to hold a consultation upon his case. But Sir Edward told them, that he had 'never taken physic since he was born, and would not now begin; and that he had now upon him a disease, which all the drugs of Asia, the gold of Africa, the silver of America, nor all the Doctors of Europe could cure,—Old Age!' Yet human nature has not always been content to believe that there is no remedy for this disease; men have often wasted the oil of life, and grown old faster than there was need, in vain researches for some medicine that should recall their youth.[231] Were we to judge

---

[229] John Cleves Symmes (1780–1829) retired from the army at the close of the War of 1812, having reached the rank of captain. In 1826 he published his *Theory of Concentric Spheres,* which set forth his novel belief that the earth and the other planets are composed of concentric spheres, separated by vacant space and open at the poles, and that each sphere should be habitable.

[230] Sir Edward Coke (1552–1634) was an influential English jurist during the reigns of both James I and Charles I. His refusal to begin taking medicines in his old age, since he had managed all his life without them, is reminiscent of the stress he placed on precedent in law.

[231] Hawthorne was challenged constantly by the idea of an elixir of life and treated it at length in "Dr. Heidegger's Experiment" and *Septimius Felton.*

merely from the great advances that have been already made in science, such a medicine might not seem beyond the reach of the philosopher. But it *is* beyond his reach, because the Creator has absolutely debarred mankind from all inventions and discoveries, the results of which would counteract the general laws, that He has established over human affairs.

(*August, p. 520*)

LITERARY CRITICISM

The Puritan: A Series of Essays, Critical, Moral, and Miscellaneous

We know of no recent work, which we can so conscientiously recommend to that portion of the public, with which we are concerned, as this excellent series of Essays.[232] They contain much wisdom—and wisdom of such a nature, and so expressed, that we hardly see how it can fail to arrest the reader's attention, and produce a practical result. The author has a vein of humour, which, being largely mingled with strong sense and shrewdness, is never like the 'crackling of thorns under a pot.' It makes us smile, but thoughtfully. It appears to us, that this writer, more appropriately than any other, may be taken as the representative of the intellectual character of New England.

The first of the following extracts is one of the truest passages that ever was written, in reference to republican institutions; yet nobody, that we know of, has ever thought of saying it before. The young lawyers, and long-winded elderly gentlemen, who lengthen out the sessions of our legislatures, should thank the Puritan for setting their labours in so favourable a light. . . .

(*March, p. 309*)

Our Predecessor

The present number of the American Magazine, has been prepared by a new hand. In assuming the charge of this Journal, it

[232] Leonard Withington, *The Puritan: A Series of Essays,* Boston, 1836. Hawthorne wrote these notes to introduce three excerpts which Elizabeth sent him. He had evidently not seen the book, for he wrote to her on February 10, "I have given the Puritan an enormous puff—knowing nothing in the world about it, except for those excerpts."

is due to more than courtesy to pay a tribute of respect to him whose place we occupy [233]—a writer long and well known in the solid literature of New England, and whose editorial labours, for so many months, have met with good acceptance from the public. Under his care, the work has redeemed the promise of its title, and been emphatically a Magazine of Useful Knowledge. In proof of the late Editor's extensive and various reading, practical information, and sound opinions, it is sufficient to refer to what he has accomplished. A mind stored with historical reminiscences has given interest to the pages.—This praise it is fit that he should receive from others; but there is a better commendation which he may safely seek within himself—that, in a moral and religious point of view, the hurried toil of a periodical writer has not drawn from him a single line, which he need wish to blot: And for ourself, the best success, that we can anticipate, must be won by following out the principles which have guided our Predecessor.

(*March, p. 312*)

Fessenden's Poems *

An American bard, the commencement of whose literary career dates more than a quarter of a century back, is truly a remarkable phenomenon. He appears with a classic dignity among the poets of yesterday and to-day, and has a claim upon the respect of his audience, apart from the merits of his song. If, in addition to this claim, the veteran bard offers us a production which has received the applause of a former day—and if it be found to possess the rare merit of originality, and an excellence peculiar to itself—the present public should give its sanction to the favourable judgment of their fathers, with even more earnestness of praise than would be the due of a

---

* Terrible Tractoration, and other Poems.—
By Christopher Caustic, M. D.[234]

[233] Hawthorne's immediate predecessor had been Alden Bradford, who also succeeded him in the editorial chair.

[234] Thomas Green Fessenden, *Terrible Tractoration and Other Poems, by Christopher Caustic,* Boston, 1836, third ed.

younger aspirant. Such would be no more than an act of justice, in requital of the neglect that has permitted his name to fade, for so long an interval, from the list of those whose effusions are deemed honourable to their country. And his tuneful brethren (if brethren they may be called, the eldest of whom were listening to their nurse's lullaby, when his strains had already gained the applause of England and America,) should pay him such reverence as Ben Jonson, the survivor of the Shakespearian age, was wont to receive from the wits at the Mitre-tavern, and Dryden from the more modern luminaries of Queen Anne's age. The severe simplicity of our republic recognises no Poet Laureate, as an officer of state; but the poets of America might place a laurel crown upon his honoured head, and acknowledge him the leader of their choir.

Such, we think, should be the reception of the author of these poems. To many of our readers he is well known, as the Editor of the New England Farmer; [235] but comparatively few are aware, that, at an early period of life, he was a poet of greater European celebrity, than any other native American, before or since. 'Terrible Tractoration,' the longest poem in the volume, passed through two London editions,[236] in the course of a few months; and the present impression is the third that has been published in America.[237] The main design of the production was to satirize the opponents of the Metallic Tractors, certain implements which caused a prodigious sensation in the medical and philosophical world, about the commencement of the present century. But the author's fancy was too affluent, and his powers of ridicule too universal, to be confined within the narrow scope of his nominal subject; and accordingly, there was no folly nor humbug of the day, but what became the theme of his laughing muse. In the edition now before us, he has been equally successful in introducing most of the new absurdities, of which the present age is no less fruitful than any preceding one. Some of these passages it would violate the neutrality of our Magazine to extract. We therefore select a few stanzas which will sufficiently illustrate the queer

[235] Fessenden founded *The New England Farmer* at Boston in 1822.
[236] Both London editions appeared in 1803.
[237] The first American edition was issued in 1804, the second in 1806.

originality of thought, and aptness of ludicrous expression, that distinguish this poet from all others of his day. Among other notable
contrivances of Doctor Caustic—an old crack-brained visionary,
whom Nature seems to have gifted with a tenfold proportion of wit,
in lieu of the least modicum of common sense—he enumerates the
following. His patent Author's mill, by the way, would be a great
convenience to ourself, and thereby to our readers:

> 'We next crave liberty to mention
> Another wonderful invention;
> A sort of stenographic still,
> Alias a Patent Author's mill.
>
> We fill its hopper with a set
> Of letters of the alphabet,
> And turn out eulogies, orations,
> Or themes for July celebrations,—
>
> News, both domestic and extraneous,
> Essays, and extracts miscellaneous,
> We manufacture by the means
> Of said superlative machines.
>
> This last invention also reaches
> To making Congress members' speeches;
> Would they adopt it, though we've said it,
> T'would cent per cent enhance their credit.
>
> We hammer'd out a lawyer's jaw mill
> Which went by water like a saw-mill
> With so much clamour, fire and fury,
> It thunderstruck the judge and jury.'

Among the minor poems, there is one, now for the first time published, entitled the Cultivator's Art. We extract a paragraph, which
is full of ideas so infinitely grotesque, that they actually become
sublime.

'We farmers are a sort of stuff
Tyrants will always find too tough
For them to work up into slaves,
The servile tools of lordly knaves.
Those men who till the stubborn soil,
Enlighten'd, and inur'd to toil,
Cannot be made to quail or cower
By traitor's art or tyrant's power,
They might as well attempt to chain
The west wind in a hurricane;—
Make rivers run up hill by frightening,
Or steal a march on kindled lightning—
The great sea-serpent, which we've read of,
Take by the tail and snap his head off—
The firmament on cloudy nights,
Illume with artificial lights,
By such an apparatus as
Is used for lighting streets with gas—
Or, having split the north pole till it's
Divided into baker's billets,
Make such a blaze as never shone,
And torrefy the frozen zone—
With clubs assail the polar bear,
And drive the monster from his lair—
Attack the comets as they run
With loads of fuel for the sun,
And overset by oppugnation
Those shining colliers of creation—
The Milky Way McAdamize,
A railway raise to span the skies,
Then make, to save Apollo's team,
The Solar Chariot go by steam.
These things shall tyrants do, and more
Than we have specified, before
Our cultivators they subdue,
While grass is green, or sky is blue.'

We should be glad to enrich our pages with the full length portrait
of Miss Tabitha Towzer; but it would be doing the author injustice

to give no specimen of his powers in a more serious style of composition. We admire the thoughts, and the strong expression, of the following stanzas.

'THE EVILS OF A MISCHIEVOUS TONGUE.

'Many have fallen by the edge of the sword, but not so many as have fallen by the tongue.'—Eccl. Apoc. xxviii. 8.

Tho' millions, the sword of the warriour has slaughter'd,
    While fame has the homicide's eulogy rung:
Yet many more millions on millions are martyr'd;
    Cut off by that cowardly weapon, the tongue.

One sword may be match'd by another as keen,
    In battle the bold man a bolder may meet,
But the shaft of the slanderer, flying unseen
    From the quiver of malice, brings ruin complete.

An *insolent tongue,* by a taunt or a gibe,
    Enkindles heart-burnings and bloody affrays;
A *treacherous tongue,* when impell'd by a bribe,
    The guiltless condemns, or a nation betrays.

A *smooth subtle tongue* vile seducers employ
    The fair sex to lure to libidinous thrall;
A *slip of the tongue* may its owner destroy,
    And *the tongue of the serpent* occasion'd the fall.

Then be it impress'd on Columbian youth,
    That the tongue is an engine of terrible force;
Not govern'd by reason, not guided by truth,
    A plague, which may desolate worlds in its course.'

At the present day, there is a vast fund of what is called poetic sentiment, diffused throughout the community; and nothing is requisite but a sort of mechanism, to mould it into a new shape. But

when Mr. Fessenden began his career, an innate fire, and originality
of thought, were necessary to constitute a poet. These gifts he had—
nor has age yet robbed him of them.[238]

* (*June, pp. 403–4*)

John Bunyan's Works

John Bunyan's works, in the collected edition fill three large oc-
tavo volumes, every page of which is stamped with the peculiar impress of his mind. But the Pilgrim's Progress alone retains its popularity; which is secured to it, so long as the world shall endure, by
the human interest with which the author has so strongly imbued
the shadowy beings of his allegory. His other productions will always attract the attention of the curious reader, but have passed forever from the list of what may be called the People's Literature. In
turning over one of them—THE LIFE AND DEATH OF MR.
BADMAN,—we find a record of several wonderful incidents, which
are narrated as facts, and which John Bunyan undoubtedly supposed to be such. . . . [239]

We doubt whether the present generation has not lost more than
it has gained, by the philosophy which teaches it to laugh, rather
than tremble, at such tales as these. Here is a beautiful story of sweet
music round a death-bed. . . .

The pen of John Bunyan, nor any other pen of uninspired mortal,
never wrote a passage of more powerful simplicity and pathos, than
the next which we shall select. . . .

(*June, pp. 419–20*)

[238] Hawthorne lived in the home of the Fessendens while he was editor of the
American Magazine. He contributed a signed sketch of Fessenden's life to the
American Monthly Magazine for January, 1838 (reprinted in *Writings,* XVII, 37–59),
in which he writes in full of Fessenden's works and tells of his own stay in the poet's
home.

[239] Hawthorne's excerpts from *The Life and Death of Mr. Badman* have been
omitted here. In the whole of Hawthorne's writings he alluded to *The Pilgrim's
Progress* more than to any other book.

Life of Eliot *

The name of Eliot, 'the Apostle to the Indians,' has come down to us in traditionary honour from an early period of our annals; and in the present age of benevolent enterprise, cannot but be venerated in proportion as it is known. His life and labours are here recorded in a very pleasing and judicious narrative, bearing internal evidence of the same conscientious fidelity to truth so remarkable through-out the series of volumes of which it forms a part; and which en-ables us to read them all with undoubting confidence, and with the conviction that they are written not for effect, not for gain, but with the veritable purpose of instructing the public on some of the most interesting points of our history. This praise, indeed, belongs to whatever is attested by the authority of Mr. Sparks,—himself emi-nently trust-worthy as well as discerning; uniting more excellencies than any other biographical writer in our language,

> 'Comprehensive, clear,
> Exact and elegant,'—

in some essential qualifications unrivalled, and even unique.

The author of this work has done justice to the conduct of the first colonists of New England towards the Indian tribes. He has shown that Eliot was zealously assisted in his benevolent plans by the magis-trates and people of Massachusetts. . . .[240]

(August, pp. 495–96)

---

* Library of American Biography, Vol. 5. Life of John Eliot, the Apostle to the Indians:—By Converse [*sic*] Francis.[241]

[240] Note the allusions to Eliot in *The Blithedale Romance* (*Writings,* VIII, 166–81) and in *The Scarlet Letter* (*ibid.,* VI, 321). See also the account in *Grandfather's Chair* (*ibid.,* XII, 46–59). Hawthorne's quotations from the biography have been omitted here.

[241] Published at Boston in 1836. The series was under the general editorship of Jared Sparks.

Major Burnham's Orderly Book

We have in our possession the Orderly Book of the late Major Thomas Burnham, of Ipswich, who acted as Adjutant to a militia regiment during the siege of Boston. . . .[242]

Every document, that refers to this period of our Revolutionary warfare, is particularly worthy of attention. It was at the Siege of Boston that the American people first acted together, as one nation; and not till then do the separate streams of their history unite in one mighty current. Nothing could be more interesting than to investigate, were it now possible, the composition of the motley army which surrounded the trimontane Peninsula, and to observe the points of difference and agreement among the natives of various colonies, then, for the first time brought into mutual contact. These diverse ingredients were then, as we may say, undergoing the process of fusion, in order to form a homogeneous mass. This, of all other scenes and periods in American annals, offers the best field for an historical novel; and it is singular that no one has attempted to work out the striking and strongly contrasted picture which it presents. Mr. Cooper, indeed, in his Lionel Lincoln,[243] has hit upon the right moment; but he erred in confining his story almost exclusively within the British lines, instead of establishing his head-quarters near the earthern ramparts of Dorchester and Roxbury.

(August, pp. 503-4)

Wild Horses

In illustration of the above cut, we copy a passage from Goodrich's Universal Geography; [244] and in so doing, it would be inex-

---

[242] This seems to have been a volume in MS.

[243] *Lionel Lincoln* was published at New York in 1825.

[244] Samuel Griswold Goodrich, *A System of Universal Geography*, Boston, 1832. This comment of Hawthorne's occurs in a footnote to an excerpt quoted from the *Universal Geography*. Such complimenting of Goodrich is by no means in agreement with the fiery denunciations in his letters of a few months earlier. But it is to be

cusable not to bear testimony to the excellence of a book, to which the present number of our Magazine owes more in the way of embellishments, than we have willingly borrowed. Mr. Goodrich has advanced no mean nor unacknowledged claims to more than one species of literary reputation; but most men would have been content to stand upon the solid and elevated pedestal, which is formed by the thousand pages of this most useful and entertaining volume. The plan of the work is entirely original; and it bears the same relation to the dry and barren systems of geography which had previously existed, that a complete picture of the earth's surface, with its diversified scenery and various inhabitants, would bear to the naked outline of a map. Such a book, with the changes that the world's moral, political, and physical history may introduce into the successive editions, cannot fail to become permanent in literature.

(August, p. 512)

Editorial Notice

Owing to circumstances unforseen when we assumed the charge of this periodical, (in March last,) the present Number will probably terminate our connection with it. The brevity of our continuance in the Chair Editorial will excuse us from any lengthened ceremony in resigning it. In truth, there is very little to be said on the occasion. We have endeavoured to fill our pages with a pleasant variety of wholesome matter. The reader must judge how far the attempt has been successful. It is proper to remark that we have not had full controul over the contents of the Magazine; inasmuch as the embellishments have chiefly been selected by the executive officers of the Boston Bewick Company, or by the engravers themselves; and our humble duty has consisted merely in preparing the literary illustrations. In some few cases, perhaps, the interests of the work might have been promoted by allowing the Editor the privilege of a veto, at least, on all engravings which were to be presented to the Public

---

recalled that when Hawthorne wrote this note, he had already engaged to write the *Universal History* for Goodrich.

under his auspices, and for which his taste and judgment would inevitably be held responsible. In general, however, the embellishments
have done no discredit either to the artists or their employers. Any
causes, which may hitherto have impeded the prosperity of the
concern,[245] will probably be done away in future, and the Magazine
be rendered worthier of the public favour, both as regards Literature
and Art.

(August, p. 520)

[245] The property of the Bewick Company had already been turned over to an
administrator for the benefit of their creditors. Because of fire, there was no issue for
the month following Hawthorne's resignation, and the magazine survived only until
September of the following year.

MISCELLANEOUS ITEMS

An Obsolete Law

At the trial of a Puritan, being asked by the Clerk of the Court, how he would be tried, the prisoner answered—'by the Law of God.' 'Whereat,' says the old writer, from whom we take the fact,—'the LAWYERS gave a great hiss!'

(March, p. 266)

[*Character*]

Any character is better than none.

(March, p. 273)

Bells of Moscow [246]

One of the most remarkable bells in the world is that of the Church of Saint Ivan, at Moscow. It weighs one hundred and fourteen thousand pounds, and is never sounded except on great occasions. The bell itself remains immovable, and is rung by means of a rope fixed to the clapper, which alone is heavier than our ordinary bells. When a peal is rung, its vibrations are perceptible throughout the city, and produce a solemn impression upon the hearer, in which the effect of the distant roll of thunder is harmoniously combined with the deepest and softest tones of an immense organ.

(March, p. 276)

[246] See text, pp. 183–85.

Fashionable Wigs

It was the custom of the early settlers of New England (at least of the frontier men, about the year 1725) to wear wigs made of the scalps of Indians, whom they had slain. This strikes us as a truly Yankee idea—to keep their ears comfortably warm with the trophies of their valour—to cover themselves at once with glory and with a wig. Perhaps they took the hint of this excellent fashion from Julius Caesar, who, when the Romans had given him a laurel crown as a symbol of his fame, used to wear it constantly to hide his baldness.

(March, p. 284)

Singular Accident

A gardener at Nantes, a short time since, while clipping the branches of a fruit-tree, with a large and keen pair of shears, cut off his own arm between the wrist and the elbow. The amputation was complete, and the severed portion fell to the ground. This seems hardly credible, though the London papers give it as an authenticated fact. In Sir Jonah Barrington's Memoirs,[247] there is an account of an accident not entirely dissimilar, and far more serious, which befell an Irish labourer. He was on his way to the mowing field, with a scythe over his shoulder, and in crossing a brook, perceived a speckled trout in the calm depth of a hollow, under the bank. The trout was of immense size, and the poor man's mouth watered at the thought of such an addition to his usual dinner of potatoes; but he had neither fishing line nor spear, wherewith to capture him. It occurred to him, that, if he could hit the trout on the head, with the butt-end of his scythe-handle, the shock would stun him, and render him an easy prize. Accordingly, he uplifted his scythe high in the air, at the same time stretching his neck over

---

[247] Sir Jonah Barrington, *Historic Memoirs of Ireland; Comprising Secret Records of the National Convention, the Rebellion, and the Union, with Delineations of the Principal Characters, Connected with These Transactions,* London, 1833.

the bank, in order to take a sure aim at the unsuspecting fish. Down
came the blow with mighty force—whether it hit the trout, remains
a mystery,—but the scythe chanced to be turned across the Irishman's out-stretched neck, and while he made his thrust with the
handle, the blade cut off his head. Sir Jonah tells this unhappy oc-
currence as a fact, within his own knowledge; and we may at least
allow, that if any man could happen to cut off his own head, it
would certainly be an *Irishman*.

(March, p. 288)

[*Wars of Louis XIV*]

Of the sixty-eight years of the reign of Louis the Fourteenth,
fifty-six were spent in war.

(March, p. 300)

A Man-Mountain

Father Martini,[248] one of the French Jesuits who were formerly
sent as Missionaries to China, speaks of a mountain in that country,
which has been hewn into the shape of a man. This immense statue
is well proportioned, and so large that the features of the face may
be distinguished at the distance of some leagues. Father Kircher,[249]
another Jesuit, speaks of two mountains, likewise in China, one of
which has the figure of a dragon, the other of a tiger. As later
travellers have seen nothing of these marvellous statues, their existence is now discredited.[250]

(April, p. 315)

---

[248] Father Martino Martini (1614–61), an Italian Jesuit missionary in China, published two books on China, which were soon translated from the Latin into French.

[249] Father Athanasius Kircher (*c.* 1602–80), a German Jesuit missionary to China,
published an illustrated book on China at Amsterdam in 1667. It was translated from
the Latin into French in 1670.

[250] Cf. "The Great Stone Face."

Enormous Still

A condenser for the distillation of gin was made in 1830, for Mr. Hodges of London, the height of which was fourteen feet six inches, and the diameter eight feet. It distilled ten gallons of gin per minute, six thousand per day, and one million eight hundred and seventy-eight thousand per annum. Such a stream of alcohol, one would think, would overflow the land. Some stills in Scotland, however, produce eighty gallons every three and a half minutes—which is indeed an amazing quantity to be added to the sin and misery of this world, in so short a time.

(April, p. 326)

Scent of the Plague

The Plague is said to smell like mellow apples, or, as some think, like May-flowers.[251] We did not know that either apples or May-flowers smelt so plaguy bad.

(April, p. 326)

Polemical Divinity

At the siege of a walled town, in one of the Spanish wars, a Catholic priest shot eleven men with a musket, from behind a battlement. Each time that he fired, this good priest made the sign of the cross in the air, with his musket, pronouncing a blessing on the man whom he aimed at—and then let fly. Thus the enemy received,

---

[251] The source of this note is Bacon's *Sylva Sylvarum* (*The Works of Francis Bacon,* V, 125): "The plague is many times taken without manifest sense, as hath been said. And they report that, where it is found, it hath a scent of the smell of a mellow apple; and (as some say) of May-flowers: and it is also received that smells of flowers that are mellow and luscious, are ill for the plague; as white lilies, cowslips, and hyacinths." See nn. 218 and 263. For other evidence of Hawthorne's interest in the plague see text, pp. 202–3 and 251 and also the story "Lady Eleanore's Mantle."

at once, a benediction for his soul and a bullet for his body. Several of the New-England clergy have taken arms, in our Indian wars and in the Revolution; but with less philanthropy than the Catholic priest, they distributed only their bullets to the enemy, and kept their benedictions for their friends.

(April, p. 332)

Wild Turkies and Deer

At the settlement of a Virginian backwoodsman, a flock of thirty wild turkeys came and fed very sociably with his hogs; who, as there was plenty of food for both, manifested no swinish ill-breeding towards their guests. But the backwoodsman took his rifle, and standing in the door of his cottage, shot one of the turkeys. The survivors, who knew nothing of the dangers of civilisation, manifested no terror at the report of the rifle, nor seemed disturbed when their companion fell dead among them. In this manner, the backwoodsman shot twenty-seven of the thirty turkeys; when the three others, seeing that something was amiss, took flight into the forest. Thus it is that all Nature's wild children are taught, by systematic injuries, to flee from civilized man.

The same backwoodsman had tamed a young deer, which, in the winter, used to feed and sport with his children. In Summer and Autumn, the deer went into the forest, in search of food that she loved better than the bread from the children's hands. At intervals, she would return to visit the backwoodsman's family, accompanied by one or more wild deer, with whom she had become acquainted in the forest and invited them to the settlement. When the wild deer saw the cabin, they would make a stand, snuff the air, and try to satisfy themselves what strange object this might be. Meantime, the backwoodsman had seized his rifle, and getting within sixty or a hundred yards, let fly—and down fell the poor citizen of the forest with a bullet between his antlers. In this way, the treacherous tame-deer—for we cannot help thinking that she was a traitress, and knew what she was about—lured fourteen wild ones to their death.

(April, p. 334)

Forced Abstinence

A person was recently confined in one of the Ayrshire coal-mines, in Scotland, by the caving in of the pit; and twenty-three days elapsed before his release. When the place of his imprisonment was discovered, the air was so impure, owing to the gaseous exhalations of the mine, as to cause sickness in those who breathed it. It is supposed that this unhealthy air, by lowering the condition of the vital functions, and thus lessening the waste of the body, was instrumental in enabling the man to subsist so long without food. There was a pool of water in the cavern, whence he drank for the first ten days, but then happened to lie down at a distance from it, and was too weak to reach it again. When found, he was a mere skeleton; the backbone could be distinctly felt through the abdomen. He was carefully nursed, and for several days, appeared likely to recover; but experienced a relapse, and finally died. It is an axiom of Hippocrates, that death is ultimately certain, after a complete abstinence of seven days, whatever care may be taken of the patient.

(April, p. 334)

Rubies

Among the crown jewels of Pegu, there was formerly a most magnificent ruby. Such was its size and splendour, that the inhabitants of Pegu considered it a subject of national glory, that this inestimable precious stone was in the possession of their king. In the hyperbolical language of the East, it was said that, if the great ruby of Pegu were to be thrown into a river, its intense and brilliant red would turn the water to blood. When the Burmahs conquered Pegu, they searched in vain for the great ruby; nor could they, by any tortures or threats of punishment, discover where it was concealed. The king of Pegu, a small, weak, and paralytic old man, was stripped naked and shut up in an iron cage, in the city of Rangoon. In this situation he continued twelve years, and was never permitted to leave his iron cage, except on occasions of festival, when he was brought out to adorn the triumph of his conquerours. It was observed that the old king held continually in his hand a lump of pitch, which was supposed to be a charm or talisman, such as the superstitious people of that country are in the habit of carrying about their persons. At length he died, and his body was thrown out to be devoured by dogs and birds of prey. A Burmah soldier, perceiving that the hand of the dead king still grasped the lump of pitch, had the curiosity to force it from him with his spear, and examined it. It enclosed the long-sought ruby, which the poor old king had thus preserved for twelve years—prizing it as much perhaps, as he did his kingdom.

The Burmahs set a superstitious value upon rubies. It is, or was, the custom of many of them to make an incision into their flesh, generally in the arm or leg, and to put a ruby in the wound, which soon heals over it. There the gem remains, throughout the possessor's life, and is considered a charm of wonderful efficacy. Whenever the English fought a battle with the Burmahs, they used to examine the dead bodies, and, if they observed a rising in the flesh, would cut into it, in search of rubies.

(April, p. 336)

A Benefactor

Laud, Archbishop of Canterbury in the reign of Charles the First, was perhaps the greatest benefactor that ever New England had. True; he meant nothing of the kind; yet, without his priestly tyranny, the Mayflower would never have been chartered—the hallowed feet of those old ministers and godly men would never have stepped upon the Rock of Plymouth—and Winthrop and all his associates might have worshipped in the parish-churches where their fathers did. New England would have remained long a wilderness, and at last have been settled by mere worldly adventurers, the most desperate of their generation, instead of the wisest and holiest. Their descendants would not have possessed that distinctive character which brought about the Revolution. Liberty would have had no cradle; and the world would have been hindered in its march, perhaps for centuries, but for the timely aid of the Archbishop. Allowing this estimate of his influence to be greatly overstrained, he yet stands a memorable example of the providence by which Error [*sic*] is made to do for Truth, what Truth could not so well do for itself. Errour fights in the dark, and inflicts the heaviest blows on its own party in the battle; all its strength, as appears by the final result, goes to eke out the weakness of the adversary. For more than errour, in addition to great infirmities of temper, Archbishop Laud does not seem to be accountable. He did not, so far as we can judge from his private diary, sin against his own conscience. At his death, he showed the spirit of a martyr; for, when about to be beheaded, looking through the boards of the scaffold, he saw some of the crowd underneath, and desired that the chinks might be closed up. 'I desire not,' said the fallen Archbishop, 'that my blood should be upon their heads.'

(April, p. 338)

[*Indian Corn*]

INDIAN CORN is of very uncertain origin. Some writers say that it is from the East, others from America. The former sustain their opinion on the grounds that it has long been known in Europe by the name of *Ble de Turquie,* or Turkey grain, and that varieties of it have been brought from the Isle of France and from China. Those who assign its origin to America say, that the early navigators found it cultivated in Mexico, and Brazil, and in all parts where they first landed; and that each region had a name for it, such as maize, flaolli, and others. It is affirmed, that it still grows wild among the Indians in Paraguay. The fact is undisputed, that,

immediately after the discovery of America, the cultivation of Indian Corn spread rapidly in other parts of the world. We would
willingly vindicate the claim of our own country to the honour of
having bestowed this grain on the rest of the globe—esteeming it
an invaluable and truly Yankee esculent, whether eaten in the
green ear, in Johnny cakes or loaves from the oven, or in puddings,
boiled or baked.[252]

(April, p. 348)

Dancing Horses

At equestrian exhibitions, horses are often made to dance. They
keep perfect time to the music, and flourish their four legs with as
much grace and facility as Celeste ever did her single pair; which,
of course, shows double skill on the part of the quadruped. But it is
said to be frequently the case, that horses drop down dead in the
performance of the dance. One equestrian company has successively
lost several valuable animals, in this way. As the physical exertion,
during the dance, does not seem to be great, the fact must be ac-
counted for by the tension of intellect, with which the poor horse
adapts his motions to the music. Frenchmen live by dancing, but
horses die by it:—as the frogs said, what is sport to us, is death to
them.[253]

(April, p. 351)

General Picton's Helmet

The battle of Busacos, in Spain, was fought in the night. Sir
Thomas Picton,[254] the British general, being suddenly aroused from
bed, forgot to lay aside the coloured cotton night-cap, in which he

---

[252] Cf. Joel Barlow's "The Hasty Pudding."

[253] See the sketch on the "Influence of Music on Animals" (text. pp. 199–201).

[254] Sir Thomas Picton (1758–1815), lieutenant general in the British army during
the Napoleonic Wars, had an important part in the battle of Busacos, Spain, in September, 1810.

had been taking a comfortable snooze. Wherever the battle raged hottest, there was seen the gallant general, in this queer sort of helmet.

(May, p. 356)

Combustion of a Professor [255]

The American Journal of the Medical Sciences gives an account of the spontaneous combustion of the Professor of Mathematics in the University of Nashville. He felt a sharp pain in the ankle, and began to strike the spot smartly with the palm of his hand; the pain, however, grew more acute, and compelled him to utter loud cries. On examining the spot, he discovered that his leg had actually caught fire, of its own accord, and that there was a flame of the bigness of a ten-cent piece, and of the colour of quicksilver. He extinguished the conflagration by pressing his hand forcibly upon the part; but an ulcer ensued, which was several months in healing. This occurred in January, 1835. Heretofore, no instances of spontaneous combustion have been known, except of persons addicted to the use of alcohol; but the Professor is a gentleman of the strictest temperance, and in no respect of a fiery disposition. He is subject to derangement of the digestive powers, and has somewhat enfeebled his constitution by a too devoted pursuit of science. Should this strange accident often occur, it will be the part of prudent men to take out policies of insurance against the Loss or Damage of their own persons by Fire.

(May, p. 360)

[*A Lilliputian Book*]

The English Bijou Almanac [256] contains an annual calendar, six portraits of distinguished personages, and poetical illustrations of

---

[255] The issue of the magazine for May, 1835 (I, 388), had carried a similar article entitled "Spontaneous Combustion of the Human Body."

[256] *The English Bijou Almanac for 1836*, London, 1835.

them; the length of this ponderous volume is one inch, and its breadth not quite so much. It would make a singular figure by the side of one of the vast folios, that were in fashion one or two centuries ago, each of which, if its solid contents were subdivided, would supply paper enough for at least five thousand such volumes as the Bijou. One of these books would adorn the library of Lilliput; the other, that of Brobdinag [*sic*].

(*May, p. 360*)

Tonquinese Soldiers

A woman, being condemned to death at Tonquin, underwent her punishment with so much fortitude that the soldiers, who were present, devoured her body, hoping that this food would inspire them with similar courage.

(*May, p. 362*)

Saint Ursula

Such was the purity of St. Ursula, that, if any unclean carcass were buried near her grave, the earth, it is said, would throw it up again.

(*May, p. 366*)

Moorish Peculiarities, Taken at Random

Tangier is a good specimen of a Moorish city; at a distance, its mosques, lofty towers, and the battlements and turrets of the Alcassaba, or castle, give it an imposing appearance; but within the walls, the stranger sees a miserable collection of houses, looking the shabbier by contrast with two or three splendid mansions belonging to foreign consuls. The shops are mere stalls. The streets are so narrow, that a passenger in the middle can easily touch the walls on each side; and the houses so low, that he can reach the roofs without standing on tiptoe. The inhabitants are very subject to Elephantiasis. In ancient times, this disease used to cause the joints to separate, and the limbs to drop off; so that only the trunk and head remained. The countenance assumed the savage and frightful aspect of a wild beast. At present, the legs only are affected; they swell to the size of an elephant's; and the similarity gives the disease its name. From the knee downward, the leg is discoloured and ulcerated, and the skin thick and rough, crackling like parchment. The general state of health does not appear affected, and the disorder is so common that it occasions little anxiety. Its causes are supposed to be poorness of living, dampness, and the bad quality of water.

In Tangier, and throughout Morocco, the Sultan alone has the privilege of carrying an umbrella. Should any inferiour person venture abroad with one, it would be high treason, and his head would be the forfeit. The habitation[s] of Moorish saints are distinguished by a small white flag, or rag, stuck on a pole; and Christians must keep their distance from the sacred precincts. A military patrol walks all night through the streets of Tangier, shouting the watchword every five minutes. Before day-light, the Mueddin bellows, with a sepulchral cry, from the summit of a mosque, enjoining the true believers to awake and pray; this vociferation is three times repeated. The Moorish Judges often hear causes in the open street; little deliberation is used; and the sentence, whatever it be, is immediately carried into execution. The bastinado is the ordinary punishment for slight offences; and decapitation for more serious crimes. When a person is to be decapitated, he is stretched on his back, his arms and legs are held down, and the executioner, with the dexterity of frequent practice, passes a long and sharp knife through his neck. So many undergo this death, that it has lost its terrours. There is, or was formerly, a mode of punishment by tossing the criminal into the air. Three or four stout negroes were the executioners, and performed their office with such skill, that he was sure to come down on his head, shoulder, or in any other position that had been prescribed by the sentence.

In some of the cities of Morocco, the streets are roofed over, and thus form a succession of long, dark, narrow passages. The shop-keepers sit cross-legged among their goods, so that they can lay their hands upon any article, without the trouble of getting up. The Jews suffer great persecutions in the Moorish cities. They are distinguished by small black scullcaps on their shaven heads. A Moorish child may often be seen to kick an old gray-bearded Jew, or smite him on the cheek; while the Jew addresses the little fellow as his lord or master, and entreats permission to pass on. Were he to return a blow for those which he receives, his hand would be cut off. Many of the Jews are good mechanics, but almost all are miserably poor. Renegadoes, or deserters from Christianity, are in even a worse condition, and are despised equally by Moors, Christians, and Jews. On the death of one of these wretches, neither Christians nor Moors would own him; and his body lay long in the street unburied.

In one of the Moorish cities, there are seventeen Jewish synagogues. The Jews keep a yearly festival, in commemoration of the sojourn of their fathers in the wilderness. During eight days, it is unlawful for them to sleep under a roof. The Jewish women are very beautiful; they dwell in greater seclusion than the Moorish females; and many of them, till the age of eighteen or twenty, are never seen in the street, and perhaps do not once cross the threshold of their homes. Yet they seem cheerful and happy—probably because they are never idle. The Moorish ladies, when they go abroad, are enveloped in a white *hayk,* somewhat resembling a shroud; it completely conceals their face and form, but discloses their bare legs—contrary to the fashion of Europe, where ladies conceal their legs, but show their faces. Beauty among the Moors consists in corpulency, and a wife is valued according to her weight, and the circumference of her waist. A lady who weighs a ton, and whose girth is equal to that of a hogshead, may aspire to be Sultana.

There are no wheel-carriages in Morocco, nor any roads suitable to them; and all the travel is performed with camels, horses, or mules. The camel goes only half as fast as the horse or mule, and his motion is not easy to the rider. In travelling, it is necessary to take a tent, or perhaps two, with bed and bedding, provisions, and a load of articles for presents, and to be attended by a military escort. In the villages, the houses are composed of low walls of stone or plastered reeds, with loosely thatched roofs. Large troops of ferocious dogs are kept in every village, not from any liking which the Moors entertain towards these brutes, whom, on the contrary, they abhor as unclean animals; but they are necessary as a defence against the Arabs and Breber robbers. Wandering tribes of Bedouins are frequently met with, dwelling in tents; they possess flocks of sheep and goats. Such is the scarcity of water, that the situation of a well is as universally known, as that of a city in other parts of the world. In the Moorish country, there is a singular method of preserving grain. A cellar is dug to the depth of seven or eight feet; the floor is covered with mats and straw; the sides are lined with reeds; a layer of straw is placed on top, then a slab of stone, and lastly the earth is heaped in a mound over the whole. In these granaries, which are called Matamores, wheat or barley may be kept perfectly good for five years, and other sorts of grain even longer. There is but a very imperfect knowledge of agriculture, and no more food is raised, than barely suffices for the scanty population. Famines have occurred, during which the half-starved wretches were compelled to eat dogs, cats, rats, roots, bones, and the most disgusting offals.

In the streets of the cities may be seen auctioniers [*sic*]—jugglers playing various tricks—story tellers, surrounded by an audience—and Moors seated at chess. At funerals, the body is borne on a bier, in a coffin resembling a large chest of varnished wood; and the mourners follow, chanting a sepulchral verse. If the dead person be of the poorer class, he is enveloped in a white cloth, and buried without a coffin. In cases of illness, a conjurer is sometimes called in. He writes his prescription on a white plate; the ink is suffered to dry, and is then washed off with water, which must be drank as a medicine. It may be said in favour of this custom, that it is one of the safest possible ways in which a doctor's prescriptions can be swallowed.

The Brebers, who infest Morocco, and are hated by the Moors, are supposed to have come originally from Syria, and to be descendants of those Philistines who were driven from their country by David, when he slew Goliath of Gath.

(May, pp. 368–69)

Public Loans

The system of public loans, by which war is carried on, is founded on the principle, that future generations ought to sustain a part of the burden, which is supposed to be incurred for their benefit. No country can make war with merely its habitual revenue.

(May, p. 369)

American Gipsies

Gipsies are known in almost all countries of Europe—an idle, vagabond race, without settled homes, living by theft, beggary, fortune-telling, and the mending of pots and kettles. They are of uncertain origin, but show the same characteristic marks, wherever they are found. No attempts have hitherto succeeded in reducing the Gipsies of Europe to the habits of civilized life. It has been supposed that there are none of this singular race in America, where, in our woods and wildernesses, their wandering propensities might have had boundless space for exercise. Yet, in fact, there is a colony of Gipsies, who were brought to America by the French, in early times, and whose posterity now live and flourish on the shores of Biloxi bay, in Louisiana. A philosopher, contemplating the points of similarity between the European Gipsy and the American Indian—both untameable—one the wild man of civilized countries and the other of the forest—might have imagined that the two races would at once have mingled, and the Gipsy have found a home in the Indian wigwam. On the contrary, ever since their settlement on this side of the Atlantic, the Gipsies appear to have thrown off their hereditary characteristics. No difference can be perceived between them and other descendants of French colonists, except in personal appearance; their complexion is much darker, and their hair is coarse and straight. They still call themselves Gipsies, or Egyptians, but are industrious, orderly in their habits, and retain nothing of their ancestry, except the name.

(*May, p. 372*)

The Looking-Glass

In her youth, a woman goes to the glass to see how pretty she is; in her age, she consults it, to assure herself that she is not so hideous as she might be. She gets into a passion with it, but dies before she can make up her mind to break it.

(*May, p. 372*)

Spider's Den

There is a species of Spider in New South Wales, which forms a den in the ground, having an aperture of about an inch in diameter. Over this aperture is a lid, composed of web and earth, so incorporated as to form a solid substance; it has also hinges of web, and when shut down, fits so accurately to the mouth of the den, as not to be discovered without the minutest inspection. A person was accustomed to feed one of these spiders, and became well acquainted with his habits. When visited by his friend, the spider would lift the trap-door of his den, come forth, and partake of the food that was brought him; and, when satisfied, would retreat into his dwelling, shutting the door after him. We are inclined to think that this spider is the only creature, except man, that has constructed a door, turning on hinges.[257]

(*May, p. 384*)

[257] See the spiders in *Doctor Grimshawe's Secret.*

[*Small Wit*]

Nothing is so intolerable as a little wit and a great desire of showing it.

(*May, p. 386*)

A Question

It is said by naturalists, that the population of a sea-coast is physically a more powerful race than those who inhabit the interiour of the same country. But how is this opinion to be reconciled with the the physical prowess of our half-horse and half-alligator giants of Kentucky,[258] thousands of whom never smell a sea-breeze in the whole course of their lives?

(*May, p. 386*)

Rich Skeletons

In the old Peruvian mines, skeletons of Indians are said to have been found, covered and intertwined with fibres of silver, and the inward parts filled with lumps of the same metal. The original owners of these dry bones were supposed to have perished, hundreds of years before, and as their flesh decayed, silver had grown around them, till, when found, they looked like silver corpses. Some men, possibly, would desire nothing better than such a transformation; provided it might take place while they were alive. Undoubtedly, it would make valuable men of them.

(*May, p. 389*)

[258] Here is evidence that Hawthorne knew the tall-tale tradition of the Southwest that had grown up around such figures as Mike Fink and David Crockett.

Theory of Tides

A Pythagorean philosopher affirmed that the ebbing and flowing of the sea was the respiration of the world, which he supposed to be a living monster, drawing in water instead of breath, and heaving it out again.

(May, p. 389)

Brazilian Ignorance

The descendants of the Portuguese settlers, in the interiour of Brazil, think that there are but two grand divisions of the earth— America and Portugal. One of these people, by no means more ignorant than his countrymen generally, inquired if Napoleon were not a general in the Portuguese service, who had rebelled against the king. Napoleon, we doubt not, would have been vexed, could he have conceived that his earth-pervading fame had so vaguely reached this portion of the globe. Another Brazilian, in giving a description of England, spoke of its noble river Mississippi, which was so wide that the eye could not see across it.

(May, p. 389)

Female Protection

At Cairo, under the government of the Mamelukes, if a criminal fleeing for his life, could reach the door which led to a Harem, he cried out—*fy ard el harym*—'I claim the protection of the women.' His life was then secure. Recently, in our own country, a body-guard of petticoats has been found a surer protection than the civil authority.

(May, p. 389)

Marriage, and Long Life

It has long been the opinion of those who have paid attention to the subject, that marriage, in both sexes, is conducive to length of life; and an European philosopher has lately made observations, which render the fact indubitable. His researches, together with what was previously known, give the following remarkable results. Among unmarried men, at the ages of from thirty to forty-five, the average number of deaths per annum is twenty-seven in a hundred; but of married men, at the same period of life, the deaths are only eighteen. For forty-one bachelors who attain the age of forty, there are seventy-eight married men who do the same. As age advances, the difference becomes more striking. At sixty, there are only twenty-two unmarried men alive, for ninety-eight who have enjoyed the benefits of matrimony;—at seventy, the proportion between the bachelors and married men is eleven of the former for twenty-seven of the latter;—and at eighty, there are nine married men for three single ones. The same rule holds good, in nearly the same proportions, with regard to the other sex. Married women, at the age of thirty, taking one with another, may expect to live thirty-six years longer; while, for the unmarried, the expectation of life is only thirty years and a half. Of those who attain the age of forty-five, there are seventy-two married women for fifty-two old maids. These estimates, it must be understood, are based on actual facts, by observing the difference of longevity between equal numbers of individuals, in single and in married life.

Should it be asked, how it is that marriage conduces to longevity, it may be difficult to give a satisfactory reply. Its mode of operation is probably rather mental and moral, than physical. As regards the male sex, the quietude of domestic life—its peaceful cares, if we may use the expression—and the calm sense of virtuous affections, and satisfied desires—would be likely to keep the soul from wearing out the frame too soon. The course of a married man's life is generally regular; his wife's influence tempers his masculine character, and makes him less wild and adventurous; he feels that he is not exclusively his own property, and therefore is not ashamed to be careful of himself. His spirit is tamed down, and does not hurry him into vicissitudes, whether of good or evil fortune. He has bidden adieu to all feverish passions. On many accounts, his health is exposed to far less peril than before; and, in sickness, he has the tenderest of nurses. Finally, he totters a long way, down into the vale of years, because supported by a careful arm, when he otherwise might sink. Compare such a life with the ill-regulated and reckless course of too many unconjugated men, and here is at least one cause for the briefer span of the latter class. Our reasoning, however, is not equally applicable to old maids, who, nevertheless, are subject to the same law as their male counterparts.

(May, pp. 390–91)

[*Wine for the Indians*]

The Hudson's Bay Company have a post on Rainy Lake, for carrying on trade with the Indians of the Northwest. Their supply of spirits for one year (and probably it was their ordinary annual supply,) was sixty kegs of what are called High Wines—or alcohol of such strength, that each keg was equal to four kegs of rum. Mr. Cameron, the chief agent, said, that, though the streams were high from the melting of the snows, yet they should run as high with liquor, if the Indians required it. Thus all the sparkling rills, where the sons of the wilderness once quaffed the pure element, are now made to overflow with poison.

(May, p. 392)

[*Books*]

Not one-fourth of the books published pay their expenses.

(May, p. 398)

Americanisms

A *span* of horses is the usual expression, instead of a pair, in New York, throughout New England, in Upper Canada, and probably in the Southern States. The word is derived from the Dutch language, and originated from the Dutch settlers of New York; it is also in use at the Cape of Good Hope, where the inhabitants are partly of Dutch extraction. 'I guess'—'I calculate'—'Tarnation'— phrases which have been called purely American, were originally brought hither by emigrants from Suffolkshire, in England. The word, *'riley,'* has been supposed of American coinage. A Yankee landlord apologizing to some Englishmen, because the water in a jug was so *riley,* his guests were inclined to laugh at him; till one of them hinted that the word was still commonly used in Devonshire.

(June, p. 404)

A Man's Wife

A witness in the case of Riot, testifying how the mob hustled him and bore him off his feet, said,—'If I touched ground, I wish I might never see my wife again.' Lord Chief Justice Jeffreys,[259] who was on the bench, told the witness,—'Now whether that be a curse that thou layest upon thyself, or no, I can't tell.' [260] It is remarkable, that jokes upon matrimony, are never out of date, nor grow stale by repetition; the one here extracted has lain in a musty old book these hundred and fifty years; yet were a judge to repeat it to-morrow, it would still set the court in as hearty a roar as it doubtless did in old Jeffrey's time. And after all, there is no great wit in it. Are we to conclude, that, since matrimony is so easily laughed

---

[259] Lord Chief Justice George Jeffreys (1648–89) is known for holding the "bloody assizes" of 1685 and for giving James II advice which led to the imprisonment of the seven bishops.

[260] Hawthorne quoted these sentences from Howell, *A Complete Collection of State Trials,* X, 53. The witness was one Mr. Rippon.

at, it must in its nature, be very ridiculous? If so, we hope, in our time, to be laughing-stocks as well as our neighbours.

(June, p. 408)

Be Short

These two words were written, in large letters, over the door of Cotton Mather's study, as an intimation to his visiters to be as sparing as possible of his precious time. The same inscription might be profitably posted up in many other places—for instance, in front of a pulpit, for the admonition of long-winded parsons; and, above all, it should be printed conspicuously, in letters of gold, on the walls of our legislative chambers.

(June, p. 424)

Botany Bay

Until within a few years, this colony was the Paradise of evil-doers. Murderers, on the day of trial, might be seen carousing with their friends in a pot-house, in the presence of the constable. Thieves, fashionably dressed, walked arm-in-arm to trial, with the constable following respectfully behind, like a servant; while the bystanders offered their best wishes for the escape of the rogues. Receivers of stolen goods came to receive sentence, in splendid carriages, and attended by servants in livery. Such phenomena naturally resulted from the fact, that the mass of the inhabitants were familiar with vice, and had themselves been convicted criminals; so that sin was without its recompense of shame.

(June, p. 428)

Indian Juggler

Major Long [261] received, from a French trader, an account of a singular feat which was performed by an Indian Juggler. On a dry

[261] Probably Stephen Harriman Long (1784–1864), explorer and author.

prairie, and at a distance from any stream or spring, this man offered to fill an empty keg with water. Being promised a keg of whiskey, in consideration of his performing this seeming miracle, the Indian first turned the water-keg with the bung-hole downward, in order to convince the spectators that it was really empty. No water ran out. He then began to dance, lifted the keg toward heaven, and enacted various other mummeries; till presenting the keg to another Indian, he invited him to drink. It was then passed round among the spectators; and all, the trader himself not excepted, were convinced that the keg really contained good and pure water. Let our readers exercise their ingenuity to guess how this water came there.

(June, p. 432)

Infection

Some people dying of the plague in England, their bodies were buried together on a hill. Nearly a hundred years afterwards, five persons happened to be digging there, and uncovered some decayed fragments of linen. Recollecting the tradition that this was the burial-place of those who died of the pestilence, they threw the earth back into the hole, as speedily as possible. Nevertheless, they all sickened of putrid fever, and three of the number died.[262]

(June, p. 439)

Doll's Eyes

It would scarcely be believed, that the manufacture of these little articles causes the circulation of several thousand pounds per annum. Children's toys, however trifling they may appear separately, are matters of great importance, when it is considered how many hands they set in motion, and how many mouths they are the means

---

[262] Miss F. N. Cherry has suggested ("A Note on the Source of Hawthorne's 'Lady Eleanore's Mantle,'" *American Literature*, VI [Jan., 1935], 437–39) that this passage may have contributed something to the conception underlying Hawthorne's story "Lady Eleanore's Mantle."

of feeding. Mr. Osle, when examined before a committee of the House of Commons, stated that he had seen a large room, filled with merely the legs and arms of dolls, which were piled in stacks from the floor to the ceiling, so as scarcely to leave space to pass between them. He received an order for five hundred pounds' worth (between two and three thousand dollars) of glass eyes, which were to be inserted into the heads of dolls. Whenever we see a company of these little figures, staring at us from the windows of a toyshop, we should give them credit for having bestowed bread on many a poor family, that must otherwise have gone without it.

(*July, p. 458*)

South American Carriers

When a road was to be constructed across the Andes, in South America, a petition against the project was presented by numbers of persons, who had long gained a livelihood by carrying travellers in baskets, over those difficult passes of the mountains, where none but themselves could tread. This is a striking instance of the unreasonableness of those who demand, that public improvements, which would be vastly for the benefit of the many, should be rejected for the advantage of a few.

(*July, p. 458*)

Relicts of Witchcraft

The pins, which the New England witches were said to have thrust into the bodies of those whom they afflicted, in 1692, are still preserved among the records of the court, in Salem.

(*July, p. 458*)

A Good Rule

A man and his wife should never both be angry at once.

(*July, p. 464*)

Witch Ointment

Lord Bacon, in his philosophical works, gives the following recipe for the manufacture of an ointment, by the use of which the 'midnight hags' were supposed to acquire the faculty of flying through the air. We trust that none of our readers will make the experiment.

'The ointment which witches use is made of the fat of children, digged out of their graves, and of the juices of smallage, cinque-foil and wolf's-bane, mingled with the meal of fine wheat.' [263]

After greasing themselves with this preparation, the witches flew up [the] chimney, and repaired to the spot, in some church-yard or dismal forest, where they were to hold their meetings with the Evil One. Cervantes, in one of his tales, seems to be of opinion that the ointment cast them into a trance, during which they merely dreamt of holding intercourse with Satan. If so, witchcraft differs but little from a nightmare.[264]

(July, p. 470)

Asthma

This disease is proverbially capricious; its severity, in one case, will be lessened by the same circumstances that would greatly heighten it in another. Dr. Johnson, who was afflicted with asthma, was frequently obliged to retire from the residence of his friend Mr. Thrale,[265] at Streatham, where the air was pure and fresh, to his

[263] This quotation comes from Bacon's *Sylva Sylvarum* (*The Works of Francis Bacon*, V, 152). Hawthorne was evidently well acquainted with Bacon, for he drew Bacon's *Works* from the Salem Athenaeum Library on October 2, 1828, August 25, 1829, and June 2, 1832 ("Books Read by Nathaniel Hawthorne").

[264] In an article entitled "The Sources of Hawthorne's 'Young Goodman Brown' " (*American Literature*, V [Jan., 1934], 342–48), Miss F. N. Cherry has suggested this article and in turn the story "El Coloquio de los Perros" by Cervantes as possible sources of Hawthorne's tale.

[265] Johnson's friendship for Henry Thrale began in 1764 and lasted until the death of Thrale in 1781. During the year 1765 in particular Johnson spent much time at the home of his friend at Streatham.

own lodgings in the narrow precincts of Bolt-court; because he could breathe more freely in the smoke of London. An asthmatic gentleman, while building a house in an elevated and beautiful situation, lived in a cottage at the foot of the hill. When his mansion was finished, he removed into it, but was so afflicted with asthma, that he was compelled to return to the cottage. Another person, being advised to travel for the relief of an asthma, found a certain village, the air of which suited him so well, that in the course of a few weeks, he was able to ascend a hill at a brisk pace, without stopping to take breath.

(*August, p. 485*)

Turkish Idleness

A Turk never works, if there is a possibility of his being idle. 'I have never seen one stand,' observes Commodore Porter,[266] 'if by any possibility he could be seated. A blacksmith sits cross-legged at his anvil, and seats himself when he shoes a horse. A carpenter seats himself when he saws, bores holes, or drives a nail, planes, dubs with his small adze, or chops with his hatchet, (I believe I have named all his tools,) if it be possible to do so without standing.' How different are these customs from our own. In America, hardly any workmen, except shoemakers and tailors, sit down; and even clerks stand up to write—a practice which, perhaps, might be advantageously adopted by literary men. But intense mental exertion (except it be oratorical) seems to require a sedentary posture.

(*August, p. 492*)

Fire Worshippers

There is a sect in Hindostan, who call themselves descendants of the ancient Persians, and, like their ancestors, pay adoration to the

[266] David Porter, *Constantinople and Its Environs, in a Series of Letters, by an American, Long a Resident of Constantinople,* New York, 1835, I, 217. After a long career in the United States navy, Porter (1780–1843) was consul at Constantinople from 1831 to 1839 and minister to Turkey from 1839 to his death.

sun, the moon, and stars, but especially to fire, esteeming all these objects as visible emblems of the invisible Deity. Like the Roman Vestals, they keep a perpetual fire in their temples, feeding it with odoriferous woods, of great value. Private individuals, when rich enough to sustain the expense, likewise keep these fires in their house, and thus transmute their wealth into the perfumed smoke which arises from the costly woods. Niebuhr affirms, that he saw, in one of the temples of these people, at Bombay, some fires which had been kept perpetually burning for two hundred years, and had probably been all that time supplied with odoriferous fuel. Such is their veneration for the element of fire, that they will not permit a candle to be blown out, lest the breath of man should pollute the purity of the flame. It has been remarked, that if there could possibly exist an idolatry founded on reason, and which did not degrade the Divine Majesty by the symbols of its worship, it would be that of the adorers of fire, and of the eternal lustres of the firmament. There is, in truth, nothing that can be seen or felt, which combines so many symbolic attributes of splendor, terror, and beneficence, as fire.[267]

(August, p. 494)

Girdle for the Earth

The English cotton manufacturers, though they cannot, like Shakspeare's fairy, 'put a girdle round the earth in forty minutes,'[268] might perform this feat in little more than a month. It is stated that the 'wrought fabrics of cotton, exported in one year, would form a girdle for the globe, passing *eleven* times round the equator;' and also, that 'the yarn spun in a year would, in a single thread, reach fifty-one times from the earth to the sun.' If all this

---

[267] This was a forestudy for the sketch "Fire Worship," published in *The Democratic Review* for December, 1843, and included in *Mosses from an Old Manse*. In the later sketch Hawthorne elaborated on the idea that fire may well be worthy of worship.

[268] *Midsummer-Night's Dream*, II, i, l. 175.

yarn were to be wound in one huge ball, it would form a good-
sized planet by itself.

(August, p. 499)

A Musical Ear

As an argument to induce a gentleman to patronise itinerant
musicians, it was stated that another person had attended their performances, although he was deaf. 'And so would I,' replied the
gentleman, 'if I were as deaf as he!'

(August, p. 502)

Duelling

By the old law of Massachusetts, duellists were to be punished by
fine, imprisonment, setting in the stocks, or whipping. In case of a
fatal result, the dead body was to be buried either at the place of
combat, or in the most public highway, with a stake driven through
it. The body of the slayer (after hanging) was to be treated in the
same manner. These were good and wise laws, where (as was the
case among our forefathers) the state of public sentiment would
permit them to be executed. The deep ignominy of the punishment
was well adapted as an antidote to all notions of false honour.

It appears to us that the present tone of the public press in regard
to duelling, though doubtless well meant, is of very evil tendency.
A bloodless duel becomes a topic of ridicule and jest-breaking in
every newspaper throughout the Union. Unless one of the duellists
be left dead or mortally wounded on the field, both must expect to
be universally hissed, like two unskilful gladiators in the Roman amphitheatre.

Most young men would deem it far more tolerable to undergo
the most solemn and weighty expressions of public abhorrence, for
murder committed in a duel, than to encounter such 'grinning in-
famy,' for stopping short of murder. This we conceive to be one of

the reasons, why duelling in America is a more bloody business than anywhere else in the world. In England, where, in theory at least, every gentleman must hold himself responsible to a challenge, or lose his place in society, nothing is more rare than a fatal duel. The reason is, that, while the custom of private combat continues in apparent force, it has in reality been so refined away, that its more horrible features are almost obliterated. Duelling (except in the few cases of mortal injury and animosity) is there a mere ceremony; but, by that mere ceremony, the antagonists incur no public ridicule, and are supposed to vindicate their honour. It is time that we should adopt the same refinement. Doubtless, if duelling could be entirely put down by the force of law, or of public sentiment, it would be infinitely the better way; but, that being manifestly impracticable, it should be our endeavor to make the custom fade away from realities, and become gradually a phantasm.

(August, p. 504)

Town-Whipper

This personage was annually appointed, while whipping-posts yet remained in New England; and his office was one of considerable labour and emolument.

(August, p. 504)

Price of Victory

The only king, that we ever heard of, who seemed to understand that blood is a high price to pay for glory, was Louis the Twelfth, of France. When he heard of the death of the gallant Gaston de Foix, in the arms of victory, at Ravenna, in Italy, he exclaimed, 'I would to heaven, that I could give every inch of the soil of Italy, and, by that sacrifice, restore life to Gaston de Foix, and the brave men who have perished with him! God forbid, that we should achieve many such victories, at the price of so much blood!'

(August, p. 510)

Duels

In the sixteenth century, during a space of only twenty years, the King of France bestowed eight thousand pardons on duellists, who had killed their antagonists.

(August, p. 515)

Complexion

Ladies who wish to preserve a fine complexion, (as what lady does not?) must take care, especially if they dwell near the sea-shore, not to venture out in the evening at twilight, nor in the morning at day-break. But the latter caution is superfluous.

(August, p. 516)

Improve

The use of the word improve, as in the following phrase—'*improved* as a tavern,' (instead of occupied, or used as a tavern,) is a Yankeeism. It originated with Dr. Cotton Mather. The Doctor's hand writing was very difficult to decypher; and the printer of one of his publications mistook the word *imployed* for *improved*. Cotton Mather's verbal authority being of great weight, this mistake had the effect of giving a new (but not *improved*) meaning to the word.

(August, p. 517)

Big Kettle

In a convent at Pisa, there is a cast-iron kettle, fifty feet high, and one hundred and forty feet in circumference. It is affirmed that soup for six thousand paupers is daily prepared in this vast cooking utensil. We should apprehend, however, that such an ocean of soup would be apt to prove rather watery, and that a poor man must either drown himself in it, or depart unsatisfied. Charity, to be truly efficient, should have a personal feeling; for, if it embrace too many objects, it will probably become meagre and unsubstantial, like a soup for six thousand paupers.

(August, p. 518)

Temperance in Iceland

Till within a recent period, there was no part of the civilized world where intoxicating liquors were so little used as in Iceland. The inhabitants were abstemious, indeed, because their poverty refused them the means of being otherwise; but to this forced abstinence may be attributed many of the simple virtues, which have always flourished in that frozen and dreary region. At present there seems reason to apprehend a change for the worse. Brandy has become much cheaper than formerly, and is more generally used; the annual importation being estimated at about a thousand barrels, which would allow somewhat more than two bottles to each inhabitant of the Island.

(August, p. 518)

APPENDIX

Books and Authors

The following is a list of the authors and works drawn on or mentioned in Hawthorne's six issues of *The American Magazine of Useful and Entertaining Knowledge*. Notes on the less familiar books have been made full enough for identification. Numbers in parentheses following the various items designate the pages of the magazine on which the references occur; numbers in brackets indicate pages in this volume where the references appear in the text.

Abdy, Edward Strutt, *Journal of a Residence and Tour in the United States of North America, from April, 1833, to October, 1834,* London, 1835 (415, 444).

Adams, John, letters to John Jay, May 30, June 1, 2, 1785 (483 [46]).

―――― *A Dissertation on the Canon and the Feudal Law,* in *The Boston Gazette,* Aug., 1765; London, 1768 (482 [43]).

Allen, Zachariah, *Practical Tourist; or, Sketches of the State of the Useful Arts, and of Society . . . in Great Britain, France, and Holland,* Providence, 1832 (461, 464, 487).

The American Gardener's Magazine (297).

The American Journal of Science and Arts, Benjamin Silliman's (314 [88], 332 [169], 340, 365, 393 [189], 410 [195], 450, 456).

The American Journal of the Medical Sciences (360).

The American Monthly Magazine (277, 286).

The American Quarterly Review (479).

The Annual Report of the Board of Managers of the Prison Discipline Society of Boston, 1826 ff. (287).

Arnott, Neil, *Elements of Physics; or, Natural Philosophy, General and Medical,* London, 1827; Philadelphia, 1829 (322, 461).

Audubon, John James (380, 429 [a long excerpt from Alexander Wilson's *American Ornithology,* I, 123-25, is here erroneously attributed to Audubon]).

―――― "Observations on the Natural History of the Alligator," *The*

Edinburgh New Philosophical Journal, II (April, 1827), 270–80 (474).

Augustine, Saint (319 [99]).

Babbage, Charles, *On the Economy of Machinery and Manufactures,* Philadelphia, 1832 (292, 295, 304, 326, 389).

Bachman, J., "Migrations of North American Birds," *The American Journal of Science and Arts,* XXX (1836), 81 ff. (450).

Bacon, Francis, *Sylva Sylvarum* (326 [232], 389 [188], 422, 468 [202], 470 [253]).

Barrington, Sir Jonah, *Historic Memoirs of Ireland; Comprising Secret Records of the National Convention, the Rebellion, and the Union; with Delineations of the Principal Characters, Connected with These Transactions,* London, 1833 (288 [230]).

Barrow, John, *Excursions in the North of Europe, through Parts of Russia, Finland, Sweden, Germany, and Norway in 1830 and 1833,* London, 1834 (336, 432).

——— *A Visit to Iceland, by Way of Tronyem, in the Summer of 1834,* London, 1835 (512, 513).

Belzoni, Giovanni Battista, *Narrative of the Operations and Recent Discoveries within the Pyramids, Temples, Tombs, and Excavations in Egypt and Nubia,* London, 1820 (323).

Blackwood's Magazine (346).

Bowen, Abel, MS. volume of letters and documents on the Boston Tea Party (351 [119]).

Brewster, Sir David, *The Life of Sir Isaac Newton,* London, 1831; Boston, 1832 (375).

The British Almanac of the Society for the Diffusion of Useful Knowledge, London, 1829 ff. (466).

Buffon, George Louis Leclerc, *Histoire Naturelle* (397 [192]).

Bunyan, John, *The Life and Death of Mr. Badman* (419, 420 [221]).

——— "Meditations upon a Candle," in *A Book for Boys and Girls* (412).

——— *The Pilgrim's Progress* (419 [221]).

Burgoyne, John, *The Blockade of Boston* (446 [146]).

Burnham, Thomas, "Orderly Book," MS. (503 [223]).

Burns, Robert (428).

Callender, James Thompson, *The American Annual Register; or, Historical Memoirs of the United States for the Year 1796,* Philadelphia, 1797 (491).

Carew, Thomas, "Lines" (398).

Carlyle, Thomas, *The Life of Friedrich Schiller,* London, 1825 (305 [81]).

Chateaubriand, François René (463 [200]).

Chaucer, Geoffrey, Prologue to *The Canterbury Tales* (493 [150]).

Galt, John, "On the Entrance of the American Woods" (478).

Gardiner, William, *The Music of Nature, with Curious and Interesting Illustrations,* London, 1832 (459).

Goodrich, Samuel Griswold, *A System of Universal Geography,* Boston, 1832 (512 [223]).

Gookin, Daniel, *Historical Collections of the Indians in New England,* in *Collections of the Massachusetts Historical Society,* I, 1792 (342 [111]).

Gützlaff, Charles, *A Sketch of Chinese History, Ancient and Modern,* London, 1834 (423).

Hall, Basil (405 [139]).

Hamilton, Alexander and others, *The Federalist* (356 [36]).

Hamilton, John Church, *The Life of Alexander Hamilton,* New York, 1834–40 (278, 355 [32]).

Hamilton, Thomas, *Men and Manners in America,* Edinburgh, 1833 (382 [127]).

Head, Francis Bond, *Bubbles from the Brunnens of Nassau, by an Old Man,* London, 1834 (322).

Head, George, *Forest Scenes and Incidents, in the Wilds of North America,* London, 1829 (438, 492).

Heber, Bishop Reginald, "Farewell" (356).

Herodotus, *History* (458).

Hesiod (315).

Hildreth, S. P., "Observations on the Bituminous Coal Deposits of the Valley of the Ohio, and the Accompanying Rock Strata," *The American Journal of Science and Arts,* XXIX (1836), 1–148 (340, 393 [189]).

Hinton, John Howard, *The History and Topography of the United States of North America from the Earliest Period to the Present Time,* Boston, 1834 (468).

Historical and Domestic Sketches of Corfu, with Legends and Traditions, London, 1834 (418).

Holman, James, *A Voyage round the World, Including Travels in Africa, Asia, Australasia, America, 1827–32,* London, 1834–35 (515 [209]).

Holmes, Oliver Wendell, "The Last Leaf" (494 [152]).

Homer (315, 394 [192]).

Hood, Thomas, "I Remember—I Remember" (377).

Howell, T. B. and T. J., *A Complete Collection of State Trials, 1163–1820,* London, 1816–20 (272 [64], 322 [100], 408 [249]).

Howitt, Richard, "Sonnet" (484).

Huet, Pierre Daniel, *Huetiana,* Amsterdam, 1799; reprinted in *Table-Talk; or, Selections from the Ana,* Edinburgh, 1827 (378).

Pepys, Samuel, *Diary* (366, 426 [141], 428).

Percival, James Gates, "To Seneca Lake" (457).

Philip, Alexander P. W., "On the Nature of Sleep," *Transactions of the Royal Philosophical Society of London*, 1833, pp. 73–87 (385 [177]).

Phillips, Henry, *A History of Cultivated Vegetables*, London, 1822 (384).

Pickering, Timothy, *An Easy Plan of Discipline for a Militia*, Salem, 1775 (496 [153]).

Pike, Albert, "Letters from Arkansas," *The American Monthly Magazine*, III (Jan., 1836), 25 ff. (286).

—— "Song" ("There is a wee and pretty maid") (277).

Pinckard, George, *Notes on the West Indies, Written during the Expedition under the Command of the Late General Sir Ralph Abercromby*, London, 1806 (424).

Plato (394 [192]).

Pliny the Elder, *Natural History* (315, 489, 490, 510, 518).

Plutarch (354 [31]).

Pope, Alexander, *Essay on Man* (354 [30]).

—— *Moral Essays* (496 [154]).

Porter, David, *Constantinople and Its Environs, in a Series of Letters, by an American, Long a Resident of Constantinople*, New York, 1835 (361, 467, 491, 492 [254], 500).

Pringle, Thomas, "To·the Ostrich" (428).

Purchas, Samuel, *His Pilgrimage; or, Relations of the World and the Religions*, London, 1613 (476).

Purvis, M., *On the Use of Lime as Manure*, review of, in *The American Journal of Science and Arts*, XXX (1836), 138–63 (456).

The Quarterly Review (519).

Report of the Committee of the Massachusetts House of Representatives on the Abolition of Capital Punishment, 1831, 1836 (279).

Revue Encyclopédique (299 [165]).

Reynolds, John N., *Voyage of the United States Frigate Potomac, under the Command of Commodore John Downes, during the Circumnavigation of the Globe, in the Years 1831–34*, New York, 1835 (486).

Roberts, Emma, *Scenes and Characteristics of Hindostan*, London, 1834; Philadelphia, 1836 (363, 375, 425).

Roget, Peter Mark, *On Animal and Vegetable Physiology*, London, 1834; Philadelphia, 1836 (294, 421).

S., L. H. (of Hartford), "The Mariner to the First-Seen Mountain, on Approaching His Native Coast" (302).

"The Salt Mountains of Ischil; in a Letter from an Officer in the American Navy," *The American Journal of Science and Arts*, XXIX (1836), 225–29 (393 [189]).

Schiller, Friedrich, *The Death of Wallenstein* (305 [81]).

Schoolcraft, Henry Rowe (356, 378).

Sedgwick, Theodore, *Public and Private Economy, Illustrated by Observations Made in England,* New York, 1836 (378).

Selby, Prideaux John, *The Natural History of Parrots,* Edinburgh, 1836 (455).

Shakespeare, *A Midsummer-Night's Dream* (499 [255]).

Smellie, William, *The Philosophy of Natural History,* Dublin, 1790; Boston, 1835, fifth ed. (499, 506 [209]).

Smith, Adam, *The Wealth of Nations* (402).

Spurzheim, Johann Kaspar (337).

Staël, Madame de, *Considérations sur la Révolution française,* Paris, 1818 (322, 348, 385).

Stark, James, "On the Influence of Colour on Heat and Odours," *Transactions of the Royal Philosophical Society of London,* 1833, pp. 285–312 (386 [181], 467 [201]).

Strickland, Catharine Parr, *The Backwoods of Canada: Being Letters from the Wife of an Emigrant Officer,* London, 1836 (466).

Sullivan, William, *Familiar Letters on Public Characters and Public Events, 1783–1815,* Boston, 1834 (379).

Swift, Jonathan, *Gulliver's Travels* (287, 360 [239]).

Symmes, John Cleves, *Theory of Concentric Spheres, Demonstrating That the Earth Is Hollow, Habitable Within, and Widely Open about the Poles,* Cincinnati, 1826 (518 [211]).

Temple, Edmond, *Travels in Various Parts of Peru, Including a Year's Residence in Potosí,* London, 1830; Philadelphia, 1833 (462, 473).

Terry, Adrian R., *Travels in the Equatorial Regions of South America, in 1832,* Hartford, 1834 (514).

Thomson, James, *The Castle of Indolence* (387 [183]).

Three Weeks in Palestine and Lebanon, with Views, London, 1833 (406, 412, 426).

Ticknor, Caleb, *The Philosophy of Living; or, The Way to Enjoy Life and Its Comforts,* New York, 1836 (439, 452, 454).

Timkowski, George, *Travels of the Russian Mission Through Mongolia to China,* London, 1827 (477).

Transactions of the Royal Philosophical Society of London, 1733 ff. (385 [177], 386 [181], 467 [201]).

Trelawny, Edward John, *Adventures of a Younger Son,* London, 1830 (418, 460).

Trollope, Frances, *Domestic Manners of the Americans,* London, 1832 (449 [147]).

Index of Selections

273

General Index

Abdy, Edward Strutt, 263
Abercromby, Gen. James, 125, 125n
Abstinence, 234
Acadians, 127n
Accidents, odd, 230-31
Account of an Expedition from Pittsburg to the Rocky Mountains, 268
Adams, John, 11, 41, 42-52, 263
Adams, Samuel, 44
Adrian, Emperor, 56
Adventures of a Younger Son, 271
Adventures on the Colombia River, 265
Africa, 79, 88
Albany, New York, 21
Alden, John, 42
Alexander the Great, 55, 56
Algiers, 82; pirates of, 120
Algiers, with Notices of the Neighbouring States, 268
All Fools' Day, 106-8
Allen, Richard, 65nn
Allen, Zachariah, 263
"Ambitious Guest, The," 108n
American Annual Register, The, 264
American Builder's General Price Book, The, 266
American Engraving Company, 1n
American Gardener's Magazine, The, 263
American Journal of Science and Arts, The, 88, 88n, 123n, 169, 169n, 189, 189n, 195, 195n, 263
American Journal of the Medical Sciences, The, 238, 263

American Magazine of Useful and Entertaining Knowledge, The: Hawthorne's editorship of, 1 ff.; publishers of, 1n; Alden Bradford's editorship of, 2; Hawthorne's comments on, 4, 5, 5n; editorial policies of, 4, 5, 8, 9, 13, 13n; contents of, under Hawthorne's editorship, 8, 10; neutrality of, under Hawthorne's editorship, 11
American Monthly Magazine, The, 12n, 221n, 263
American Notebooks, The, 99n
American Ornithology, 263, 272
American Quarterly Review, The, 263
American Traveller, The, 265
Americanisms, 249
Amherst, Sir Jeffrey, 125-30, 125n
Ancestral Footstep, The, 131n
Ancient Chronicles, 266
Andes, 252
Andros, Sir Edmund, 99, 99n
Anecdote, an, 146
Animal Kingdom, The, 265
Animals: ass, 208; beavers, 144-45, 200; bull, 208; camels, 241; cats, 199, 208; dogs, 192-93, 208; goat, 208; hare, 208; horses, 145-46, 195-98, 199-200, 208, 223-24, 237, 249; orang outang, 209; oxen, 113, 208; sheep, 113, 208; influence of music on, 199-201; life span of, 208-9; uses of dead, 195-98
Anne, Empress of Russia, 184
Anne, Queen of England, 186